Bal Gangadhar Tilak

Bal Gangadhar Tilak

Series Editor
Dr. M.H. Syed

Editor
M.A. Khan **N.P. Sharma**

Himalaya Books Pvt. Ltd.
'Ramdoot', Dr. Bhalerao Marg, Girgaon, Mumbai - 400 004
Tel : (022) 23863863. Fax : (022) 23877178
Email : himpub@vsnl.com

First Edition : 2011
Edition : 2016

Published by : **H.B.P.L.**
"Pooja Apartment", 4-B, Murari Lal Street, Ansari Road, Darya Ganj, New Delhi - 110 002.
Phones: 011-23270392, 23278631; Fax: 011-23256286
Email: hphdel@vsnl.com

Sole Distributors : **Himalaya Publishing House Pvt. Ltd.**

Branch Offices :

Mumbai : "Ramdoot", Dr. Bhalerao Marg, Girgaon, Mumbai - 400 004.
Phone: 022-23860170/23863863, Fax: 022-23877178
E-mail: himpub@vsnl.com; Website: www.himpub.com

Nagpur : Kundanlal Chandak Industrial Estate, Ghat Road, Nagpur - 440 018. Phone: 0712-2738731, 3296733;
Telefax: 0712-2721216

Bengaluru : Plot No. 91-33, 2nd Main Road Seshadripuram, Behind Nataraja Theatre, Bengaluru-560020.
Phone: 08041138821, 9379847017, 9379847005

Hyderabad : No. 3-4-184, Lingampally, Besides Raghavendra Swamy Matham, Kachiguda, Hyderabad - 500 027.
Phone: 040-27560041, 27550139

Chennai : New-20, Old-59, Thirumalai Pillai Road, T. Nagar, Chennai - 600 017. Mobile: 9380460419

Pune : First Floor, "Laksha" Apartment, No. 527, Mehunpura, Shaniwarpeth (Near Prabhat Theatre), Pune - 411 030.
Phone: 020-24496323/24496333;
Mobile: 09370579333

Lucknow : House No 731, Shekhupura Colony, Near B.D. Convent School, Aliganj, Lucknow - 226 022. Phone: 0522-4012353;
Mobile: 09307501549

Ahmedabad : 114, "SHAIL", 1st Floor, Opp. Madhu Sudan House, C.G. Road, Navrang Pura, Ahmedabad - 380 009. Phone: 079-26560126;
Mobile: 09377088847

Ernakulam : 39/176 (New No: 60/251) 1st Floor, Karikkamuri Road, Ernakulam, Kochi – 682011. Phone: 0484-2378012, 2378016;
Mobile: 09387122121

Bhubaneswar : 5 Station Square, Bhubaneswar - 751 001 (Odisha).
Phone: 0674-2532129, Mobile: 09338746007

Kolkata : 108/4, Beliaghata Main Road, Near ID Hospital, Opp. SBI Bank, Kolkata - 700 010, Phone: 033-32449649, Mobile: 7439040301

Printed at : M/s. Aditya Offset Process (I) Pvt. Ltd., Hyderabad. On behalf of HPH.

Preface

Biography, is now a form of literature, very much in vogue. In fact, biography is a description or account of someone's life and the times, which is usually published in the form of a book. A biography is more than a mention of personal facts (life, education, work, relationships and death), it also portrays the subject's experience of events. Technically speaking, a work is biographical, if it covers, all of a person's life. Biography writing has a long history. A biography is real. Ancient Greeks developed the biographical tradition, which we have inherited, although until the 5th century AD, when the word 'biographia' first appeared, in Damascius' "Life of Isodorus," biographical pieces were called simply "lives". It is quite likely that the Greeks were drawing on a pre-existing eastern tradition. Certainly Herodotus' "Histories" contains more detailed biographical information on Persian kings and subjects. The earliest surviving pieces, which we would identify as biographical are Isocrates' "Life of Evagoras" and Xenophon's "Life of Agesilaos," both from the fifth century BC. "Parallel Lives" by Plutarch, a Greek writing under the Roman empire, is a series of short biographies of eminent men.

The Golden Age of English biography emerged in late eighteenth century, the century in which the terms "biography" and "autobiography" entered English lexicon. The classic works of the period were Samuel Johnson's "Critical Lives of the Poets" and James Boswell's "Massive Life of Johnson". Generally American biography followed English model. By World War I, cheap hardcover reprints had become popular. The decade of the 1920s witnessed a biographical 'boom'. Later, biographical writings developed a lot and today biographies are written and compiled in the finest form of the genre. In India too, biography, as a form of literature has been evolved, cultivated and polished over the years. Here is an effort to promote this tradition further.

This series of biographies of great men, great women and celebrities in all walks of life is an adventurous academic endeavour, in its own right. A team of researchers and compilers has worked for a good period of time to accomplish the project. For this purpose, hundreds of books by eminent authors and editors have been consulted and referred to. We have benefited from various works, liberally, in order to illustrate and enrich this effort of ours. Present book is devoted to the great personality of Bal Gangadhar Tilak.

One of the tallest figures, among the first generation of modern freedom fighters. He was the most outstanding leader among the extremist congressmen. Bal Gangadhar Tilak later came to be known as 'Lokmanya Tilak'. He played a leading part in popularising the culture of patriotism. He started two newspapers, *The Maratha* in English and *The Kesari* in Marathi. He was the first congress leader to suffer several terms of imprisonment. He organised the Ganapati Festival and the Shivaji Festival. A great fighter, both in political and social fields, he played an important role in the Renaissance Movement. He devoted his entire life to the service of the country. He made excellent use of his great flair for journalism to mould public opinion in favour of his political aims and objectives. Tilak left the Indian National Congress in Surat session, held in 1907 and later organised his own party of extremists, in collaboration with Lala Lajpat Rai and Bipin Chandra Pal. Tilak, while in Mandalay prison, wrote his famous book '*Gita Rahasya*'. He also established the Home Rule League in Bombay. The British rulers called him the 'Leader of the Indian Unrest' and the Indians hailed him as 'the Prince of Patriots'.

This is a compact and comprehensive account of the above mentioned great life, which is bound to attract the attention of scholars, researchers, students and the general readers alike. Let's hope this humble effort would receive a warm welcome and due applause.

— ***Editors***

Contents

Preface *vii*

1. **An Illustrious Life** 1

Birth and Early Life • Family Background • The Backdrop • At the Threshold of Public Life • An Indian Jesuit • Six Years in Exile — Wife's Death and Extinction of Extremist Party • The Demise • The Legacy

2. **A Leader in the Making** 41

Beginning of a Political Career • First Imprisonment • Love's Labour Lost • As a Councillor

3. **An Eventful Career** 69

Early Career • Arrested Again • The Article in Question • Court Case • Two Home Rule Leagues • Legal Proceedings • Appeal to High Court • A Purse Presented • Provincial Conference at Ahmedabad • At Bombay • Sarvajanik Sabha and Congress • Defence of India Force • Triumph for Home Rulers • Home Rule League Meeting • Comments on Trial • Sentence, 1908 • Scholar and Unique Leader • Significant Writings

4. **Leader of Congress** 129

Indian National Congress • Reform of Legislative Councils • Social Reforms • Hindu - Muslim Riots • Music Question • Ganpati Celebrations • 'Moderate' and 'Extreme' Parties • Shivaji

Celebrations • Famine • Plague Measures • Arrest and Trial • Defence Fund • Imprisonment and Release • Tour to Burma • Prosecution of Globe Newspaper for Libel • Trial in Tai Maharaj Case • Festival in Honour • Dissemination of Disaffection • Swadeshi Movement • Press Prosecutions • Influence and Popularity • Dussehra Celebrations • Dissemination of Disaffection • Meeting at Nasik • Industrial Conference at Pandharpur • Congress Meeting • Split in Congress • Surat Session • Public Meetings • Conviction and Sentence • Transfer to Mandalay • After Release from Mandalay • Difference in Methods Only • Mrs. Besant's Statement • Another Move for Unity • Clause Amending Congress Constitution • Mrs. Besant's Home Rule League • Personal Activities • Provincial Conference at Puna • Bharat Itihas Sanshodak Mandali • Compromise between Extremists and Moderates • War and Loyalty • Tilak's Home Rule League • United Congress • Home Rule Propaganda • Indian Home Rule League Conference • Chairman's Speech • Another Milestone • Attitude to War • Shivaji Coronation Celebration

5. **Great Nationalist** 219

Concept of Swaraj • Precious Opinions • Ideology behind Indian Home Rule League • On Economic Front • Four-point Programme for Swarajya

6. **Significant Speeches** 269

Swaraj is My Birthright, I Will Have It • Historic 21-hour Speech • On Political Situation • On National Education

7. **Golden Words of Tilak** 293

8. **Tilak's Life at a Glance** 295

Bibliography 297

Index 301

1

An Illustrious Life

Birth and Early Life

Bal Gangadhar Tilak was born in Ratnagiri in Bombay Presidency on July 23, 1856. His great grandfather Keshavarao, named after Lakshmi Keshav, the presiding deity of the family, was a Mamlatdar (revenue officer) during the reign of the last Peshwa. Well versed in letters, an expert rider, an unerring marksman and a champion swimmer, Keshavarao combined in himself the qualities of a scholar and soldier. He was a happy man, but at the age of 40 his life suddenly underwent a change when, late in the second decade of the nineteenth century, the Peshwa rule, styled by some as the Chitpavan government, was overthrown by the British. He abandoned the mamlat, and made the performance of religious rites his main occupation for the rest of his life.

Keshavarao married a second time, after the death of his first wife. The two wives bore him three children of whom Ram Chandrarao was the eldest. Ram Chandrarao, also known as Ramchandra Pant, was yet a child of ten when the flickering lamp of Peshwa glory went out. His education was neglected, and he was married at an early age. In August, 1820, when he was only 18 years old, his wife gave birth to a son who was named Gangadhar.

Time was when Deccan Brahmins, especially the Chitpavans, were masters of the Konkan, the coastal strip lying between Bombay and Goa, and occupied high administrative posts under the Peshwa. Though they were employed by the British in the subordinate administration, they had lost their commanding influence, and were scrupulously kept out of all positions of power and responsibility. They adjusted themselves, as their fellow-countrymen did in other parts of the country, to the new situation, but a certain discontent and longing for a return to power naturally remained.

Descendants of a Mamlatdar, the sons and grandsons of Keshavarao found themselves in a similar position. Straitened circumstances of the family forced Ram Chandrarao to seek a subordinate job in the Survey Department. Professional work and a fondness for travel kept him away from home for long periods. This incidentally provided Gangadhar an opportunity for closer association with his erudite grandfather from whom he learnt his alphabets at home. He was then put into the village primary school where he finished his Marathi course of instruction. Gangadhar must have been an adventurous boy. Failing to get encouragement from his grandfather and father to prosecute his studies further, perhaps on account of the family's circumstances, he left home and walked all the way to Puna where he entered an English school.

But a severe calamity shattered all his cherished hopes. His mother, who was on a visit to Poozia to see him, suddenly died there of cholera. He withstood the shock bravely, but to his father's separation from the wife proved disastrous. He developed a philosophical attitude of mind, and became indifferent to the world, nay, to his own children — two sons and a daughter. In orthodox Hindu families, reading from the scriptures was, and is still, a regular feature of daily lite; and impressions, such as non-attachment and renunciation, strike roots deep down into one's nature at a tender age. To a soul in distress renunciation suggests itself as a spiritual remedy.

It was in this state of mind that Ram Chandrarao left for Chitrakut, which has been sanctified by association with the Ramayana and whose spiritual atmosphere still attracts many a recluse. Between 1837, in which year his wife died, and 1872, when his own earthly existence came to an end, Ram Chandrarao once, and only once, came home.

The British reprisals that followed the failure of the Great Revolt of 1857 had terrorised the people, even the "Government had issued secret instructions not to allow any one to go about in the garb of an anchorite without a certificate". It was apprehended, and perhaps rightly, that the defeated heroes of 1857, who were wanted by the authorities to be punished, were hiding themselves under the ascetic cloak. At this distance of time, it is a matter of conjecture whether Ram Chandrarao went home to secure such a certificate or whether a desire to see his dear ones got for a while ascendancy over his non-attachment. He noticed an agreeable change in the family, and saw the face of a grandson born a year before the Revolt.

This child, son of Gangadhar Pant, was named Balwantrao, and he later became known as Bal Gangadhar Tilak, whom a grateful nation reverentially calls Lokmanya Tilak or Tilak Bhagwan. During his long absence from home, Ram Chandrarao served for some time under the deposed Peshwa as a superintendent of stores, but he never returned to the worldly life and passed the rest of his days on the banks of the Ganga in Banaras.

After the death of his mother in 1837 and the disappearance of his father, Gangadhar, who was then only a boy of 17, was sorely perplexed. It was obvious that he could not pursue his studies, but how was he to find the wherewithal to support the family? He was forced to prepare himself for a profession and took the job of a teacher in a Marathi school on Rs. 5 per month. He was fond of Sanskrit and Mathematics, and by self-study acquired proficiency in both. By sheer dint of labour, resourcefulness of mind and devotion to duty, he earned rapid promotions and rose to the position of an assistant deputy inspector of schools. In a speech bidding him farewell at the time of his transfer from the Ratnagiri High School to Puna, a colleague of his, Dr. Bhandarkar, spoke of him thus:

> "The erudition, imaginativeness, compassion, independence of thought, and tirelessness of Gangadhar

Pant are worthy of emulation. He is a repository of grammar and a storehouse of Marathi".

Unlike his father, Gangadhar Pant did not allow himself to be lost in spiritual exaltation and surrender. He was an author, a moneylender, a shareholder in a mill. The three books that he wrote — a history of England, a textbook of arithmetic, and a handbook of grammar — were purchased by the Education Department of the Government for schools.

Gangadhar's wife, Parvatibai, was a kind-hearted and intensely religious woman. After having borne him three daughters, a longing for a son naturally grew in her. Saintly in her habits, she would not think of taking her meals without saying her prayers. She made her delicate health the worse by frequent fasting. And when Balwantrao was born to her, she believed that her penance and prayers had been rewarded by the Sun-God. She fondly called the child Keshav, after his great grandfather and out of gratitude to the family deity, Lakshmi Keshav. But the endearing domestic sobriquet Bal became eventually his real name. No longer quite fit to steer through the journey of life, Parvatibai died in 1866, when Bal was only ten years old.

His father, himself a teacher, gave Tilak a good grounding in Sanskrit, arithmetic and Marathi. His memory being encouragingly retentive, he was taught, while yet a child, to recite sacred Sanskrit verses. Once Tilak provided his father an opportunity which made him jubilant. The father's reading of the sonorous cadences of Bana Bhatta's famous work, Kadambari captured the heart of the son, and he asked for the loan of the book. "Startled at the request, but unwilling to dispirit the son by a curt refusal, Gangadhar Pant promised to give the book on one condition". He was given a knotty problem in arithmetic and asked to work it out. He worked at it for an hour and a half, and amidst the applause of his mother and sister won the prize.

In 1866, he was admitted into the Puna City School, where he made more than satisfactory progress, completing three standards in two years. To a conventional martinet, Tilak was a rebel; he was not popular with his teachers and often quarrelled with them. He had inherited a liking for Sanskrit and mathematics textbook, Scott's Kenilworth. And for his vigorous pranks his fellow-students called him "Devil".

Yet his banters were innocuous, his manners gentle. His lifelong friend Upsani, said long after the two had left the college that he shared Tilak's room while both were students of Law at Bombay, and "I do not remember a single occasion when he gave expression to any unworthy thought".

He jealously guarded his character, and even an insignificant reflection on it pained him deeply. As a rule, he did not dine out, and it is said that when a teacher once ignorantly accused him of doing so, he was red with rage, and left the classroom. Two of his professors, Wordsworth and Chhatre, whose memory he enshrined in his mind, brought to bear on their work a moral and intellectual equipment of high order. At the college, as at the high school, Tilak persisted in his summary method of study: he would not take notes, nor burn the midnight oil. He hurriedly did his daily lessons, often without his mind in them. But when he set himself a task, he accomplished it with surprising thoroughness. In a Sanskrit poetry competition, organised by one of his teachers, Professor Jinsiwale, (the subject was Matra Vilap — Mother's Sorrow) Tilak's verses were adjudged the best. He kept up his interest in Sanskrit which was aroused in his childhood, and composed many verses, but the poet in him did not go beyond the college walls. Sometimes his enthusiasm for extra reading was so much stirred up that he cut himself off from everything else and virtually plunged into serious study. Once he took it into his head that he should draw up a synopsis of the reigns of the Queens Mary and Elizabeth. He studied a dozen standard authors, and prepared a comprehensive precis, which was copied out by his classmates for their benefit.

A treatise on a grammatical point which he developed with similar assiduity also won him praise. Among the subjects which he studied in the higher classes, Hindu Law interested him most. His study of the books on Hindu Law by English authors whetted his appetite for a deeper knowledge of the subject, and he went through the original works of Yajna-valkya and other authorities. He studied all the important Acts enacted by the Government of India since 1827 and all the important works on Hinduism with their commentaries.

This vast reading beyond the prescribed law books he did, not for passing the examination but in order to understand the complicated structure of Hindu society as seen through the eyes of the law. A thorough knowledge of Hindu society, its customs, its gods, its heroes, provided him, in his public career, rich material for political agitation. He began and completed his education at Puna, but for one term he strayed to Bombay and joined the Elphinstone College.

There Professor Hawthornwaite taught Mathematics, but his teaching did not impress Tilak, and he went back to Puna where he graduated in 1876 in the first class. The next year, he studied for the M. A. examination, but failing to pass it, began to study law and took the L. L. B. degree in 1879. Five or six years later, after he had already made teaching a mission in life, he again appeared at the M. A. examination, and again he failed.

A University degree was a rare possession in those days, and a graduate's field of activities, whether professional or public, was a town rather than a village. In the case of Tilak, lack of congeniality in the family at home (in the village of his ancestors) was an additional cause which perhaps prevailed upon him to choose Puna as his new home. It is here that he began life, in a humble way, as a missionary in the cause of education, and it is here that he rose to the eminence of an undisputed political leader of India.

Much of what was foretold in Tilak's horoscope never came to pass, but as if it was decreed by destiny, litigation, which he inherited, became his shadow till the last days of life. It began with family feuds as far back as 1865, involving his grandfather in several suits about ancestral landed property.

They, lasted, in one way or another for over 35 years, and denied Tilak that warmth and affection of home whose sweet memories man cherishes most. Never in his life could he stay so much as a week in Konkan — Konkan which for generations inspired Mahratta youths and stirred them to action. The longest he stayed at home was for four days in 1889, and that too in a mood of detachment and renunciation. What was he to do with his share of the ancestral property? That was his problem, for he had already made up his mind that he would have nothing to do with it himself. He found a rightful claimant in Lakshmi Keshav, the village deity.

For several decades, the family had little physical association with the property at home, and a well-established convention prompted Tilak, as one who had migrated to another place, to do a religious duty. A belief had grown among the people of Konkan that such of the sons of the soil as had gone out and prospered should get dilapidated temples in their villages repaired. The belief had been handed down from generation to generation, and had in most cases been translated into action like a ceremonial rite. Many regarded the performance of this duty as the first charge on their income. Tilak went one step further and decided to dedicate his entire ancestral property to Lakshmi Keshav.

Litigation with regard to family property, therefore, became his supreme religious duty. He fought and fought until, in 1894, the award of an arbitration allowed partition and delimitation of the land. Tilak's long-cherished wish was fulfilled, and in his will, he offered his entire share to the deity. In between these periods of family feud, Tilak was involved as a journalist in one or two other legal actions, which are described elsewhere in this book.

Even before the land was dedicated to the deity, Tilak never derived any benefit from it. His father, a self-made man, left him some property after striking a favourable balance sheet of loss and gain. Gangadhar Pant had made it a habit to write down his income and daily expenses in an accounts book which made the task of his son's biographers, probing into minute domestic details, easy. The accounts book gives an idea of the amazing industry with which he built up a little fortune for the son who was to be left an orphan at the age of 16.

Gangadhar Pant drew upon several avenues, outside the profession of teaching, to supplement his income. In 1866, according to his accounts book, he started the year with Rs. 250 and closed it with Rs. 3,900. This was, in those days, an enviable income for a middle-class family.

One of his outside sources was shares in a saw mill which was a European concern managed by one Crawford. But eventually the investment had to be struck off as a loss. One of the episodes connected with it provides a little material for the present story.

Arrangements were being made for Tilak's marriage, and the father was collecting money from all possible sources, the main among them being the refund of his shares in the mill.

He wrote to Crawford, "The marriage is near at hand", "and reform of text, unless you redeem your promise, it may have to be postponed. Pray send me at least Rs, 800 as soon as this letter reaches your hands". The money never came, and instead the company went into liquidation. The marriage, however, took place according to programme.

After completing his education, Tilak, with the assets he inherited from his father, set up an independent family establishment. He was fortunate in having in Govindrao an uncle who bestowed on him the same affection as a father does on his son. He set before Tilak the same example of industry and devotion to work as did his father. Like his brother, Govindrao also maintained the family accounts scrupulously. One of the items in the accounts of 1875 suggests that Tilak used to get in the Deccan College a monthly scholarship of Rs. 10.

Tilak's reverence for his uncle more than matched the uncle's affection for him. With the elementary education that Govindrao had received he was not able to make much headway in life, and Tilak allowed his own share in his father's property to be used for the benefit of the uncle's family. In 1897, when Tilak was sentenced to a term of 18 months imprisonment, the uncle was alive. The old man was overwhelmed with the concern expressed over the imprisonment of the nephew throughout the country and the praises showered on him. He was overpowered with emotion, and the tears rolled down his cheeks.

Family Background

Tilak's father was a Government servant and at the time of his death in 1872 was Assistant Deputy Educational Inspector. Tilak was educated in the Puna High School; took his B. A. degree with honours from the Deccan College, Puna, in 1876, and three years later obtained his L. L. B. degree from the Bombay University. It is said that, while in college, he and Gopal Ganesh Agarkar made a mutual resolution never to take Government Service and to devote their lives and talents to the education of their countrymen. In pursuance of this object they, with Vishnu Krishna Chiplunkar, opened the New English School, Puna, on the 2nd January 1880, and a little later started the *Mahratta* and *Kesari* newspapers. His political career may, therefore, be assumed to have begun early in 1880. In 1882, Tilak and Agarkar, as registered Editors and Publishers of the *Mahratta* and *Kesari* newspapers, were tried in the Bombay High Court for defamation in connection with articles which had appeared in these papers criticising the treatment accorded to His Highness Shivajirao, late Raja of Kolhapur, and on conviction sentenced in two cases to three months' simple imprisonment apiece in each case, the sentence being ordered to run concurrently.

While they were in jail Chiplunkar died. The success of their Educational institution induced Tilak and Agarkar to formulate a scheme for an Education Society, the life-members of which were to undertake to work in the Society for 20 years. The idea took, and in 1884, the Deccan Education Society came into existence with Tilak, Agarkar and others as life-members. One year later, the Society opened its own College. Shortly after the establishment of the Deccan Education Society, the life-members began to wrangle among themselves and it was decided to separate the interests of the newspapers and press from those of the Educational institutions.

In 1886, the separation was effected and under its terms Tilak and two others became owners of the papers and press. About the same time differences of opinion between Tilak and Agarkar led the latter to start his own newspaper under the name of the " *Sudharak* " which eventually became the organ of the "Reform" or " Moderate" Party.

In 1890, Tilak severed his connection with the Deccan Education Society. Shortly after, he quarrelled with his partners in the newspapers and became sole proprietor of both. He thus became master of his own time and with his wonted energy and zeal threw himself into the stream of politics. The "Age of Consent Bill" was then on the political anvil and it afforded him the opportunity of making a bid for the political leadership of his community. He attacked the policy of the leaders of the community in regard to the measure, and did not scruple to misrepresent their intentions, with the result that he caused a division in the community and became the leader of the "Orthodox" or "Extreme" Party. His attitude towards Government has always been that of an irreconcilable opponent and on each successive occasion he has, from the platform and through his organs, opposed and at Limes misrepresented its actions. His political creed may be defined as a determined and persistent effort to obtain "Self-government" for the natives and in preaching it he advocates even rebellion provided it holds out a prospect of success.

His influence among the educated extends to the radical section only; the other sections admire his ability, energy and zeal, but do not agree with his methods. His power lies in the support afforded him by pleaders and students generally. Personally, he is of small stature and poor appearance and by disposition self-willed and impatient of control. Amongst Natives he is considered to be moral and strictly honest in all pecuniary dealings; and in political matters to hold that the end justifies the means.

The Backdrop

The period 1885-1920, particularly after 1895, is mainly dominated by the political activities of the Lokmanya. Naturally a major portion of the police reports is covered by these activities. Much of the information has already seen the light. But Tilak's pen-picture from the Police has its own flavour. It shows with what suspicion Government looked to him from the beginning. The reports also show how some of the police comments are malicious and far from truth.

The report by Mr. Harry Brewiri, Assistant I.G.P., C.I.D., Puna, submitted to Government on 31st July 1902 giving his opinion regarding the charges against Tilak in the Tai Maharaja Case is, however, an important document, in as much as he expressed his opinion that (i) the charge of Forgery would not stand and that (ii) as the remaining charges were connected with personal affairs " Government should assume an attitude of neutrality". This, as well as Government report's regarding Tilak's four trials (1882,1897, 1902 and 1908) have not been included in this volume, as all the cases have been widely published.

The Labour disturbances at Bombay (June 29 to July 27, 1908) at the time of his arrest and trial were, perhaps, the first expression of the people's political discontent exhibited on such a wide scale. These disturbances, it seems, had attracted Lenin's attention and evoked his comments.

Tilak's History ticket from the Mandalay Jail is very interesting and gives some details of his jail life including his health reports. His memorials to the King, etc. from jail were traced from his history ticket only.

The London Secret Police report of his activities in England (1919) is another important document. The report says " Tilak has the strongest hope of the deliverance of India by the Bolsheviks and was delighted with the Afghanistan imbroglio and Amritsar riots". The very idea to utilise for Indian cause the possible regrouping of World powers as a result of the war is significant.

The short extract from Khadilkars editorial in the Lokmanya gives information about what Tilak urns contemplating to do when Gandhiji's Satyagraha Movement would start. This information goes to show that the Lokmanya was thinking and planning to live in England when the Satyagraha movement would start. This he wanted to do, as is reported by Khadilkar, to avoid the diversion of public attention towards his and Gandhi's incarceration. Such a diversion would necessarily result in the toning down of the National demands. This information is full of meaning and can be interpreted in more than one way.

Tilak's expectations about the probable achievements of the Satyagraha movement are also significant. His letter to Dr. D. D. Sathaye shows that he wanted his followers to fully support the *Satyagraha movement. Tilak's talks* to *the labourers in Bombay on the subject of Swadeshi point* out the importance he gave to the organisation of labour in India. He also has written a few articles on Trade Union Movement and its utility in the Kesari about the same time.

The Congress reports show how poorly Hume was supported on the organisational front in the early years of the Congress. Tilak did this though he belonged to the group of juniors in the Congress. Within the next five years it was seen that the leadership of the Congress could not keep pace with Hume, and Tilak was one of the few leaders who supported Hume's "aggressive" propaganda methods.

He appears to be one of the earliest leaders who correctly perceived the conflict of interest between the rulers and the ruled and saw the futility of petitions and protests. He in his small field attempted to organise the masses, who were dreadfully backward and perpetually under semi-starvation, for creating sanctions in the districts of Kolaba, Thana, Bijapur, Belgaum, etc. for compelling the government to apply the famine code and alter the forest laws. That is one of the earliest of mass agitations, in the real sense of the word. Thus, Tilak in effect took up such programmes which Hume had placed before the Congress. The Commissioner, Central Division, Mr. Logan in his report (1897) stated that "Tilak had flooded the country with proclamations against payment of land revenue and urging resistance to any attempt to collect it". He also says that there was a " partial mutiny amongst the police and the Village Officers were almost passive or active connivers with the disturbances".

The pen-portrait prepared by the police also shows how he trained his lieutenants to organise the masses. Through his writings and speeches he has propagated that the Congress was intended to serve the interest of the masses and not only of the classes. It is well known how after the Bengal partition he became the leader of the popular will and the cleavage between the moderates and the extremists then came to the forefront. Some of the extracts given below show how anxious he was before the Surat session to avert the breach. In fact Tilak knew best the mind of the Rulers. He knew it well that they could fight under the Congress-leadership alone, which was well acknowledged by the government as an instrument of constitutional agitation. The officials must have desired to see a rift in its ranks with a uieto to expose the extremists. Tilak was most anxious to avert this calamity.

The moderates led by Mehta, Gokhale, Surendranath and the Nationalists led by Tilak, Arvind, Khaparde had published their versions of the Surat incident at that time. The nationalist version is very clear and is found to be corroborated by the police reports even in its small details. These Police reports, are perhaps seeing the light for the first time. They deary show how earnestly the

Lokmanya strove to suggest some compromise; and how shabbily he and his young friends were treated by the office bearers of the Congress. These reports show that an attempt was made to remove Tilak forcibly from the dias but he (Tilak) brushed the man-one of the office holders of the Reception Committee aside. Gokhale and Malaviya seem to have prevented that attempt.

At the Threshold of Public Life

The year 1880, when Tilak entered public life as an educationist, draws a demarcation line between a decade of great upheaval which reached its climax during the Viceroyalty of Lytton and another of almost complete calm which began with the taking over of the Indian administration by Eipon. On the one side of the line, during the seventies, were violent political turmoils, agrarian revolts and widespread preparations on a large scale for launching a simultaneous attack on the British authority. The Deccan too was red with discontent and virtually spitting fire. The Maharashtra peasants were sorely turbulent and had thrown a considerable part of that territory into a state of disorder and lawlessness.

Famines, which became too frequent in the seventies, were in a large measure, if not wholly responsible for the disturbed state of affairs. Large quantities of foodgrains were despatched to England from India as a result of which starvation became a normal feature of life. In 1859, the exports of rice, wheat and other grains amounted to Rs. 2,801,871, and by 1877, they rose to £ 7,988,189- as if in vengeance, "in 1876-77, when India was on the brink of one of the severest famines of the country, she exported a larger quantity of foodgrains than she had ever done in any preceding year". There was no surplus to permit exports; in fact, "if the whole population ate as much as they could, this surplus would not exist. The grain exports of India represented many hungry stomachs".

The land revenue had been raised, and the producer had to sell larger quantities of his produce in order to pay the State dues. The gross revenues of India increased from £ 36 million to £ 51 million in 18 years, after the Revolt of 1857, and the proportion of it spent in England, in the shape of Home Charges, rose from £ 7.5 to £ 10 millions.

"Large tracts of cultivable land were deprived of food crops and acquired by English companies for the cultivation of tea, indigo and jute, Independent peasants were, in those areas, reduced to a position of slavery. A special law was enacted for the recruitment of labour for the tea gardens. For its exacting provisions, the law was, in common parlance, called the Slave Law. Says R. C. Dutt: "Hateful cases of fraud, coercion, and kidnapping for securing these labourers have been revealed in the criminal courts of Bengal, and occasional acts of outrage on the men and women thus recruited have stained the history of tea gardens in Assam".

Lytton believed that appeasement of the landed aristocracy, even if it meant oppression of the peasantry, should be the policy of Government. In May, 1876, after assuming charge of India, he wrote to the Secretary of State, the Marquis of Salisbury: "I am convinced that the fundamental political mistake of able and experienced Indian officials is a belief that we can hold India securely by what they call good government; that is to say, by improving the condition of the ryot, strictly administering justice, spending immense sums on irrigation works, etc. Politically speaking, the Indian peasantry is an inert mass. If it ever moves at all, it will move in obedience, not to its British benefactors, but to its native chiefs and Princes, however, tyrannical they may be. The only political representatives of native opinion are the Baboos whom we have educated to write semi-seditious articles in the native press, and who really represent nothing but the anomaly of their own position. But the Indian chiefs and Princes are not mere noblesse. They are powerful aristocracy. To secure completely and efficiently utilise the Indian aristocracy is, I am convinced, the most important problem now before us. Fortunately for us, they are easily affected by sentiments, and susceptible to the influence of symbols".

Lytton lost no time in giving effect to this policy, and called an Imperial Durbar in 1877, which was to serve another purpose also, namely, to celebrate and proclaim to the Indian people the new title of Queen Victoria, The Durbar added insult to injury, for it coincided with a terrible famine which had already swept away five million people of South India.

In Maharashtra, the starving people, in sheer desperation, attacked the grabbing landlords, moneylenders and other oppressors. There was a great commotion in which thousands of peasants took part. It was a full-fledged agrarian revolt, and the police arrested about a thousand people, half of whom were prosecuted. But Lytton was unconcerned and went ahead with his scheme of decorating the aristocracy with new 'honours'. "Services hitherto inadequately recognised were rewarded; pensions enjoyed by ancient native families whose unquestioned loyalty had rendered them deserving of assistance were increased; numerous increased salaries for life were granted to the principal native chiefs; and to each chief entitled to a salute was presented, in the name of the Queen and with due ceremony, a large silken banner bearing on one side the Royal Arms and on the other his own".

Lytton's policy prepared the ground for rising discontent. Two eminent Englishmen, both officials, who in later years were closely associated with India's political life and aspirations, reported on the basis of information in their possession that a revolt was being vigorously organised. They were Allan Octavian Hume and Sir William Wedderburn. The former is commonly known as the Father of the Indian National Congress and the latter as one of its famous Presidents.

Reading from the situation in the country, they apprehended that the 1857-58 trouble might be repeated. Hume says the "poor men were pervaded with a sense of hopelessness of the existing state of affairs; that they were convinced that they would starve and starve and die, and that they wanted to do something, and that something meant violence". There were innumerable entries which referred to the hoarding of old swords, spears and matchlocks which would be ready when required.

The forecast of trouble throughout India was in exact accordance with what actually occurred, says Wedderburn, from his own observation in the Bombay Presidency of the agrarian rising known as the Deccan Riots. "These began with sporadic gang robberies and attacks on the moneylenders until the bands of dacoits, combining together, became too strong for the police; and the whole military force at Puna, horse, foot and artillery, had to take the field against them.

Roaming through the jungles tracts of the Western Ghats, these bands dispersed in the presence of military force, only to reunite immediately at some convenient point. A leader from the more instructed class was found, calling himself Shivaji the Second, who addressed challenges to the Government, offered a reward of Rs. 500 for the head of Sir Richard Temple '(Governor of Bombay) and claimed to lead a national revolt upon the lines on which the Mahratta power Had originally been founded".

Advised them that if they wanted their miseries to go, they should help him end the British Raj, And they responded to his call.

In Puna, Vasudev organised a secret society of youths selected from schools and colleges. Temples and secluded places were chosen for giving revolutionary lectures. The training in the art of war was given in the neighbourhood of the Ferguson or the Gultekdi Hills. Regular contact was established between the secret society and the Ramoshis.

Having assured himself of manpower, Vasudev opened negotiations with some rich men for money, telling them that their contribution would be regarded as a loan refundable after freedom had been achieved. There was no response. He, therefore, decided to collect funds by force, and did actually commit dacoities with the help of his armed band. But before his plans could take a definite shape he was captured. His own diary and autobiography, which he had scribbled during his fugitive career, made the task of the Prosecution easy, and he was awarded a sentence of transportation for life.

During the trial "cavalrymen and the police guarded the courtroom and its outside which was daily crowded with a vast multitude of spectator's". They included distinguished Europeans and Indians.

Life-transportees those days were usually sent to the Andamans, but "not sure of the prisoner's behaviour", the Governor of Bombay sent Vasudev to the fort of Aden. He was confined in a solitary cell. He managed to escape, but was again captured and died in February, 1883.

Vasudev's abortive attempt was only an extension of similar attempts made earlier. They were, according to Henry Dodwell, akin to the Wahabi movement; the latter's centre of activities was Patna and the former's Puna, The Marathas had fresher recollection than the Muslims of their independent power; in fact, but for British intervention, the Marathas would have been rulers of India after the collapse of the Mughals and of the Muslim power generally. Though, as Dodwell says, the Marathas were not fired by an equally fanatical religion, that lack was made good by the feeling of nationality engendered by Maratha history. Conspiracies were discovered in 1862. The movement, Bartle Frere wrote to Canning; "is an evident offshoot of the discontent which lost its chosen leaders in the Nana, Tautia Tope, etc. and which still smoulders in Central India and Maratha country. From all I can learn any spark such as a war in Europe or with America would have been followed by a number of concerted but separate insurrections in all parts of India between the Vindhya mountains and Tunbhudra, the movement was detected too early to become dangerous, but evidently did not die out".

The Deccan Riots were a result of the British policy of neglecting the peasant and nurturing the aristocracy. The law courts protected the moneylenders; the letter of the law being in their favour, the debtor-tenants were often dispossessed of their holdings, and made to pay to the landholders by selling their all. The stranglehold of the moneylenders became so tight that agricultural land was passing into the hands of interest-earning classes, and cultivators were being reduced to the position of serfs. When the condition became unbearable, the people rose to undo what an unjust law had done.

In 45 villages in the Puna district and in 22 in the Ahmedabad district, they forced the moneylenders to surrender the bonds and other securities, which were burnt in the open. The trouble again raised its head in 1878 when the Government was forced to take up legislation for the amelioration of the peasants, and the Deccan Agriculturists Relief Act was passed. The Act restricted alienation of land and restrained usury. Both in the Vasudev Revolt and in the Deccan Riots, the conspicuous participants were the Ramoshis.

Until the time of Lytton, Indian politics was divided into two schools of thought: one believed in the overthrow of the British rule by force and the other had no intention of removing the

British by any means, but merely wanted a share in the administration. A kind of mild constitutional agitation had begun to take shape in the Deccan more than a decade before the Great Revolt.

An institution working, in a mild way, for constitutional reforms before the Great Revolt, was the Kalyan Unanayak Mandal of Puna. The Mandal drew up a Charter of Rights for presentation to the British Parliament. Gopalrao Deshmukh, commonly called Lokahitwadi, was the leading luminary of the Mandal. (His father had fallen in the battlefield fighting for the last Peshwa). Gopalrao took up a judicial post under the British, but evinced a keen interest in politics in order to promote the country's constitutional advance. He carried on his agitation, single-handed, through the columns of the Prabhakar, a leading journal of those days. There is evidence in his articles of political sagacity, almost prophetical. In the issue dated April 1, 1849, he wrote under the title, "The Effect of British Rule", that a time would come when the people of India would become politically and culturally so strong that the British Government would be compelled to quit. He was half a century ahead of his time, and preached swadeshi and establishment of small industries. In one article, he plainly suggested that imports of foreign goods should be stopped even if the people had to wear coarse cloth.

But an organised effort, in the realm of politics of the constitutional variety, began a few years later. On August 26, 1852, a meeting of the "native inhabitants" was held in the room of the Elphinstone Institution, and on the same evening was inaugurated, mainly through the efforts of Jagannath Shankar Sheth, the first political association in the Presidency, the Bombay Association. Among members of the Association were both Indians and Europeans, but its first major activity caused a serious rift. The Association had drawn up and submitted to the British Parliament a petition asking for an "enlightened system of government". The wording of the petition was mild, but since it suggested some defects in the administration, it was construed by some of the members as an indictment of the East India Company's rule. "Soon after the text of the petition was published, the English journals that had at first blessed the movement began to fall foul of it". Some Europeans seceded from the Association, and some Indians followed suit. For many years, the Association, which was later broad-based and called the Bombay Presidency Association, exercised, under the leadership of Dadabhai Naoroji and Sir Mangaldas Nathubhoy, monopoly over the politics of the Presidency.

Dadabhai, who started his political life with an agitation against the system of recruitment to the Indian Civil Service, brought into being several associations to carry on propaganda in England for the establishment of representative political institutions in India. One of these was the East Indian Association, inaugurated on December 1,1866, in collaboration with a committee of retired English officers. Later, a branch of the Association was formed in Bombay. He made a tour of the country, and among those he met were also the ruling chiefs whose support he was anxious to enlist for constitutional reforms. Pherozeshah Mehta was one of the proteges of Dadabhai "whose sage counsel and inspiration" (to quote Mehta's own words) "had formed my character and elevated my ideals whilst I was studying law in England". Dadabhai was a moderate, but through his monumental works on India's economic condition during the British rule, Poverty of India and Poverty and British Rule in India, he became instrumental in provoking many a young man to resort to violent methods against the British Raj.

Similarly, Mahadev Govind Ranade, himself a cautious moderate, inspired the young men of Maharashtra for many years through his books. His Rise of the Maratha Empire and The Sources of Maratha History were read and reread, reminders as they were of the fact that the state of the Deccan under the Chitpavan Peshwa was far superior to its condition under British rule. For over a decade before Ranade rose to the position of a Judge of the High Court, the Sarvajanik Sabha was the medium of his political work.

Gifted speakers like Dadabhai and Ranade were few and far between in India, and realising the need of encouraging public speaking, some of the leading men of Puna formed in 1868 a society for the practice of elocution; they called it Vaktrit-vottejak Sabha. Two or three subjects, political, social or religious, were announced every year by the secretary, and candidates were invited to speak on those subjects at public meetings two months after the issue of the notice. A committee of five or six members chosen from the audience decided the merits of the speakers and awarded the prize which ranged between Rs. 10 and Rs. 50.

The Vaktrit-vottejak Sabha may be regarded as complementary to the Puna Sarvajanic Sabha which was founded on April 2, 1870, under the auspices of the Pant Pratinidhi, the chief of Aundh in Satara, with the object of promoting the political welfare and advancing the interest of the people of this and other parts of the country. The members included, besides a few Deccan Sardars and Inamdars, Government servants chiefly of the Educational and Judicial Departments, pensioners, and a few pleaders. From time to time the Sabha discussed and made representations to Government on many important subjects. But it was not just a resolution passing political body; during the five years of draught in Maharashtra (1870-75), it interested itself in the peasant problem and every year sent representations to Calcutta, signed by thousands of ryots and secured remissions. In 1873, it undertook the task of investigating the economic conditions of the Maharashtra cultivators. During 1876-77, when Maharashtra was in the grip of a severe famine, the Sabha organised relief measures and made representations to Government.

Ranade was the beacon of the Sabha, but the spirit behind it was Ganesh Vasudev Joshi alias Sarvajanik Kaka who plunged into political and social work, and cut himself off from everything else. A pioneer of swadeshi, he spun yarn daily for his own wear and opened swadeshi shops. He threw himself heart and soul into the movement, and converted people to the swadeshi creed by his own example. He was chosen by the Sabha to represent it at the Delhi Durbar, 1877 and clad in Khadi, he became in that imperial show an object of attraction. In an address which he read out at that pageant, Sarvajanik Kaka appealed to the Queen to grant to Indians the same political and social status as was enjoyed by the British people.

Another enthusiast of the Sarvajanik Sabha was Gopal Narsinh Deshpande. His field of activities was Indapur in the district of Puna, where he established a branch of the Sabha.

He was a stormy figure, he moved through the villages, enquired about conditions of the people, drew up representations on their behalf, went from house to house to collect signatures, and at his wayside lectures taught the people their duty towards each other and towards the country. A swadeshi protagonist like Sarvajanik Kaka, he would say that not a pie should go out of the country. In times of crisis and calamity, he knew no rest during the famine of 1876-77, he toured for 18 months through Gujarat, Kathiawad, Cutch and Bombay, collected donations and distributed food. Famines and the economic deterioration of the people, which were largely the result of Lytton's policy, roused the interest of the public workers of the towns in villagers and their problems. Another result of the Lytton administration was the toning up of the nationalist Press; in order to suppress it, he very hurriedly caused the Vernacular Press Act to be passed by the Legislature. This attack on the liberty of the Press sent up a wave of resentment all over the country, and an all India conference, in which Sarvajanik Kaka played a leading role, was held at Calcutta to protest against the "Gagging Act". Another law, more obnoxious than the Vernacular Press Act, enacted by Lytton was the Arms Act which made the possession of arms with a licence an offence.

Lytton's soulless and oppressive rule came to an end with the change of Government in England in April, 1880. Gladstone once again assumed the British Prime Ministership and naturally desired that the Indian Governor-General should carry out the policy of the new Government faithfully, Lytton had, therefore, to resign, and Ripon was appointed in his place. The new Viceroy made a good start in the sphere of administration and succeeded in appeasing the Moderate public opinion. At the instance of Gladstone, he withdrew the Vernacular Press Act, and announced his intention to introduce reforms in the sphere of municipal administration.

Lytton, as Surendranath Banerjee remarked, "had roused the public from its attitude of indifference and had given a stimulus to public life. In the evolution of political progress, bad rulers are often a blessing in disguise. They help to stir a community into life, a result that years of agitation would perhaps have failed to achieve".

Partly because of the congenial rule of Ripon and partly for other reasons, the barometer of political activity, which had been rising during the seventies, now dropped considerably. The Bombay Association was already a spent force.

Dadabhai Naoroji seemed to be relaxing for a while. As a biographer observes, the period between 1877 and 1881 was the quietest in his life. Sarvajanik Kaka, who provided the Puna Sarvajanik Sabha with energy, was keeping bad health and passed away in 1880.

There were, of course, some other individuals like Vishnu Krishna Chiplunkar who twinkled in the serene sky of Maharashtra. After graduating in 1872, Chiplunkar joined the Education Department as a teacher. He did not find himself at ease there, feeling as though his soul were in bondage.

While yet in Government service, he brought out a monthly named Nibandha-Mala, in which he freely criticised the Government. His essay, "Our Country's Present Situation", published in one of the issues of his magazine, was, as the author of the History of Abhinav Bharat, Dr. V. M. Bhat, observed, "full of sedition and roused revolutionary tendencies in the minds of the younger generation".

Eventually, he resigned his post under the Government towards the end of 1879, and felt a sense of relief. After submitting his resignation, he wrote to his brother: "On the 1st of October, my chains will be broken off, and I shall be a happy man again".

Such was the state of Maharashtra when Tilak, a youth of 24, appeared on the scene, fired by a zeal for public service.

It was 1880. The curtain had fallen over Lytton's misrule, and a kindly hand had lulled the agitators to sleep.

An Indian Jesuit

The first chapter of Tilak's public life opened in the field of education which he entered with the zeal of a missionary. From his work as an educationist, we get a glimpse of his unbending spirit, his tenacity of purpose, his indomitable determination, and above all the fighter in him. Fortunately, Tilak has left a written account of this period, and this part of the story can profitably take an autobiographical form.

"It was in July or August of 1879, when I was living at the Deccan College for studying for the L. L. B. examination, that Messrs. G. G. Agarkar, B. A. Bhagwat, V. B. Karandikar and myself first discussed the importance and practicability of establishing private schools on the model of missionary institutions. There was no difference of opinion as to the necessity of native private enterprise in education; but the question was how to make it successful. Self-sacrifice was evidently the only means for men in our circumstances, and though we were prepared for it, yet various difficulties were raised and discussed, as for instance, quality of work, private gains, etc. Suffice it to say that after many a private and prolonged discussion the conclusion at which we arrived was that if we applied ourselves to the task with the determination of carrying out our idea at 'any sacrifice, it was not an' impossibility, though it might be long time before it could be accomplished. So enthusiastic were we that soon after Mr. Agarkar and myself wrote to a leading gentleman in the town that for bare maintenance, the highest estimate of which came up to Rs. 75 per mensem, we were prepared to devote ourselves to education, and that, if it were possible to raise funds that would yield the necessary income, we might soon undertake to give free education. The gentleman wrote to us in reply that, though our object was a laudable one, the public would not come to assistance until we were actually in the work and had done something. We were nothing disheartened for this, as we had determined to carry out our programme at 'any sacrifice. It was at the Stage of our discussion that we learnt that Mr. Vishnu Shastri Chip-lunkar had given up service, and was in Puna, intending to start a new school. All of us resolved to go to him, disclosed our scheme, and requested him to take the lead. He consented, and it was settled to start a school by the beginning of 1880.

Messrs. Bhagwat and Karandikar, however, had by this time, begun to doubt the success of the scheme, and the possibility of even earning a decent maintenance in the profession.

Mr. Vishnu Shastri did not, in consequence, mention any names in the prospectus which he published on behalf of himself and his colleagues on the 15th December, 1879. The same prudence restrained him from describing the objects of the institution in high words—the only object mentioned being to make education inexpensive. The subsequent events showed that he was justified in being so moderate.

Messrs. Bhagwat and Karandikar withdrew; and I am now glad that they did, though at the eleventh hour; and Mr. Agarkar, having got the senior Fellowship in the Deccan College, deferred joining us for a year; Vishnu Shastri and myself were the only persons then left to open the school (the New English School) on 1st January, 1880. It was at this time that Mr. Mahadev Ballal Namjoshi came to us. He had given up his business, and was in search of something else; and Mr. Vishnu Shastri promised to take him in against many a friendly warning. We knew, he said, what his weak points were, and knowing them we could use his energies to giving proper work to him.

"Our strength was equal to the task, but as several persons, and amongst them Mr. Vaman Shivaram Apte, whom I requested to join us, had declined to do so, we had to pull on somehow or other. At the beginning of the second term, I had nearly grown hopeless of enlisting more men in our cause, when circumstances brought in Mr. Apte, who had first refused. Our salaries were however, too low and Mr. Apte continued to be a paid teacher for some months with higher salary; and it was only after the assurance of Mr. Agarkar to the effect that he too intended to join us, that he permanently joined the body. The idea of supplementing his income by doing some other work was, however, uppermost in his mind.

"Such was our position by the beginning of 1881. Five of us had come together, though not from the same motive, to conduct a school. The work was rather heavy, and as everything had to be done anew, it put a great strain on the energies of all. Each man was given the work most suited to him. There were no outside interests yet created and every suggestion was made and received in good spirit.

Not that there were no discussions, and even hot discussions, but somehow everyone felt that all were working for a common end, and the result was always satisfactory. As regards pay the doctrine of jealous equality was not yet developed. Just as each was entrusted to do what he could do best, he was allowed such salary as was necessary for his maintenance, and as could be spared by the Board. Thus, for the first year, Vishnu Shastri and myself took almost nothing, while Messrs. Namjoshi and Apte were paid more than their due fare. Everything thus went on smoothly".

For a precise understanding of the causes that led to the shining success of the New English School, a brief acquaintance with the co-actors of Tilak is necessary. Vishnu Shastri Chiplunkar was the son of Krishnashastri, well known for his learning and erudition. His house was the favourite resort of the leading lights of Maharashtra. At the Deccan College, from which he took his B. A. degree in 1872, he was considered much above the average rate of students. He belonged to a school opposed to Ranade's and, instead of trying to introduce reforms, inspired by western ways of life, he thought the best way was to rouse people to a consciousness of their own religion and their own historical glory.

His example — resignation from Government service and criticism of the authorities in his monthly Nibandh-Mala had a stimulating effect on Tilak and Agarkar. But while Tilak held identical views on social reforms, Agarkar was diametrically opposed to them. "Neglected by relatives, occasionally insulted by those whose help he had to seek", he grew up in poverty and believed there was something wrong with society. Partly his early bitter memories and partly the convictions he developed later were responsible for his reformist leanings, which grew, and, as a subsequent chapter will show, became one of the causes of his acute differences with Tilak, who tenaciously clung to things purely Indian. A student of Logic and Moral Philosophy, Agarkar had lost much of his faith in religion. After passing his M. A. examination, an opportunity came his way to ward off poverty and lead a comfortable life. But he stuck to the mission of his life on which he had made up his mind in conjunction with Tilak, and wrote to his mother thus: "You may be waiting, mother dear, for your son to become an M. A. and lift you up from all the misery that haunts you. But I have decided to turn my back on money and happiness and dedicate my life to the service of the country".

Namjoshi was recommended to Tilak and his colleagues by Ranade. He had no academic career, but his "versatile powers, keen perception, sound experience and tactful, pushing nature more than compensated for his lack of higher education". His indefatigable energy and resourcefulness helped his colleagues get over many crises and they gave him the title of "our foreign secretary".

But Apte's approach greatly differed from that of his colleagues. He associated with the school largely as a paid servant. He had a creditable academic career, and immediately after doing his M. A., taken up the post of a headmaster in a Mission school. His ambition to enter the Education Department remained unfulfilled. He was offered by Government the modest post of an assistant master in an Anglo-Vernacular school, which he refused. The founders of the New English School found him to be a useful man for their institution, and appointed him as its superintendent.

In September, 1882, the Education Commission, recognising the importance of the school, afforded it an opportunity of placing its views before the Government. The management authorised Apte to give evidence on its behalf before the Commission. In his statement Apte said: "We have undertaken this work of popular education with the firmest conviction and belief that, of all agents of human civilization, education is the only one that brings about material, moral arid religious' regeneration of fallen countries and raises them up to the level of most advanced nations by slow and peaceful revolutions; and in order that this should be so it must be ultimately in the hands of the people themselves".

The Commission was much impressed with the way some enthusiasts were conducting the school in a spirit of self-sacrifice. Its President, Dr. William Hunter expressing his opinion about the school said: "Throughout the whole of India, I have not witnessed a single institution which can be compared with this establishment. This institution can rival arid compete with success not only with the Government High Schools in the country, but may favourably compare with the schools of other countries also". In 1884, when its percentage of passes in the Matriculation Examination reached 89, the Private Secretary to the Bombay Governor sent a letter of congratulations to the school authorities.

Now, to continue the autobiographical account, "It was our determination to devote ourselves to the work accepting only a bare maintenance. The phrase 'bare maintenance' is rather vague; so I must state what was our idea of it. Our highest estimate of the same, when we imposed this mission upon ourselves, never rose higher than Rs. 75 per month.

In our enthusiasm we went still further. We could well see that in the beginning we could not get even Rs. 40 per month. When it was asked how many would be content with what we might get, some withdrew from the project, Mr. Agarkar and myself still remaining firm. During the first years of the School, each of us could hardly get Rs. 30 or Rs. 35 per mensem".

The sacrifice and selflessness of the promoters of the institution bore fruit and it made rapid progress. The school was started with 19 boys, and by the end of January, 1885, there were about 1,200 students on the rolls. About 15 per cent free and half-free scholars were admitted, and there were monthly scholarships of the total value of Rs. 50, paid from the school proceeds. The school succeeded every year in securing at least one of the two University Jagannath Shankar Sheth Sanskrit Scholarships.

There were in those days many Christian missionaries working in India for the advancement of literacy and education. There were differences of opinion as to their real motive, but their steadfast devotion to the cause of education had an inspiring effect on Tilak and his colleagues. In the town of Puna alone, the missionaries had established a network of schools: The Free Church Mission Girls' Vernacular School, Bishop's High School, St. Vincent Roman Catholic High School, the Free Church Mission Institution, the Mission Orphanage and the Christian Boys' Middle Class, St. Mary's Girls' High School, the Zanana Mission Anglo-Vernacular School for Girls, the Free Church Mission Anglo-Vernacular Boys' School.

Before Tilak entered the field of education, a feeling had been growing that Christian missionaries, though seemingly benevolent, had virtually become masters of the education of Puna children. The missionaries' conversion activities were very mild, and they met with little success. Nevertheless, there was resentment, and religious-minded, self-respecting Indians felt the want of a national system of education. The New English School, in a way, was considered as a counterblast to the mission schools.

Six Years in Exile — Wife's Death and Extinction of Extremist Party

Tilak was yet confined to the Sabarmati gaol but the decision to send him to Burma had already been taken. A Home Department note advised against sending Tilak to Mandalay as that place, the note suggested, was associated "with lenient treatment of Lajpat Rai". The Home Member of the Government of India thought Insein jail, ten miles from Rangoon, to be "the most suitable". But it had a damp climate, and he said that "if Tilak's complaint, which I understand is diabetes, requires a dry climate, I am afraid there is no large suitable jail in Burma except Mandalay". The choice therefore fell on Mandalay.

On September 14, in the morning, Tilak was put on board the R.I.M.S. Habdinge for Rangoon. That was the last day of the Ganpati festival. There was great enthusiasm at Belgaum, and the police authorities issued certain orders to regulate the celebrations. These were duly obeyed. But in the afternoon, an oral order was made prohibiting shouting of slogans like "Vande Mataram", "Tilak Maharaj ki jai", and "Shivaji Maharaj ki jai". But as this new order was not embodied in the proclamation made earlier, it was disregarded by processionists. The police construed this attitude as defiance of orders, and thrashed several boys and beat up others.

Seventeen persons were arrested, and the carts carrying the idols of Ganapati and effigy of Tilak were detained. The carts were allowed to go after Tilak's effigy had been removed.

In the State of Limbdi, the police prohibited sale of Tilak's photographs. All the copies in possession of a student were seized, and he was asked not to sell in future Tilak's or any political leader's pictures. Every shopkeeper in the town of Limbdi was compelled to remove Tilak's portrait from his premises.

There was a word of sympathy everywhere for Tilak's family, but few came forward to render real help. In the first week of September 1908, a women's meeting was held in Bombay for the purpose of expressing feelings of sympathy towards Mrs. Tilak in her mental distress. About 700 ladies participated in the meeting, among them being three or four Muslim ladies in purdah. The meeting, which was presided over by a leader of the Swadeshi movement in the Punjab, Mrs. Sarla Devi, passed a resolution consoling Mrs. Tilak. On September 21, a week after Tilak's departure for Rangoon, the newspaper offices received after midnight an official communication informing them that the sentence of transportation passed on Tilak had been commuted by the Bombay Government to one of simple imprisonment "in consideration of his age and condition of health", and that the fine of Rs. 1,000 had been remitted. This seemingly merciful order deprived Tilak of some of the advantages accruing to a transportee, who was entitled to greater remission. A transportee lived in perfect freedom in the Andamans after furnishing some security; but Tilak had to pass six long years in a room measuring 20 x 12 feet. In vain did he once again represent to the authorities against this revengeful mercy.

In October, 1909, on account of an outbreak of cholera in the Mandalay jail, he was removed to Meiktila prison for a brief period.

On August 7, while he was yet in the Sabarmati gaol, a petition was made to the Full Bench of the Bombay High Court for permission to appeal to the Privy Council, but it was refused. This was followed by another petition to the Judicial Committee of the Privy Council for special leave to appeal, but that too was dismissed. A third attempt was made.

This time, a petition was drafted for presentation to the House of Lords asking that the order of the Judicial Committee might be reviewed by the Magisterial Council of the Peers in Parliament "to the end that by a presentation to the King justice might be done. But as the projected petition necessitated its presentation by a Peer, a memorial was presented to the Secretary of State for India by a solicitor of Tilak. Among the grounds of the appeal, the most conspicuous was that the "evils of the trial were aggravated by the fact that it was the trial of a political offence in the most populous province of the Empire where the liberty of the subjects was not yet provided with those safeguards which had long existed in the United Kingdom. The solicitor demanded "that the unlawful sentences passed upon Tilak may, either by a pardon or by a remission, be reduced to the proportion which they would have been if there had been a fair trial".

The Government of Bombay through whom the petition was submitted returned it saying that it should be addressed to the King Emperor of India. And when the instruction was carried out, the solicitor, E. Dalgado of London, got this reply from the India Office: "Your petition to the King on behalf of Bal Gangadhar Tilak has been laid before His Majesty, who has been pleased to direct that it should be referred to the Secretary of State for India, who regrets that he has been unable to advise His Majesty to accede to your prayer".

Early in May, 1909, Tilak's principal lieutenant, G. S. Khaparde, who was in London then, wrote to him asking whether he would agree to conditional release. Tilak turned down the suggestion; he would prefer death in jail to living outside like a dead man. In his reply to Khaparde (May 29, 1909), he said:

"I have received your kind letter dated 6th instant on 28th instant the question, viz, whether I would accept any conditions and if so what, is indeed an awkward one".

"I shall tell you my mind about the acceptance of any conditions. If the conditions are the same as those offered to me in 1898, I would not hesitate to accept them. I do not care for demonstrations and such other honours. I would gladly forgo them. But once out of jail, I must have the same liberty of action as every citizen enjoys under the law of the land. That was secured to me by the conditions of 1898, and I accepted them in consequence. But I do not think the same conditions would be offered now. They will, if offered at all, be harsher now; and I do not see how I can accept them. I have now nearly completed one year of my punishment, and after five years more I shall be, at any rate I hope to be, amongst you as a free citizen. Do you think I should surrender this chance, distant as it is, by voluntarily incapacitating me (by the acceptance of the conditions) for any public or political work for ever?

"I am already 53 years. If heredity and average health be any indication of the longevity of a man, I do not hope to live at best for more than ten years more. Of these five, say, are available for unrestrained public work, which, if I accept any condition of the kind you mention, I shall have to live as a dead man. To say the least I do not like that kind of life".

It is true that my activity is not confined to politics; and I can do literary work even if I be prohibited from taking part in politics. I have considered this view fully, and have come to the conclusion that it is inconsistent with all my antecedents.

In fact I shall be undoing my life's work thereby. You know that I have never lived exclusively for my family or for myself alone, but have always endeavoured to do my duty to the public. Now judge what would be the moral effect of my effacing myself from public life, for the sake of five years' personal comfort.

"From these remarks you might think that I may accept a condition imposing restriction on my public activity for a short time, say, six months or a year after my release. But I shall rather like to be in jail for that period than be out a disabled man. The stun total of the above remarks is that I would like to be a free citizen as soon as released. The Government have already secured power to keep me out of public work for five years more and it will be quid pro quo and not mercy if, by releasing me now, they secure my permanent abstention from public activity".

On his return from Mandalay in 1914, Tilak did not have a word of complaint about living conditions in jail. But Subhash Chandra Bose, who was lodged in the same prison in 1925, says: "I often used to think and wonder how in those circumstances Lokamanya could go in for prolonged intellectual work for over five years. Only one who had attained complete self-mastery, who was altogether indifferent to pleasure and pain and heat and cold, could rise above such dismal surroundings. Lokamanya was all alone in that horrid cage—the only society that he could get was the none too desirable company of the jail officials whenever they dropped in. Even the ordinary prisoners of the jail were not allowed to associate with him.

"Even in small matters Lokamanya's freedom inside jail was restricted. He could not have had more than two books at a time. His correspondence was subjected to censorship. When he had interviews with his people or with Mr. Khaparde officials used to be present, the conversation would be followed closely and he would be pulled up at times. All these pinpricks must have told severely on his sensitive mind".

"In this connection I am reminded of an anecdote. A certain Government official came to see Lokamanya in prison and said, 'How are you, Tilak?' The omission of the prefix 'Mr. was too much for Tilak and in a rage he went for the official. The official was first taken aback for he did not expect to find such a keen sense of self-respect in a prisoner, but he ultimately got out of the scrape by apologising'.

Tilak was fond of gardening and there are trees which exist today which are reported to have been planted by him.

"He was suffering from diabetes and had to adhere to a very rigid diet. I have heard from the officer who was in charge of the jail at that time that he lived practically on barley or on wheat. He was allowed to receive ghee from his people, but hardly anything else. A Marathi-speaking convict was sent to Mandalay from an Indian jail, and he used to cook for Lokamanya.

"I still wonder how in those circumstances Lokamanya Tilak could produce a magnificent work like Gita-Rahasya".

Tilak was entitled to an interview every three months and when, in December, 1908, two of his relatives went all the way from Puna to Mandalay to avail themselves of the first interview, they were deeply disappointed. The time allowed them was so short that they were left wondering whether it was at all an interview. They had, however, the satisfaction that they had seen him, and would at least be in a position to tell his dear ones that he was in good spirits. He was not allowed to write private letters, and there was no communication between him and his family. He was allowed no newspapers. For six years, he did not know what was happening in the world outside the Mandalay Central Jail.

And, poor Mrs. Tilak; she was in good health but domestic worries and constant anxiety about her ailing husband overpowered her courage and fortitude, and she died early in June, 1912. The news was conveyed to Tilak by telegram by his nephew, Dhondo Pant When he read the telegram, there were hardly any signs of grief on his face. He immediately sat down to write a letter (dated June 8, 1912). In this letter, which was allowed to be delivered, he said:

Your wire was a very great and heavy blow. I am used to take my misfortunes calmly; but I confess that the present shook me considerably. According to the beliefs ingrained in us it is not undesirable that the wife should die before her husband. What grieved me most is my enforced absence from her side at this critical time. But this was to be, I always feared it, and it has at last happened. One chapter of my life is closed and I am afraid it won't be long before another will be.

The task of looking after the physical and intellectual development of my sons falls on you now with greater responsibility. Let them remember that I was left an orphan when I was much younger than either of them. See that their time is not lost in useless grief. The inevitable must be faced boldly".

Tilak in jail was a greater hero than outside and revolutionaries both in India and abroad constantly used his name to inspire young men. They were asked to emulate him and to make a more determined attempt to strike at the British authority.

After the announcement of judgement in the Tilak case, Shyamji Krishna Varma, one of the pioneers of the Indian revolutionary movement in England and who was inspired by Tilak's suffering and sacrifice, started in London his famous paper, the Indian Sociologist, which carried on, for a long time, propaganda against the British rule. He was later joined by scores of others, and after the arrival of Har Dayal, that celebrated leader of the Ghadar movement during the first World War, Indian revolutionaries were to be found working against the British in many countries, and preparing for an armed revolt in India.

In India, a number of political workers, suspected of association with Tilak, were arrested. Members of the All India Volunteer League were harassed and victimised. Some of them were taken into' custody. Tilak was president of this organisation, although, on account of his preoccupation with other activities, he was able to do pretty little for it.

In the Central Provinces, Tilak's imprisonment was used as an incentive to bring into being several secret organisations, the chief among them being the Arya Bandhav Samaj. The aim of the Samaj was "to drive out the British by war, by collecting a secret army of thousands of Indian young men".

It reminded its members of the teachings of the Gita: "If you are killed in war, you will go to heaven. If you survive, you will rule the earth". Members of the Samaj invited Muslims to join; and some actually were enrolled. Hindus were encouraged to take part in Muslim festivals and fraternise with that community.

In the city of Hoshiarpur (Punjab), Amarnath, an admirer and follower of Tilak, started a paper to propagate his views; the paper was named Tilak. The first issue of the paper appeared in April, 1909, and in June it was suppressed. The press was also confiscated. The district magistrate in his order said: "The Tilak is a menace to the public peace; the paper, which is extremely scurrilous, finds a ready sale in Lahore and elsewhere".

In many places, a number of organisations were started and called after his name. His speeches and writings were published in several Indian languages. In the Punjab, that enterprising and courageous leader, Sufi Amba Prasad, published an Urdu version of them and suffered for this act.

Political advance in the constitutional sphere was, however, halted; nay, it received a setback. At the Congress sessions, there was now greater display of loyalty to the British Government. In a speech he made at Puna in July, 1909, Gokhale urged loyal cooperation with the British rule for two reasons: "One that, considering the difficulties of the position, Britain had done very well in India, the other that there was no alternative to British rule and could be none for a long time.... They could proceed in two directions; first, towards an obliteration of distinctions, on ground of race, between individual Indians and individual Englishmen, and secondly, by way of advance towards the form of government enjoyed in other parts of the Empire. The latter is an ideal for which the Indian people have to qualify themselves, for the whole question turns on character and capacity, and they must realise that their main difficulties lie with themselves".

Again at Bombay, in October of the same year, he told the Students' Brotherhood: "The active participation of students in political agitation really tends to lower the dignity and the responsible character of public life and impair its true effectiveness".

This was undoing what Tilak was attempting to do. At the Congress of 1909, even his name was not mentioned. The authorities had already wiped out the Extremists a year before.

In December, 1908, they were to hold the first meeting of the Extremist Congress at Nagpur, and while announcing it its promoters repudiated an archist cult. But the Chief Commissioner of the Central Provinces disallowed the meeting, under Section 144 of the Criminal Procedure Code. The reception committee asked for an opportunity to explain its position and enquired the reason for the official attitude. No answer was given.

A more stringent law, the Criminal Law Amendment Act, was enacted and some workers of the Extremist Party were arrested and deported without trial. Of the two principal lieutenants of Tilak in the Party, Aurobindo quietly left British territory and engaged himself in spiritual pursuits, and BC Pal proceeded on a tour of Europe. Thus, ended the Extremist Party so assiduously built up by Tilak.

The End: The man who calculated the age of the Vedas also calculated nearly precisely the span of his life. In 1909, in a letter he wrote to his friend Khaparde from the Mandalay jail, he casually said: " If heredity and average health be any indication of the longevity of a man, I do not hope to live at best for more than ten years". Eight or nine years later, his health began to fail, and he once said in a moment of exhaustion: "People cannot possibly realise that I feel so weak. When the moment comes, I lecture. But the body is all the while breaking under the strain. The lecture over, I retire from the crowds and sleep over my fatigue. Only my will supports me. The body is done in".

In 1920, in the month of July, he had a severe attack of malaria. But he soon recovered and proceeded to Bombay to appear in the Tai Maharaj Case, which, in one form or other, continued to worry him for two decades. There a drive along the seashore brought him a chill which developed into high fever. None, however, expected the worst, and in celebration of his sixty-fourth birthday, public meetings were held and congratulations poured in from all over the country.

From Monday, July 26, his fever took a serious turn and he developed signs of pneumonia; the base of his right lung was affected. The whole of Tuesday was a day of anxiety.

Friends and relatives gathered round his bed. But he was cheerful, and chaffed his son for having come to Bombay on this pretence and his daughters upon being rather too fond of their parents home. And when someone asked him if he would like to leave any instructions regarding his affairs, he said, "I am not going to die these five years, be sure of that".

On Wednesday morning, his temperature was normal and pulse regular. This was a happy sign. He asked for plain water, and the doctors gave him water mixed with sugar.

He remarked jocularly that the Bombay Corporation might be suffering from diabetes to offer only sweet water. The diabetes patient for twenty years now lacked in sugar! There was also a complication in the stomach, which began to be-distended, and, with great difficulty, the doctors led him out of the crisis.

At this stage, when he was desperately struggling for life, a copy of the Gita was brought to him, and he uttered his favourite verses.

The next three days were very critical. He lost consciousness and became delirious. On Tuesday at about 5 pm, he had an attack of angina pectoris which threatened to be serious and fatal, but the doctors' timely efforts again pulled him out of the danger.

In his delirium, he frequently spoke of his country's poverty, about the Congress and about Swaraj — "Has the Special been arranged? Have you wired to Mr. Patel? Five hundred rupees to the editor, plus motor allowance! What will these lordlings do for the country? He murmured of the Punjab wrong. Often he got excited, as in his speeches, and talked wildly. As if this dying leader was for the last time inspiring his people, he repeated several times — "1818-1918, one hundred years, what a life of servitude!" His last words were: "Unless Swaraj is achieved, India will not prosper. It is required for our existence". And he spoke no more.

On Friday and the whole of Saturday, he continued in a state of unconsciousness with an uncertain and irregular pulse and a weak heart at 10-30 on Saturday night, his heart began to show signs of exhaustion and his breathing became hard. After midnight, the lingering hope began to vanish fast, and at 12-50, the doctors announced that "the Lokamanya is no more". His sons, daughters and grandchildren and a host of friends and admirers, who had passed long hours by his bedside, burst into a fit of sobbing. There was a drizzle of rain, the night was dark and the giant city of Bombay lay asleep, not knowing the disaster that had overtaken it.

Never before in the history of Bombay had such a scene of universal grief been witnessed. People began to flock to Sardar Graha, where the departed leader had been staying, from 7 in the morning and by 8 the surroundings were so thickly crowded that the late-corners had to go back disappointed, without having a glimpse of his remains. Then the body of the Lokamanya was brought out and put on the balcony so that it could be seen by the crowds from a distance.

At 2 pm, an hour after the scheduled time, the funeral procession, about a mile and a half long, started from the Sardar Graha. A conservative estimate put the figure of the mourners at two lakhs. It was a cosmopolitan gathering of all communities and classes.

Tilak was a Brahmin, and some of his friends and relatives decided that only Brahmins should lift the bier. When Gandhi came forward and bent low to lift the bier, someone tried to obstruct him. Gandhi stood up for a moment and said, "Public men know no caste". He bent down again; and lifted one end of the bier. The convention was broken, and their bier was in turn shouldered by Shaukat Ali and Dr. Kitchlew along its route to Chowpatty.

The longest funeral procession (according to the Indian Social Reformer) "witnessed in Bombay was that of Dadabhai Naoroji. But Tilak's totally eclipsed it. Most of those who followed Dadabhai's remains to the Tower of Silence were English-educated men". But the vast multitude which accompanied Tilak's bier consisted not only of educated people but of men from all walks of life.

At sundown, the body was placed on the pyre of sandalwood on the sands of Chowpatty. Once again, there were loud sobs. And as the flames consuming the mortal remains of the great leader leapt up, thousands of voices were raised:

"Tilak Maharaj ki jai; Tilak is immortal".

The Demise

Tilak was so disappointed by the brutal incident of Jalianwala Bagh massacre that his health started declining. Despite his illness, Tilak issued a call to the people not to stop their movement no matter what happened. He was ready to lead the movement but his health did not permit him. Tilak had become very weak by that time. In mid-July 1920, his condition worsened and on August 1, he passed away. As soon as this sad news spread, a veritable ocean of people surged to his house. Over 2 lakhs people gathered at his residence in Bombay to have the last glimpse of their beloved leader.

The Legacy

After Tilak's death on August 1, 1920, on the first day of Gandhi's first non-cooperation campaign, Gandhi paid his respects at his cremation in Mumbai, along with 20 people. Mahatma Gandhi called Tilak "The Maker of Modern India". The court which convicted Tilak bears a plaque that says, "The actions of Tilak have been justified as the right of every individual to fight for his country".

2

A Leader in the Making

A significant event prompted Tilak's rise in political arena. Early in 1890, the retiring Governor of Bombay, Lord Reay, figured rather prominentiy in the press of the Presidency. He was to be given a warm sendoff and efforts were being made to perpetuate his memory. One section of the press was critical of his administration while, the other was all praise. Among the latter was the Kesari, which, in its issue dated March 25, 1890, said: "Whatever the traducers of Lord Reay may say to the contrary, it must be admitted that though His Lordship might have committed a few mistakes, yet the Bombay Presidency has, without doubt, made much advance during his administration, which has been such as to be for ever remembered for the various good tracts evinced therein by His Excellency, such as zeal for public interests, a leaning towards popular rights and privileges, regard for public opinion, thorough watchfulness of disposition in private. Lord Reay will shortly retire from office, and it is the duty of the public to show its regard and gratefulness to His Excellency and to raise a suitable memorial to him with united exertions".

But the other section of the press maintained that the Reay Government was found wanting in justice in the case of Mamlatdars, and the Governor did not deserve any felicitations. Although Tilak's papers had been more critical of the Government than others, he could not ignore the fact that Governor Reay had shown extraordinary courage by setting up a Commission of Enquiry against Crawford in the teeth of bitter opposition from his officers and the entire Anglo-Indian press. Therefore, at the Provincial Conference, Tilak spoke in support of the resolution which "gratefully appreciated the conduct of the Government of Bombay and congratulated it on having done its duty by vindicating the purity of public services and removing the cause of a long-standing scandal". Tilak knew that it was the Government of India which, in spite of all pleadings of the Bombay Government, stood in the way of the Mamlatdars' reinstatement.

The following comment of the Bakul, a Marathi weekly of Ratnagiri, typifies the tone of criticism adopted by the opposition press: "What business has the Provincial Conference to pass this laudatory resolution? Those who were in charge of the resolution have taken upon themselves a serious responsibility. Are they prepared to defend the Bombay Government in all the proceedings of the Crawford Case? But we are not much surprised at the people of Puna. Those who dismissed the Secretary of the Puna Sarvajanik Sabha for having had talks with Mr. Crawford are capable of bringing before the Conference a resolution whitewashing the local Government!"

The Crawford episode was followed by another controversy. Lord Reay was succeeded by Lord Harris, and the Bombay Provincial Conference decided to present an address of welcome to the new Governor, who accepted to receive it.

There was jubilation in political circles, and elaborate preparations were set afoot. After long deliberations and longer discussions, the draft of address was prepared and then circulated to the office-bearers and principal members of the Conference. In the meantime, the Governor cancelled the engagement. The immediate cause of cancellation was the Conference Secretary Namjoshi's failure to keep an appointment with the Governor. Namjoshi had his difficulties, and as the Mahratta (dated June 29, 1890) remarked, "the number of serious workers" in the Conference was "very small, and one or two persons had generally to bear the whole burden". The cancellation caused deep disappointment and the press variously commented upon it. Some papers, like the

Prated '(June 30) showed extraordinary courage by asserting that "in declining to receive the address of the Conference, Lord Harris has shown disrespect to the people of the Deccan and thereby hurt their feelings. For this act of childishness, the people are likely to hate Lord Harris".

Others like the Phoenix (July 2) censured Namjoshi for his irresponsible behaviour. The Pratod, older than the Kesari was a very fearless paper of Maharashtra, and in later years, its editor suffered imprisonment.

At the 1890 Political Conference, Tilak transcended the limit which convention had set on speeches and proposed a resolution condemning the excise policy of the Bombay Government and demanding adoption of the principle of local option. He gave facts and figures to prove that consumption of liquor was on the increase, and challenged the Government statement which sought to make out a case that it was taking all possible efforts to discourage the drink habit. He suggested that power to start or close a liquor shop should vest in municipalities, local boards or village panchayats and not in the Excise Department whose one job was to increase the revenue of the state year after year.

The new vigour that he introduced into his speech at the Conference was kept up, and on September 28, the Mahratta editorially commented: "While there has been a good deal of tall talk on our part through Congresses and Conferences, and a great deal of rosy assurances from rulers of the land, little has been really achieved during the past six years, either by way of political or industrial prosperity. The attitude of the various local Governments with regard to the question of the working of the jury system in India was the subject of comment throughout the press of the country not long ago. We have had a number of despatches on the question of the enlargement of the basis of nomination and representation on the Legislative Council, but the question still hangs fire, and it is uncertain whether we shall have anything tangible in that direction in the definite future.

Next December, the Indian National Congress will enter upon its sixth year, but what demand of the people has been granted? The answer is very discouraging".

Within a year of his participation in the deliberations of the Political Conference, Tilak made an impression on the members as a leader in the making and was elected as one of the secretaries, which office he occupied for several consecutive years, the other two secretaries being Dinshaw E. Wacha and Chimanlal H. Setalwad. In 1891, it seemed as if the Conference was completely under his thumb.

One of the items of the agenda was the much-discussed Age of Consent Bill, and since it was a highly controversial measure, a suggestion was mooted by some that Puna should not be the venue of the Conference that year. But Tilak, with the following of the majority of delegates put his foot down and eventually, the Conference, as usual, met there. In the city of Puna, the delegates were elected by municipal wards; this democratic procedure was adopted in order to bring home to the Government the attitude of the people at large towards the Age of Consent Bill. And when Tilak rose to move the resolution on the Bill, there were spontaneous gestures of approval, and an overwhelming majority of the delegates voted for it.

Ever since the Bombay Provincial Conference came into existence, Puna had been the venue of its annual meeting, and this fact led many to declare that the Bombay Provincial Conference was in reality a Maharashtra conference. The assertion was not wholly untrue because at the annual gatherings, while the Maharashtrian districts were over-represented, others were either represented inadequately or went completely unrepresented. The proceedings of the Conference were conducted in Marathi, which again gave cause for complaint. The representative character of the Conference was questioned by several journals, but as one of them, the Gujarati, said for this the promoters were not to blame.

They sent invitations to the leading citizens in each district, and did what they could to secure adequate representation of all districts. An important province like Gujarat, the paper observed, sends no representative at all. This indeed is very discouraging and shows in a convincing manner how its people are apathetic in political as in other matters.

At the 1891 Conference, which was again held at Puna, the speeches and resolutions made an advance in tone and tenor.

They brought to the fore the sufferings of the people in a more direct form than at the previous gatherings. The resolution on salt tax asked the Government to so amend the definition of the word "manufacture" in the Salt Act as to exclude all processes of cleaning and purifying from the scope of the Act. A graphic picture was presented of how the poor people had been put to great hardship and were liable to come into the clutches of law if they simply cleansed and purified impure salt for domestic purposes.

Another resolution expressed regret at the oppressive policy of the Government in imposing harsh restrictions on free grazing in open forest areas. But as is apparent from a comment on the Conference of 1891, Tilak was not satisfied with the pace of political progress:

> "The rulers apparently hold that the suggestions which the people make about administrative reforms are impracticable. We hold otherwise, and unless we strengthen our case each year, it is impossible that solutions of the several administrative problems can be brought nearer".

Beginning of a Political Career

A year before he actually resigned from the Deccan Education Society, it had become clear to Tilak that it would be impossible for him to stay in that organisation without compromising his principles. His resolve to devote his life to the service of the country was irrevocable, and therefore, early in 1889, when his differences with his colleagues began to touch breaking point, he decided to take part in politics. On the 17th day of March, he got an opportunity of working for the Indian National Congress. On that day a public meeting was held to press the claim of Puna to be the venue of the year's Congress.

Tilak and Namjoshi were selected to contact the leaders of Bombay, which had already been nominated as the host of the coming Congress, and to induce them to retire in favour of Puna. But Bombay was adamant, and the next best thing that Tilak and his colleagues did was to collect a sum of Rs. 10,000 as Puna's contribution to the Bombay Congress two months later, in May,

1889, was held the second annual session of the Bombay Provincial Conference. The Conference had come into existence only a year before. A renowned educationist and journalist, Tilak was well known in the public life of Puna, and he participated in the Conference as one of the front-rank leaders.

The Conference was a mild, innocuous body. But if it lacked political fervour, there was none in the country which had a programme of progressive politics. A very modest constitutional agitation had recently begun in the country, and if Hume accelerated its speed in one year, in the next it was pushed back by the reactionary attitude of certain rulers. The constitutionalists had established a convention of loyalty to the British Crown, and therefore, no political organisation or individual ever said that the British were foreigners and that the British rule should be replaced by Indian. To say so would have constituted, as Tilak himself remarked in later years, sedition. But while the Bombay Provincial Conference played the same humble role in early years as any other organisation in the country did, it took up popular causes and carried on campaigns. It was a new development in India's public life.

One of the resolutions adopted by the Conference in 1889 protested against the excise policy of the Bombay Government. Since continued pursuance of this policy eventually compelled Tilak to launch a Temperance Movement in 1908, it is necessary to give a brief account of the agitation carried on in the Bombay Presidency and in India generally.

Every week some journals, as if by turn, appealed to the Government to restrict the sale of liquor, but, on the contrary year after year, more shops were being opened by the authorities. The question assumed national importance, and in 1888 the Congress passed a resolution saying "that, having regard to the fact that a serious increase in the consumption of intoxicants has taken place under the system of Abkari and Excise now prevailing in India, the Government be respectfully urged to adopt some such improved system as shall tend to discourage insobriety".

In 1889, the House of Commons advised the Government of India to take into account the popular feelings in framing its excise policy. The Government accordingly caused a despatch to be published in the Gazette of India, dated March 1, 1890, in which it was laid down as a policy that local opinion would be given due consideration. But the provincial governments conveniently ignored the despatch and continued to make liquor even more easily available, if only to add to their revenues. Again and again the press, the Provincial Conference and the Congress had been urging upon the attention of the authorities that "stringent measures should be taken by the Government in granting licences to retain liquor shops and that no such shops should be established anywhere without taking the sense of the inhabitants of the place. But the resolutions of these bodies were not backed by any practical agitation, and the Bombay Government like some other provincial administrations went its own way. It was not prepared to forego a considerable portion of revenue from excise.

In the nineteenth century, and in fact up to the Partition of Bengal which engendered a new spirit, protestations in carefully guarded language were considered enough. So, is keeping with the tradition, the other resolutions which the Bombay Provincial Conference of 1889 passed (i) proposed certain amendments, based on the principles of local self-government in the Bombay Village Sanitation Bill; (ii) deprecated the policy of Government as regards education; (iii) demanded reduction in the salt tax; (iv) recommended that higher appointments in the police service should be opened to Indians; (v) urged the Secretary of State for India to extend the tenure of office of the Bombay Governor, Lord Reay, who was much better than his predecessors there and counterparts in other provinces.

The leading men of the Presidency pursued the last resolution, and held public meetings in different places to eulogise his service to Bombay. Decisions were taken to perpetuate Eeay's name as one of the most righteous and enlightened rulers India has had.

Such was the political life in Maharashtra when its poor helplessly murmured against the salt tax, and the political organisations only passed resolutions. But an Englishman named R. D. Rusden was so much moved by the burden that this tax caused those living in grinding poverty in India that he wrote from Manchester a very angry letter to the editor of the Mahratta which that paper published in its issue dated July 21, 1889, and which nearly landed the editor in gaol. The letter has a great historical value in as much as it completely anticipated, by its revolutionary suggestions, the Salt Satyagraha of Gandhi which came off four decades later.

The letter, headed the "Salt Tax", said:

"I am very glad indeed that the Provincial Congress has taken up the Salt Tax question. I hope as a consequence of that to hear of an important and if possible exhaustive discussion of that matter in the next Congress; in fact, it is only there that it can be properly discussed and with that complete knowledge which produces conviction. At a distance, where thousands of minor facts and many practical matters are of necessity unknown and even unsuspected, it is not possible to discuss such a question fully, and it often seems to me like a piece of conceit or presumption on my part to write about it at all whilst so many men in India must be so much more capable and so much better informed; but then they will not speak, and if these big dogs absolutely refused to bark, it is evident that even the 'thrice mewing of the Blinded Cat' may rise to the dignity of a public voice and prove of some small public value.

I should think your 'policy' as regards the salt tax should be to agitate for its total extinction as opposed to mere 'reduction'—that is what our anti-corn law men did and you know they won in the end.

I think the time has come to say to the Government: This is an abominable tax; we don't want any reductions; it is wrong in principle; it falls most severely on the most poor, it is a tax on a necessity of life, whatever salt tax the ryot pays he eats so much less salt in consequence. A large proportion of what is called death by famine is really murder by salt tax; the whole thing is hateful and shameful and scandalous, and we insist upon the sweeping away of the tax; and if you do not repeal it, we will try and make it so hot and disagreeable for you that before long you will have to drop it whether you like it or not. Speak clearly in this way; never mind your loyalty which some of you think a good deal too much about throw it to the dogs; 'loyalty' to a Government that imposes a salt tax is only another word for neglect of the most vital interests of the people; speak clearly then and emphasise your words by organising a 'plan of campaign' against the salt tax. You cannot, it is true, boycott the use of salt whatever its price, but you advise your people to avoid the tax by preparing their own salt, wherever the presence of salt earth or salt water enables them to do so, and you can encourage them to do this by raising funds for their protection and defence in case of need, and I think other ways of action in this line will suggest themselves to you by which you could raise such a buzzing around the ears of the Government and such a disagreeable state of mind among 100 millions of your people that the Governors of India would be compelled to attend to it. As I have often written, it's no use going to a Government with a plea of justice.

They know all about that, the principles of justice are like the principles of Christianity, very well-known, but never acted on, certainly not by Government, but go to them and show by good evidence that unless a certain course is taken there will be danger for the 'Rulers'. See how quickly they change and how very dear some hitherto quite neglected interests become to them. And yet they are not villains, by no means, they are only men. But such is man. Don't let us despise him, poor fellow. He has got a lot to do and only 60 or 70 years to learn to do it in, no wonder that his mind seldom gets more than half formed and that he makes such a mess of most things".

The Government of India took a serious view of the letter and called for legal opinion of the Advocate-General whether a prosecution of the editor of the Mahratta could be launched.

The Advocate-General, in a long note, carefully examined the article, and said that there was no room to doubt that it was capable of inciting disaffection and rebellion against the Government and that prosecution, if launched, should succeed. Later, it was thought that the prosecution was likely to serve the purpose of the writer more than the Government's, for the Mahratta, unlike the Kesari, was not a widely circulated weekly.

If we picture before our mind's eye the political leaders of those days and their activities, we may safely conclude that none would have come forward to organise a no-tax campaign like the one suggested by Rusden; none perhaps except Tilak would have had the courage to publish a letter which suggested a rebellion.

The Provincial Conference, as other organisations, was aware of the hardship caused to the poor by the salt tax, and protested against it. But action, like the one suggested by Rusden, was considered beyond the pale of practical politics.

How could those religiously adopting resolutions of loyalty to the Queen adopt a course leading up to rebellion? But in the Provincial Conference. Tilak found a body through which he could gradually convert people to 'extremism' of the kind advocated by Rusden. Some years later, it was the Provincial Conference whose active workers actually manned Tilak's Extremist Party.

First Imprisonment

Other chance, not of his seeking, introduced Tilak into journalism. Hardly had the School completed one year and made itself self-supporting when some of its sponsors thought of starting an English and a Marathi weekly. The suggestion was mooted by Chiplunkar and Namjoshi, the former had already made a name as the fearless editor of the Nibandh-Mala, and the latter also owned and edited a paper called the Deccan Star. Namjoshi's press was in a bad way, and had been mortgaged with one Sathe. Tilak was indifferent to the new proposal, but when it was avidly put forward by others, he agreed to cooperate. There was no money to buy a press, but Namjoshi got Sathe to agree to part with his press on the condition that payment would be made by instalments. The possession of a press was considered a great achievement and within a few hours after the bargain had been struck, the new owners themselves carried the entire establishment to the School premises. In his later life, Tilak referring to this incident, used to say that he had carried the type cases on his shoulders.

They all seemed to be in a tearing hurry and without loss of time, preparations were started for publishing the two papers. "At Apte's invitation", says Tilak, "Namjoshi's Star was converted into Maratha" It appeared under its new name on January 2, 1881. Two days later the Marathi weekly, Kesari saw the light of day.

The papers were jointly conducted by Chiplunkar, Tilak, Agarkar and Namjoshi; for the editing, Tilak and Agarkar were made mainly responsible. Although the papers belonged to an educational institution, they began to evoke within a few weeks of their appearance, a keen interest in politics. A few samples, quoted below from their early issues give an idea of their courageous writing. In the very first year of their publication, they were described in official records as "unfriendly to Government". They dealt also with literature, religion, law, history and economics but Tilak mostly wrote on religion, law and political issues, but what put them ahead of their contemporaries was their tone when they wrote on Indian States and criticised Government measures.

In dealing with Indian States, the writers were actuated by a feeling of affection and regard; the States were considered remnants of the indigenous rule of which large parts of the country had been deprived by the British.

The Kesari, in its issue dated March 15, 1881, expressed its concern at the contemplated destruction of 400 guns belonging to the Gaikwad of Baroda, as a precautionary measure. "It is difficult to understand", said the paper, "what makes the Government afraid of such guns of inferior workmanship in the possession of the Native Princes. Is this the sort of confidence reposed in their integrity and loyalty? If the people are really disloyal, is this the sort of punishment to be dealt out to them? If another rebellion should really take place in India, would the rebel leaders find any difficulty in providing themselves with guns? It is not meet that the Government should in this way unnecessarily alienate the hearts of the people".

The Mahratta, after deploring in earlier issues the Government of India's decision to defray the costs of the Afghan War out of Indian revenues, the Viceregal visits to the heights of Shimla, the Arms Act, etc. wrote in its issue dated April 24, 1881: "Students of history who have with a careful eye watched the progress of the English in India and studied their relations with Native Princes must have observed that the so-called paramount power has on every occasion made an attempt at thrusting itself on the Native Princes and by some political trick reduced Native States to mere dependencies, continuing to exist only during the will of the

Political Agent. This work of reduction was completed when Her Majesty the Queen declared herself the Empress of India. At the Delhi tamasha, all the Native Princes were forced to attend the State Durbar and this suzerainty was most cunningly established".

"The occasion for the note was provided by an incident in the Indian State of Janjira where a British Civilian was sent from Bombay to investigate and report upon certain accusations. The paper added: "We humbly ask what right the British Government had to interfere with the internal administration of a state which neither was a tributary nor a dependency of the British town".

The Maratha, which was Tilak's responsibility, gradually toned up its editorial writing, and began to be looked upon with suspicion by the Government. An official comment said that the Mahratta "frequently quotes paragraphs and articles of a violent and democratic nature from the English Radical".

In order that we may more appreciatively be acquainted with the leader in the making, an extract from another of his articles, which appeared in the October 30, 1881, issue of the Mahratta, may be quoted:

> "There is much truth aye, we may say that is the" whole truth in the remarks that we are misgoverned because we allow ourselves to be so, India has been under British rule for more than three score years, and yet we do not find independent and vigorous constitutional agitations set on foot to convince our rulers of the manifest hardships, we have to suffer owing to the present form of Government. The flowers of our universities have chosen to fetter their freedom of action by accepting Government service, and the ignorant masses, notoriously unused to agitation, are without any intelligent leaders to guide them. Hence, it is that Government Acts pass uncontradicted, though the masses groan under them; hence it is that the opinion of the Native Press is passed in contemptuous silence. The masses must begin to move or be taught to move by constitutional means, the task must be undertaken by independent educated natives,

and not by closet-patriots. It is indeed a shame that with our thousandfold grievances, we should lag behind. Organisation, agitation, moral courage, are exactly what we want, and what we have to learn. And these can, like all others, be learnt by agitating, combining, etc. Let us, therefore, commence to move and more persistently, that is successfully. Till then, no strength, no redress, no privilege!"

Both the Mahratta and the Kesari, and especially the former, took keen interest in the affairs of the states of the Indian ruling Princes, vigorously pleading the cause of the rulers against the paramount power of the British Crown.

Among others, who more prominently figured in the columns of the papers, was the Maharaja of Kolhapur, who supposedly by design, was sought to be got rid of by his own Minister and the British Resident. They had declared that the Maharaja was not in a sound state of mind, and this statement, uneasiness among his subjects and sympathiser, who refused to believe it and thought that the British authorities, in conjunction with the Minister, Rao Bahadur Madhavarao Wasudev Barve, were intriguing against him. A feeling of hatred for the British rather than any great regard for the Indian ruling chiefs seems to be the reason why the people unhesitatingly believed all rumours that were circulating about the ill-treatment of the Maharaja at the hands of his Minister and the Paramount Power. The newspapers played a prominent part in confirming what word of mouth had already dinned into their ears. The Anglo-Indian Press and what was known as the Native Press were divided on the issue; the former eulogised Barve as a selfless and able administrator, the latter condemned him and took up the cause of the Maharaja.

In order to mobilise public sympathy, which of course was already there in an abundant measure, a public meeting was held under the presidentship of Rao Bahadur Gopalrao Hari Deshmukh on November 24, 1881, at which a well-known lawyer, Nana Bhide was the principal speaker. In his two-hour speech, Bhide claiming to be in possession of the full facts about the affairs of Kolhapur, succeeded in arousing public resentment against the Minister and the Paramount Power. The meeting passed a resolution suggesting that the Maharaja should be immediately put under the guardianship of some trustworthy persons.

The anti-Barve propaganda reached its climax when confidential correspondence—supposed to be his private letters was found circulating among the leaders of the place, including the editors of the Mahratta and the Kesari. Ranade, who was a legal luminary of sober and cool temperament, saw the correspondence, kept it with him for one month, and did not doubt its genuineness. The letters suggested that a plan to poison the Maharaja was being hatched. For a news-journal, nothing was more welcome than a correspondence of this nature. The Dynanprakash, a contemporary of the Kesari, could no longer resist the temptation and published the entire correspondence. The Kesari did not publish it yet, but in its issue, dated December 20, 1881, it referred to a Statement of Barve and Nana Bhide's replies thereto. The paper wrote;

> "Mr. Barve states that the young Maharaja of Kolhapur has become insane, and though every means has been tried to cure him, lie has not recovered; that there is no hope of his recovery, and that the Khardekarin lady will have to adopt another son; that the young Maharaja's natural father and grandfather are mad; that the Maharaja showed signs of insanity about the time when he went to Rajkot".

The Kesari started the new year 1882 with a prayer, in its first issue, for a more prosperous career. But Destiny willed otherwise. After the Dynanprakash had published the correspondence, and after satisfying himself that it was genuine, a member of the editorial staff, quoted these letters at some length in the Mahratta and the Kesari and challenged Barve to a fight in the court of law. Barve, who had already been contemplating doing something to arrest the mounting propaganda against him, accepted the challenge and obtained Government's permission to file a suit.

But it transpired later, too late in the day, that the correspondence was imaginary and had been manufactured by some designing person. And mass psychology being what it is, when this fact went round, nobody was prepared to believe it, for how could the credulous deprive himself of the fascinating picture he had formed in his mind? He also would not believe what was now an established fact, that the Maharaja, an adopted son, had really shown signs of insanity ever since 1877 and was often subject to delusions and suicidal tendencies. The editors of several papers were prosecuted for carrying on a defamatory propaganda against Barve, among them being Tilak as editor of the Mahratta and Agarkar of the Kesari. The article, which was the subject matter of the prosecution case, was not written by either of these two, but in keeping with time-honoured convention, both accepted full responsibility for it. Tilak had the letters with him and, when he was convinced that they were imaginary he consigned them to the flames, and sent a letter of apology to Rao Bahadur Barve. But the case had gone far ahead in the court, and lest withdrawal at this stage should be construed as a weakness Barve stuck to his suit. The editors made his task easy by pleading guilty, and he succeeded in securing their conviction. Tilak and Agarkar were each sentenced to four months simple imprisonment.

Conditions in jail were awfully bad, and the journalists lodged there were treated like ordinary criminals. In a brief sojourn of 101 days in jail, nineteen days were remitted for good behaviour. Tilak lost 25 Ib in weight. "The room allotted to them measured 13 square feet; the appliances provided were of the dirtiest sort; the food was nauseating; the blankets given for covering their bodies were the homes of dangerous insects". For the first 25 days, they were allowed neither to read nor to write.

The public mind, which had for many months been fed on a different material, was still not prepared to accept the sentence of imprisonment as a proper dispensation of justice.

People openly declared that bureaucracy had ultimately succeeded in wreaking vengeance on Tilak and other editors.

Protest meetings were held, and sympathy was expressed for the brave men who had walked into jail for a cause. Such men as Mandlik and Wordsworth sent a petition to the Governor, Sir James Fergusson, for remission of the sentence but he expressed his inability to interfere in the course of justice. This heightened the feeling of respect and love that was developing for the fearless journalists. And when the day of their release, October 26, 1882, arrived, hundreds of people thronged at the jail gates and received the patriots, as they were styled in the chorus of applause. They were taken in a carriage through the city, and the progress of the carriage was punctuated with public functions on the way.

When they were leaving Bombay for Puna, students gathered in large numbers to pay their homage. An excited crowd awaited the heroes arrival at the platform of the Puna Railway Station. There was enthusiasm and the atmosphere seemed to be charged with triumphant zeal. As in Bombay, a public welcome was accorded them at several functions in Puna.

Ever since the start of the case, Tilak more than others had endeared himself to many people. In the early stages of the case, a merchant of Puna—a complete stranger to Tilak — ran to the court with a purse of Rs. 5,000 as soon as he heard that a security had been demanded from Tilak.

In his later life, whenever in a reminiscent mood, Tilak gratefully talked of this merchant and said how profuse and plentiful was, as a rule, the harvest of a little public service.

In the defamation case, people spontaneously raised funds for the defence while pleaders were willing to conduct the case free of charge. Puna students staged a drama in aid of the fund; in this G. K. Gokhale, then a student of the Deccan College, played a feminine role.

There was resentment in the public mind; the Mahratta, the Kesari and other papers had often been drawing attention to misdeeds of the British agency in the Indian States and to the exacting British rule itself. The Mahratta wrote unsparingly on the "poverty-stricken conditions of the people". It brought home to the readers how the "Merchant Princes of Manchester" were fleecing India. In June, 1881, the assumption of the control and management of the Gaikwad's contingent by the British was paraded as a breach of faith. In these affairs, the conduct of the State Minister, Sir T. Madhava Rao was commented upon with disapproval.

With this background, it is easy to understand why public resentment, instead of being allayed by the revelations made at the trial, was actually accentuated. There was discontent all round;

there was no dynamic leadership to mobilise it. The Kolhapur episode, however, laid the foundation on which the superstructure was yet to be built.

Love's Labour Lost

The Kolhapur Case considerably enhanced the popularity of Tilak and Agarkar in the public mind, and incidentally proved advantageous to the School; it was now easier to collect funds. The next three years, 1883-85, according to the account left by Tilak, were spent in organising the institution. The important event of this period was the support of the late Abasaheb Ghatge, Chief of Kagal, and the honour of a visit which His Excellency Sir James Furgusson was subsequently pleased to pay to our institution (13th February, 1884). In the declaration of aims and objects which we made before His Excellency, we clearly set forth that for a small yet decent remuneration we were prepared to establish a network of schools throughout Maharashtra, and that it was our ambition to start a private college to secure a continuous supply of graduates, actuated by the same motives as their teachers. In short, self-denial and self-reliance had been our watchwords by this time. They were the mainsprings of our actions; and it was for these moral reasons our work came to be so much valued.

As a preliminary to giving practical shape to their ambitious plan, the promoters held a public meeting in Puna on October 24, 1884 at which the decision to establish the Deccan Education Society was taken. The Society was intended to be a cosmopolitan body, which is evident from the fact that the public meeting was presided over by Sir William Wedderburn and on the motion of Tilak the following among others, were elected to constitute the Board of Managers: Rao Saheb, V. N. Mandlik, Sir William Wedderburn, Prof. Wordsworth, Justice Telang. The aims of the Society were stated to be to facilitate and make education inexpensive by starting, affiliating or incorporating at different places, as circumstances permitted, schools and colleges under native management or by any other ways best adapted to the wants of the people. The bye-laws of the managing board were framed on the model of the regulations of missionary bodies. All life members were to receive equal pay, and had equal rights; but, as the monthly salary fixed was not very high, it was provided that under special circumstances, gratuities might be granted to life members either monthly or in lump sum, in addition to their monthly salaries.

A further provision for accidents, etc. was made by assuring the life of every member for Rs. 3,000". The sum originally proposed by Tilak was Rs. 5,000, but it had to be reduced for want of funds. All these provisions were made on the understanding that this would leave no motive for any one to seek work outside the Society.

In fact, in an anxiety to protect members interest, provisions made for them exceeded those the missionary institutions made for their workers. Tilak drew up a comparison between the two: "As we are proud to call ourselves Indian Jesuits, it may not be uninstructive to compare the provisions we had made with those of the missionary bodies. The Jesuits are never married, and it is no wonder if their regulations are more stringent than ours. But even the provision which the American Mission makes for its members is less liberal than ours.

This Mission gives only a bare maintenance to members—those that are married being allowed double the allowance of a single member; while some special grant is made for children. We have embodied all these in our bye-laws, and a life policy in addition; and it is but natural to expect that the members of our Body should show as much, if not greater, devotion and zeal in our cause, as the Members of the American Mission do in theirs". Better provisions begot greed, and it was the departure from the principles enunciated in the beginning which forced Tilak to sever his connection from the Society.

Barely two months after the inauguration of the Society an Arts College was established, on January 2, 1885. Within a short time, the Society secured endowments of the value of about Rs. 80,000. The institution was named the Fergusson College after the then Governor of Bombay. Both the institutions were registered for grant-in-aid by the Education Department; and, as Tilak says, "our position was thus in every way improved. During the next five years, the Institution had been so far established and organised that the work in the School and the College was reduced mostly to routine; and our material and moral position was better than we expected".

Encouragement from Government in other ways was not-wanting, and when the Society asked the authorities for a plot of land for the College building, space was readily made available. The College was recognised by the University of Bombay for the previous examination provisionally for three years. Again, official pleasure was sought, and the foundation stone of the building was laid by Sir James Fergusson on March 5, 1885. The site provided by Government was later given up and the building actually was erected on a better site secured through Tilak's efforts from the daughter of the Gaikwad.

But the two journals created a problem. They and the educational institutions were pulling in different directions. The Kesari and the Mahratta were coming up as fearless papers, while the Society was formed purely as an educational institution for which Government cooperation was considered desirable. Therefore, though the promoters of the Society continued to be the proprietors of the press and the journals, the latter were considered to be a distinctly separate branch of common business.

It had been Tilak's ambition to give Maharashtra as many schools and colleges of the type he and his colleagues had built up as was practicable, and when a hint was thrown out by the Government that the Society might take over the Government institutions as well, the members' joy knew no bounds. The Society had been conducting its institutions very economically, and high officials of Government in the education department often discussed how much more the officially run institutions really cost the Government. The suggestion, however, did not materialise.

And, even if it had materialised, the arrangement would not have lasted long, for among the members of the Society themselves the spirit of sacrifice was gradually vanishing, and Tilak who was the moving spirit of the Institution was finding it difficult to pull on with some of his colleagues, who had now become ambitious and desired to earn more from the Society which was now quite prosperous.

Then, the differences between Tilak and Agarkar were growing over the issue of social reform. Agarkar was for a complete overhaul of the Hindu religious and social customs, rituals and practices, and advocated that new laws should be legislated by Government for the desired reform, Tilak argued that the people should be convinced of the need for, and converted to the reform rather than forced by law to observe it. He was not prepared for a violent shake-up of Hindu society. Concensus of opinion among the members favoured Tilak's view, and Agarkar formally ended his connection with the journals in October, 1887, though in his individual capacity he continued to contribute special articles to the Kesari.

For a more vivid picture of the inside working of the institution which eventually led to the dissociating of Tilak from it, we had better turn to his own account.

The financial position of the School and College, by this time, had far improved, and we felt sure of our ground there in; but not so in the press. It paid itself, and a considerable part of its debt, but the writers got nothing. This was a state of things not to be long tolerated. Some of us had already ceased to write for the papers and devoted our time to more paying pursuits, while others had to devote the whole of their time to the press without receiving anything.

Again, as the press and the papers were as yet the property of all, no individual member had perfect freedom to express his personal views in the editorial columns of the papers.

For the first few years after the papers were started, we worked on the principle that the views expressed in the editorial columns must represent the views at least of the majority of members and should be commonly acceptable; but as the individuals became more marked, this arrangement was found to be more unworkable.

From those and similar other causes, after many discussions, it was considered desirable to separate the press from the papers. But as the proposal was not feasible it was given up, and a second resolution was passed to completely sever the connection of all members-from the press and the papers I was sent to the press to make the accounts; and so great was the belief in the bankruptcy of the concern that Agarkar once refused to give to the press a loan of Rs. 500 from our funds, though the School and the Press were then conducted by the same members. The accounts were made up, and in October, 1886, the press and papers with all their liabilities were formally given over to Mr. Kelkar. The offer was first made to Mr. Agarkar, but he declined to take it on account of, as he said to us, the liabilities and also because it was not the aim of his life to turn out an editor; He said he would rather close them than go over there. I was against closing a concern started by us, especially when the vernacular paper had become so successful and popular; and offered myself to conduct the papers, in case no one was willing to undertake the responsibility, Mr. Kelkar, however, undertook to conduct the concern; but as the management was to be entrusted to Mr. Hari Narayan Gokhale, who would come over only on my promise to support, Mr. Kelkar requested the Board to declare me as 'the next hypothecated member for the press', and the Board passed a resolution accordingly on August 22, 1887.

The press and the papers were thus formally handed over to Kelkar, who was left at liberty to settle his terms with Mr. Hari Narayan Gokhale, while I was declared as the next hypothecated man for the purpose of general advice and assistance.

When we thus separated the press, it was believed that we had got rid of one cause of difference and diversion; and we could thenceforth apply our undivided attention to the School and the College. There was thus a sense of relief for a time; but it was destined not to be permanent. Some of us began to feel that we had committed a mistake. Mr. Kelkar had so conducted the papers as not to hurt any member or interest but this was not enough. To some, it was a loss of possible honour or gain. Mr. Agarkar especially lost his opportunity of publishing his opinions in the editorial columns; and some of the social subjects which came up for discussion in the press, soon after, caused the want to be felt more intensely. He was told that he could express his views under his signature and in communication columns.

But that was not to his taste. At last even the papers were offered to him, but he did not like to take the financial responsibility upon him. Whereupon he was told that he could not use the papers for preaching his hobbies and throw the financial responsibility on our shoulders. He knew (and the sense of the Board was once informally ascertained) that the opinions expressed in the Kesari were mostly approved by the majority; but still gradually he came to believe that the Kesari was ruining the body by alienating the sympathies of the Reformers.

> "This open division in the camp encouraged for opponents arid their support encouraged Messrs. Agarkar and (Hari Narain) Gokhale, who supposed that they had influential sympathies. The majority of the members thus came to be talked of by these two as social conservatives. The bitterness of feelings increased and each party scandalised the other. All further progress thus came to an end, and the net result of the whole was a new paper started by Messrs."
>
> *Agarkar and Gokhale in October, 1888*

In regard to the work of School and College, "singleness of purpose gave way to diversity of pursuits and interests; and these brought in differences in views and aims, where there was harmony before. Differences on questions of principles, once already decided and accepted, naturally led to hot discussions. Party-feeling led to jealousies and the latter ripened into rancour, making reconcilement a practical impossibility. The patriotic and independent position of 1881-1883 came to be talked of with scorn. The new life members had but dim perception of why and how the sacrifice principle was adopted by us. I tried to gauge the strength of the Body on the Jesuitical principle, and I found it in the minority".

Differences among members, once begun, went on increasing, Tilak insisting on austerity, and some others, who eventually became a majority, getting impatient to share the prosperity of the institution. In order to get the best of a member for the institution, outside work was tabooed. Now a desire to earn more had substituted this principle. And the final break came over this issue.

G. K. Gokhale, who was also a member of the Society and had for sometime been working for the Sarvajanik Sabha Journal, thought of accepting the post of secretary of that association with two or three hours work every day. Tilak objected to such diversion of energy and pointed out that even Government did not allow its servants to do anything else, and that for a body like ours, it would be carrying the principle of private work too far to allow members to contract such definite engagement outside the Body. The secretaryship, Tilak said, was offered to himself before, but he declined to accept it as long as he was connected with the Deccan Education Society, and suggested that Gokhale should do the same. He also stated "that there was still ample enough scope for Gokhale's energies in the duties of Professor of English Literature in the Fergusson College; and that if we wished to compete with other colleges, we must at least show that we were not behind in reading work".

His arguments were, however, of no avail. The Board was equally divided on the question, and after an unpleasant scene, Gokhale came to be appointed secretary of the Sabha in June, 1890. Tilak again pressed for a solution of the question with the result that a vote of censure was passed against him in the Council on October 14, 1890. He was disgusted, and informed the Council that he had decided to resign from the Society, and the next day, he submitted his resignation.

By constantly insisting on the settlement of the question of outside work and salary, he said, "I have alienated the sympathy of almost everyone and rendered myself extremely unpleasant; so much so that I am regarded almost an obstacle in the way of others and every fault of mine, however, trifling is at once caught hold of and magnified to an incredible extent".

The resignation came up for discussion at the next meeting of the Council which was held on November 21, 1890. So revengeful and exacerbated were some of the members that there was in the Council an atmosphere of impeachment rather than of sympathy. When the chairman formally moved a resolution of regret at Tilak's withdrawal from the Society, two members of the Council stood up and proposed that Tilak should be called upon to explain, by December 6, why he had resigned. Eanade suggested that differences between Tilak and the others should be settled by arbitration. But this proposal was opposed by Apte who felt sure that arbitration would be of no avail. In the opinion of Dr.

Bhandarkar, which he had expressed on the letter of resignation itself, "the differences between Tilak and other members of the Society had a long history behind them, and though there might have been some deflection from the fundamental principles on which the Society was originally founded, Tilak's imputation of dishonesty to the members of the managing board could not be overlooked". The Council deferred its decision, and meanwhile sent all papers relating to the resignation to the managing committee for a report. The Council reassembled on February 2, 1891, and adopted a resolution characterising Tilak's charges as baseless. Some counter charges were framed against him, one of them being that while he objected to outside work in case of others, he engaged himself in the activities of the Indian National Congress. Tilak's answer to this was:

> "The charge is entirely groundless. The Congress work was undertaken by me when I was on leave, and was thinking of resigning from the Body. It is true that I rejoined in June, 1889, and did not give up the work undertaken before. But that was because the work was of a temporary nature. Those that have ventured to bring this charge against me entirely forget the fact that I did not take up any Congress work in previous years, though it had long been in existence. Neither did I do any outside work during the first nine years of the School, though when the School was started in 1880, it was entirely in my hands to fix morning hours for tuition and leave the afternoon for pleading work".

The Council met again and confirmed its previous resolution. As a member of the Deccan Education Society, Tilak's emoluments were not much, but they were necessary to help to keep the family going. His resignation not only deprived him of the opportunity of serving a cause, but also of the means of his livelihood. He was not yet the sole proprietor of the Kesari and the Mahratta, and, even if he were, the papers did not yield enough to enable him to make the two ends meet.

After Agarkar had withdrawn from the two journals, Tilak, N. C. Kelkar and H. N. Gokhale jointly conducted them. Gokhale looked upon the enterprise purely as a business proposition, but for the other two, profit was not the only consideration.

The Kesari was now the most popular weekly of Maharashtra. It had come to be regarded as a political institution; it helped people to form their opinions on the current social and political problems. There were not many newspaper readers those days, and that explains why the circulation of the Kesari Marathi contemporaries did not go beyond 400 or 500 copies, but the Kesari, though younger to many, had a net sale of over 4,000 copies. It was easily able to pay its way, and earn some profit as well, but its English counterpart, the Mahratta, was not making headway.

In September, 1891, the sole proprietorship of the Kesari and the Mahratta passed into the hands of Tilak. But what a proprietorship! The papers during their life of a decade had incurred a debt of Rs. 7,000, and Tilak preferred to take over this debt against the alternative of closing down the institution. The press, went to the share of Kelkar and Gokhale.

There was no solution yet to his personal problem of livelihood. He put in an advertisement in the press announcing that he had opened law classes and inviting students to attend his lectures. The venture was successful and yielded him about Rs. 150 every month. As the institution expanded, the services of more lecturers were needed, and he engaged his old colleagues, Kelkar and H. N. Gokhale, from whom he had separated only recently. "The more difficult of the subjects, viz. Hindu Law, Evidence Act, Contract Act and Equity, Tilak used to teach himself. His lectures on Hindu Law were reputed to be very learned, critical and exhaustive". Even the practising lawyers were attracted to his classes and joined it with those studying for the L. L. B. examination. He had planned to prepare a digest on Hindu Law, but the ambition remained unfulfilled. Other activities left him little time to undertake the work.

Some friends made him interested in another enterprise for which he was hardly suited. He was advised to start a ginning factory. He had no money to invest in the new venture, but succeeded in securing two other partners, and at last a factory was set up at Latur in the Nizam's dominions. The journals and the law classes already occupied most of his time, and his going to Latur to look after Hie factory was out of the question. His nephew watched his interests there, but the factory's accounts showed no gains, and six years later, in 1897, when Tilak started on his second term of imprisonment it was closed down.

As a Councillor

In spite of the combined opposition of the Moderates, the European community and the Anglo-Indian press, Tilak was twice elected to the Bombay Legislative Council, first in 1895, and again in 1897. The Reforms Act of 1892 had provided for an elective element in the Legislatures, and in Bombay Presidency, eight seats were thrown open for election. In the first elections under the new Act, the Central Division of the Presidency was somehow left unrepresented, and since this division included Puna, the storm centre of politics, an agitation was carried on against the omission.

The agitation had its effect, and before the next elections came off in 1895, the Central Division was allotted a seat, and Tilak's friends persuaded him to contest it. Two months before he had been elected to the Puna City Municipality, and they were sure that he would win the Council election. The Moderates were opposed to Tilak's candidature, and put up a Government servant of high position to contest the election. His name was Jathar, and he believed that the District Boards of the Division, which constituted the electoral college, would not dare cast their votes against him.

Then, men like Ranade and Gokhale personally canvassed for him. There was yet another man, named Garud, in the field. Garud was a pleader and counted on his personal popularity which he had achieved through his professional work.

These two had monetary backing too. But Tilak had many supporters, who worked for him ungrudgingly, believing that it was a public cause for which they were working. They succeeded with Tilak getting 35 votes as against Garud's 26, and Jathar's only two.

Tilak's election came as a rude shock to the Anglo-Indian press, which was never tired of hurling abuses at him. His main adversaries were the Times of India and the Bombay Gazette. They suggested to the Governor that Tilak's election should not be approved. The 1892 Act, while introducing some elective element into the Councils, gave no power to the representatives of the people. They had no power to make any alteration in the budget. They could only make speeches, and those too within certain defined limits. Even the provision of elected representatives was a farce, because the Governor had the power to reject the election of any member. The fear that an election might be rejected, compelled members to exercise control over their tongues. The Anglo-Indian press regarded Tilak an undesirable member, and they would not tolerate his taking a seat in the Council.

The Bombay Gazette asked Government to veto Tilak's election. The paper denounced him as a "rabid journalist and a discredited agitator".

When the fury of the Anglo-Indian papers did not abate, the Kesari made a reply in which it said: "Our contemporary, the Bombay Gazette, suggests that in case Mr. Tilak, who is the editor of two rabid journals, is elected for the Central Division, Lord Sandhurst should exercise his right of veto and squash the election. If Government vetoes the election of a representative chosen by a constituency, the attempts to reform the Legislative Councils and the slight good done by the Indian Councils Act of 1892 will be nullified".

But the authorities acted wisely, and Tilak's election was approved by the Governor on June 12, and he took his seat in the Council, on August 7, after taking the customary oath of allegiance to the Queen. He made a speech, and quite expectedly it was a departure from the common run of speeches made by the 'Honourable Members' who kept themselves within well-defined limits so as not to offend the Government. Tilak crossed the limits and made an all-out attack on Government's taxation policy. Before entering upon his new task, he made a throughout study of the Budgets of previous years, and equipped himself with facts and figures. He said that since 1870, the revenue receipts of the Bombay Government had gone up quite considerably, without corresponding increase in the income of the people. The burden of ever greater taxation was crushing the people. The Government did not spend the extra revenues on works of public utility, but spent them on the bureaucracy. The criterion of examining the budget, he said, should be "how far the revenue has increased during the last 25 years and what portion of it has been devoted to the material development of the Province". But the budget figured gave a surprising answer, he said and added: "The revenue of the Presidency has increased by about 5.5 crores of rupees during the last 25 years. Land, Forest, Abkari have all been made to yield as much as possible even to the inconvenience of the people; and yet out of the revenues so realised only a small portion has been devoted to the material improvement of the Province".

He was a member of the Council, when he carried on what was called a "no-rent campaign", and his colleagues were astonished that an Honourable Member should associate himself with such questionable activities. The 1892 Act gave Indians no power, and he had no faith in it. If he entered the Legislature it was to carry the anti-Government agitation into that 'august body'. An extra seat for the Central Division was no bait, and he told the critics: "An additional membership is, as I view it, no sop or gag intended to stop honest and fair criticism. But if it is, I should certainly give it up rather than consent to draw the curtain over the gross negligence or the palpable errors of officials, however high they may be".

During the course of two years, the Council met barely for eight days, and worked for less than 36 hours. That was the short span of Tilak's legislative career. He asked questions, he made long speeches, and he broke the established convention under which members made only mild speeches in the presence of the Governor who presided over the Council. The first term being over in 1897, he again contested the seat and won it with camparative ease. But his activities during the 1896 famine and the recent plague made the Anglo-Indian press and the European community his sworn enemy. Again, the Anglo-Indian press began to shower abuses on Tilak and sternly warned Government that a man like him had no business to sit in the Council. Their advice was ignored, and Tilak's election was approved. But a month later, he resigned from the Council after his conviction for sedition. For the same reason, he resigned from the Municipality also.

3

An Eventful Career

Early Career

The great Indian leader, Bal Gangadhar Tilak was born in a middle class Chitpavan Brahmin family. His father, Gangadhar Ramchandra Tilak served as an Assistant Teacher at Ratnagiri and later on as Assistant Deputy Educational Inspector at Thana and Puna. Gangadhar was a well-known Mathematics Teacher of his time and was well-versed in Trigonometry and Grammar. He did not live for a long time. Bal was hardly sixteen when his father died in 1872. He continued his studies and passed the Matriculation four months after his father's death. Thereafter, he joined the Deccan College and passed B.A. with honours in 1876. He qualified in Law in 1879 from the Bombay University.

During his school and college days, Tilak was not an ordinary student. He participated in several extra-curricular activities and gained much popularity among the students. He was, however, not happy with the prevalent educational system and, given time and opportunity, he made up his mind to suggest modifications in the system. While studying law, he made friendship with Agarkar, who later on became Principal of the Fergusson College. Both of them deliberated upon the idea of opening a model institution. They also decided not to accept government service, but to start a private High School and College for the purpose of imparting cheap and healthy education to the younger generation.

In these efforts, they were joined by Vishnu Krishna Chiplunkar, popularly known as Vishnu Shastri and M.B. Namjoshi. The former had resigned from government service as he could not pull on with his supervisors and had shifted to Puna with a plan to start a private academic institution. He was a very fine Marathi prose write of the time. So the four young men, Tilak, Agarkar, Chiplunkar and Namjoshi started the New English School in Puna for boys belonging to middle class families. It was indeed a novel experiment in the field of education at a time when the development of educational system under the Raj was in primitive stages. It was a step which was to lead the younger generation towards socio-economic progress in that region.

Tilak did not wish to confine his activity to the development of education. He was keen to see that the public should not remain unaware about numerous happenings in the region and in the subcontinent as a whole. He had the desire to give vent to his feelings in the press with a sense of complete freedom. He detested and opposed any kind of restraint on free-will, of course with a sense of responsibility. This could only be achieved if he had his own press. Therefore, he started two newspapers, the *Mahratta* and the *Kesari* and he along with Chiplunkar made a mark in the field of native journalism. Besides Chiplunkar established two printing presses, the *Arya-Bhushan* for the use of the two newspapers, and the *Chitrashala* for the purpose of encouraging fine arts. In a short time, the New English School as well as the *Kesari* and the *Mahratta* became the leading institutions in the field of education and journalism in the Deccan. The faith of the people in this region greatly increased in these social agencies and consequently Tilak, Chiplunkar, Agarkar and their associates in this work became household names. This kind of social encouragement afforded them academic impetus which prompted them to put in more work by burning midnight oil.

The line of action taken up by the *Kesari* and the *Mahratta* landed these newspapers into trouble. Unmindful of the consequences, they published some articles severely criticising the treatment accorded to Shivaji Rao, the Maharaja of Kolhapur and the Karbhari of the State, M.W. Barve. The laws of the Raj took the severest course and as editors of the two papers, Tilak and Agarkar were tried for defamation in the court of law. They were sentenced to simple imprisonment for four months. This kind of legal decision became the popular talk among the public in the Deccan and naturally it greatly enhanced the social prestige of the two editors. The English School and the two newspapers gained much popularity among the sensitive Maratha population of the Deccan region.

This kind of behaviour of the Raj did not upset Tilak, rather is generated a new spirit of working hard towards better and noble achievements in his career. At this point of time, V.K. Chiplunkar died and his untimely death greatly shocked Tilak and his associates. Their social programme received the on going process in 1884, when Tilak and Namjoshi laid the foundation of the Deccan Education Society of Puna, with themselves as its first body of life-members.

In these efforts, he was assisted by Professors V.B. Kelkar, Dhrap, M.S. Gole, H.N. Gokhale, Bhanu and Patankar. They were instrumental in the foundation of the Fergusson College in 1885 under the auspices of the Deccan Education Society. The life Members gave an undertaking to serve as professors for twenty years. Day by day, the College began to develop in a huge and spacious campus given to it. Lord Reay fulfilled an earlier promise given by Sir James Fergusson.

Tilak joined the Congress in 1889 after resigning from the Deccan Educational Society and he was a devoted adherent of the Congress movement all through his life, although it is curious that he was never the President of the Congress I remember very well at the Calcutta Congress of 1917 over which Dr. Besant presided, Tilak's speech supporting lie resolution on self-government and also in the Amritsar Congress of 1919. Although at that time he had opposed Dr. Besant in many particulars, he tried to be a harmonising factor. But from the beginning, Tilak was anxious to transform the Congress into a body working all the year round and not merely a holiday gathering of people of all shades of political.

Very soon, the differences between the Moderates and the leftist group developed and Surendranath Bannerjee, Phirozeshah Mehta and Gokhale were ranged on one side and Tilak on the opposite side. Naturally, therefore, the authorities took advantage of the Rand murder in 1897 and prosecuted Tilak for sedition, and his notorious trial began before Mr. Justice Strachey. Notwithstanding that Mr. Asquith appeared for Tilak in the appeal from Strachey's Judgement, he was convicted. While Tilak was in jail, the section appertaining to sedition was amended thus proving that Tilak was illegally sentenced. It fell to the lot of Tilak to test the law of sedition as he was again tried for the same offence in 1908 and once more in 1916. Remarkably, Tilak's release from imprisonment was due to the efforts of men like Max Muller who drew attention to the fact that an erudite scholar like Tilak was under-going rigorous imprisonment for alleged sedition. During the second prosecution, Tilak spoke for over twenty hours and his speech was, though not perfect in style, so penetrating that, in the language of the *Modern Review*, the judge, jury and prosecuting counsel shrank into insignificance before the lowering personality of Tilak who delivered, according to the journal, a brilliant discourse on the law of sedition.

A remarkable characteristic of Tilak was his loyalty to his friends which was demonstrated in the Bapat Case and the Jagannath Maharaj Adoption Case during the course of which Tilak was charged with fabricating evidence and forgery. Justice Beaman however made it clear how vindictive the attitude of the Government was. All the subordinate judicial authorities consistently took an antagonistic view and it remained for the High Court to expose the campaign to tarnish the reputation of Tilak.

It is wonderful to realise that during the course of the criminal litigation and when he was suffering from many trials including the death of his eldest son from bubonic plague, Tilak published his well-known work on *The Arctic Home in the Vedas.* In the civil litigation, the Privy Council vindicated the action of Tilak. In the sedition trial, Tilak was sentenced to six years imprisonment and sent to the Mandalay Jail.

All these difficulties and tribulations, however, did not prevent Tilak from pleading for Swaraj, following, in this respect, the efforts of Mazzini of Italy; and Tilak had always had the international factor prominently in mind. As a journalist and as an author, in addition to his being a deep Vedic scholar, Tilak became the protagonist of prohibition and Swadeshi and Swaraj. During his stay in the Mandalay Jail, he wrote the *Gita-Rahasya* which has been translated into most of the Indian languages and into English; and during his incarceration not only did be make a deep study of Oriental and Western philosophy but he began the study of the German language so as to understand the work of German savants.

C.P. Ramaswami Aiyar, *Biographical Vistas: Sketches of Some Eminent Indians.*

Tilak's role now was in a wider field: as Secretary of the Bombay Provincial Conference, he acted in a disciplined way. He was instrumental in organising its first five sessions. In 1893, when the communal riots broke out, Tilak offered his services and greatly criticised the policy of Divide and Rule adopted by the bureaucracy under the Raj. He was critical of the policy of Lord Dufferin. His criticism was not to be cowed down by the repression of the bureaucracy. Indeed through the columns of the *Kesari,* he voiced his own comments of the existing political situation and the feelings of the masses which wanted nothing but justice to various causes having deep linkage with the constitutional reforms. His social doings made him a popular and respected leader and he was twice elected a member of the Legislative Council and the Fellow of the Bombay University. In 1895, he headed the poll at the general election to the City Municipality of Puna and won the esteem of his colleagues as a sound practical worker.

His popularity in politics has deep linkage with his interest in the revival of old religious worship in the form of the Ganpati and the Shivaji festivals. In fact he had come to the conclusion that a veneration of old gods and heroes would generate the spirit of patriotism among the youths of the country and would raise their moral standard.

The run for spurious imitations of foreign ideas and customs and the consequent spirit of irreligiousness among the younger generations were, in his opinion, exerting a disastrous influence upon the moral character of the Indian youth; and if things were allowed to drift in this way, the ultimate result, Mr. Tilak believed, would be a moral bankruptcy from which no nation can ever hope the rise. It was a very grave problem, and even the Government of India had turned their attention to it at that time. The official panacea, however, was the teaching of moral textbooks in Indian schools, which Mr. Tilak in several articles in the *Maharatta* severely criticised. Mr. Tilak thought that to make Indian youths more self-reliant and more energetic, they must be taught greater self-respect, and that could only be done by making them respect their religion and their forefathers.

Excessive and aimless self-debasement may perhaps be a good thing in an ascetic or a philosopher, but it does mischief in practical life. Superfluous patriotism may sometimes lead to excesses, but it will also do some good; while self-denying abjectness will only lead to lethargy and death. This is, in brief, Mr. Tilak's social and political philosophy; and however opinions may vary as to its correctness, nobody can deny that he has followed it consistently. Mr. Tilak has often been accused of hypocracy and inconsistency in matters of social reform. He is a practical reformer in his own way. He had educated his daughters, postponed their marriages till the utmost limit sanctioned by the Shastras, advocated relaxation of caste restrictions, and generally sympathised with the social reform movement; and yet he attacked the social reform party. Superficial observers are staggered at this strange incongruity of behaviour, while his opponents attribute it to a desire to gain cheap popularity.

The fact is, his conduct in this matter was entirely the result of his strong convictions. He desired social reform, but did not believe in the men or the methods that were then employed in carrying it out. The so-called social reformers of the past generation were not, in his opinion, the men who possess the aptitude or the moral qualities requisite for a successful reform movement. Hence, his criticisms are generally directed to the men and not to the object aimed at. This is the real key to Mr. Tilak's attitude as regards social reform. His principle of criticism is in fact the same with respect to political as well as social questions. He may approve of a Government measure and yet criticise the conduct of officials who carry it out; similarly he may desire a particular reform and yet strongly condemn those who want to pose as its ministers.

In 1895, Mr. Tilak came to be associated with the Shivaji Commemoration movement. A stray article of his in the *Kesari* of 23 April 1895 gave such an impetus to the public desire to subscribe for the repair of Shivaji's tomb at Raigad fort in the Kolaba district Rs. 20,000 were in a short time collected, mostly from small contributions. Festivals also began to be celebrated at many places since that time on Shivaji's birthday or coronation day. When it was resolved to hold the eleventh National Congress in Puna, in the Christmas of 1895, Mr. Tilak was, by the united voice of all parties in Puna, chosen its Secretary, and had as such to do almost the whole work of organisation in the beginning. He worked till September, when differences as to whether the Social Conference was to be held in the Congress pandal led to bitter party quarrels and compelled Mr. Tilak to retire from the work. He did not, however, cease to take interest in the Congress, but on the contrary did much from outside to make it the great success it was.

As life member of the institution, Tilak performed his duty in a disciplined way. He was in favour of a Jesuitical mode of life and advised others to lead a simple life with devotion towards the cause assigned to them. After some time, there was difference of opinion between Tilak and his colleagues on observances if certain principles in running the institution. The opposition's point of view was not up to Tilaks taste and he, therefore, resigned. Undoubtedly, he was a superb teacher of Mathematics, Sanskrit and Science and his leaving the institution was a great academic loss to the institution.

Soon after this, Tilak started a Law College in order to prepare students for the High Court and District Pleadership examinations. Several students of the region were beneficiaries from this new academic experiment of Tilak. At this point of time, he took charge of the *Kesari* and Professor Kelkar remained editor of the *Mahratta.* Soon after Kelkar left and Tilak began to manage both the papers. The *Kesari* specially flourished much and soon its circulation was enviable in our country.

Mr. Tilak was not a man to waste the whole of his time in ephemeral writing. He now resolved to turn his leisure to some account and devoted himself of his favourite books the "Bhagavad Gita" and the "Rigveda". As a result of has researches in the chronology of the Vedas, he wrote a paper on the antiquity of the Vedas as proved by astronomical observations. He sent a resume of this paper to the International Congress of Orientalists which was held in London in 1892, and published the whole paper next year in a book form under the title "The Orion; or the Researches into the Antiquity of the Vedas. Mr. Tilak in this book traces the Greek tradition of Orion and also the name of that constellation to Sanskrit Agrayana or Agrahayana; and as this latter word means the beginning of the year, Mr. Tilak concludes that all the hymns of the Rigveda containing references to the word or the various traditions clustering round it must have been composed before the Greeks separated from the Hindus and at a time when the year began with the Sun in the constellation of Orion or Mrigashirsha, i.e., before 4,000 BC. It is impossible to do justice to his wide research and masterly argument in a sketch like this, but everybody who has a curiosity on the subject ought to go through the book himself.

The book was highly praised by European and American scholars, and Mr. Tilak's conclusions may now be said to have met with universal acceptance. Many Orientalists, such as Max Muller, Weber, Jacobi, and Whitney have acknowledged the learning and the originality of the author. After the book was published, Mr. Tilak carried on for some time a friendly correspondence with Prof. Max Muller and Weber on some of the Philological questions discussed by him, and the result was that both parties agreed that there was much to be said on each side. Professor Whitney of America, only a short time before his death in 1894, wrote an able article in the Journal of the American Oriental Society in which he highly analogised Mr. Tilak's theories. Similarly, Dr. Bloomfield, of John Hopkins University, in an anniversary address, spoke about Mr. Tilak's book in these terms:

'But a literary event of even greater importance has happened within the last two or three months an event which is certain to stir the world of science and culture far more than the beatific reminiscences. Some ten weeks ago I received from India a small duodecimo volume, in the clumsy get-up and faulty typography of the native Anglo-Indian press. It came with the regards of the author, a person totally unknown to fame I had never heard his name; Bal Gangadhar Tilak B.A. L.L.B. Law Lecturer and Pleader, Puna. The book is published by Mrs. Radhabai Atmaram Sagoon, Bookseller and Publisher, Bombay. The title is 'Orion of Researches into the Antizuity of Vedas.' It will be understood that the entry of the little volume upon my horizon was not such as to prejudice me in its favour, and secondly, I placed it where it might be reached without too much efforts in the drowsy after-dinner hour, to be disposed off along with much second class matter, such as reaches a scholar through the channels of the Postal Union. Nor was the preface at all encouraging. The author blandly informs us that the age of the Rigveda cannot be less than 4,000 years before Christ and that the express records of the yearly Hindu antiquity point back to 6,000 before Christ.

Having in mind the boundless fancy of the Hindus through the ages and his particularly fatal facility for 'taking his mouthful' when it comes to a question of numbers, I proposed to myself to continue to turn the leaves of the book with the amused smile of orthodoxy befitting the occasion. But soon, the amused smile gave way to an uneasy sense that something unusual had happened. I was first impressed with something leonine in the way in which the author controlled the Vedic literature and the occidental works on the same; my superficial reading was soon replaced by absorbed study and finally having been prepared to scoff mildly, I confess that the author had convinced me in all the essential points. The book is unquestionably the literary sensation of the year just before us; history the chronic readjuster shall have her hands uncommonly full to assimilate the results of Tilak's discovery and arrange her paraphernalia in the new perspective.

Tilak did not expect the people to copy every incident in Shivaji's life, as the times had radically charged. It was the spirit which actuated Shivaji in his exploits, not the exploits themselves, that was held up as a model and an example to the rising generation. Tilak was well aware that the British Press in India was trying to make mischief by labelling the festival as a deliberate attempt on his part to stir up the Hindus against the Muslims. He warned his Muslims countrymen not to fall into the Anglo-Indian trap. "The Shivaji festival" he declared, "is not celebrated to alienate or even to irritate the Muslims. Times have changed and the Muslims and the Hindu are in the same boat as far as the present political condition of the people is concerned". The people understood and followed him implicitly. The political movement of the towns had begun to reach the villages.

Tilaks' involvement in the Tai Maharaj Case is a tragic saga of his career. His friend. Balia Maharaja, made him a trustee of his estate and he was also asked to take care of the interests of his young wife after his death. Other trustees were G.S. Khaparde, Kumbhojkar and Nagpurkar. The document of the will had these words: 'My wife is expecting a baby. If she gives birth to a daughter, or if a son is born but lives only a short time, then for the purpose of continuing the name of my family, with the *vichara* (consent and consultation) of the trustees, a boy shall he placed, as often as may be necessary, for adoption, on the lap of my life, in accordance with the *shastras* (religious practices), and the trustees shall, on behalf of that son, carry on the management of my movable and fixed estate until he attains his majority.

After a few months, when Baba was no more, his wife gave birth to a son, who died two months later, Tilak was still in prison. When he was released, he took up the complex problem of adoption by Tai Maharaj. The estate left by the Baba was in heavy debts and creditors were pressing hard for payment. Indeed Tilak spent money from his own pocket to satisfy a few creditors. He however, suggested strict economy on several items of expenditure as he felt unhappy to see many resources being wasted away. The widow of the Baba did not like the economy measures suggested by Tilak. She was advised by several hangers—on that her status would be reduced to that of a pensioner. She was also advised to get rid of these trustees and adopt a boy of her own choice. She therefore secretly began negotiations to adopt Baba Maharaj of Kolapur who was four years older than herself. In this kind of decision, she sought the support of Nagpurkar, one of the trustees of the estate.

Under these circumstances, Tilak and Khaparde took a different line of action. They in fact were pained to learn about this kind of adoption which, they would argue, ruin the economic status of the estate. They suggested to Tai Maharaj that she should adopt a boy from the Babre branch of the family of Aurangabad, in the Nizam's dominion. A suitable boy named Jagannath, just seven years old, was found suitable for adoption. In a huge gathering of learned men who performed the religious rites and prominent citizens, the boy's father put him in the lap of the widow and Jagannath was adopted in a formal way. All the relevant papers of adoption were signed by the parties concerned and were witnessed, thus completing the boy's adoption.

But Tai Maharaja, on returning to Puna, was unhappy and restless and began to resentment against adoption. On 29 July 1901, she applied for revocation of the probate granted to Tilak and other trustees. Now the litigation started. The grounds of her application were: (i) that the grant of probate to Tilak and others had become void and inoperative through the birth (and subsequent death) of a son to Tai Maharaj and (ii) that the executors had become unfit to act in the said trust, so necessitating the appointment of new trustees. Aston, the District Judge, decided in widow's favour, held the adoption disapproved and revoked the probate. He also stated 'Mr. Tilak's disposition and whole behaviour was untruthful'. He committed Tilak to the City Magistrate to be dealt with according to the Criminal Law. He was convicted.

Tilak felt much indignant as his self-respect was outraged and his personal honour sullied. He at once appealed to the Bombay High Court, and Aston's decision the matter of probate was reversed. In the charge of perjury, Tilak was convicted and sentenced to eighteen months' rigorous imprisonment with a fine of Rs. 1,000/- which was reduced to six months by the Sessions Judge. Liter on, Tilak appealed to the High Court and he was found innocent on every charge. Meanwhile, Tai Maharaj died, but the case was continued in the name of her daughter, Shantabai. It was decided against Tilak who now appealed to the Privy Council in London and finally won the case in 1915. The execution of the decree of the Privy Council was somewhat delayed but ultimately the estate was handed over to Jagannath in February 1917.

It appears that several government officials were much prejudiced against Tilak who had to suffer in this case. The blatant attack on Tilak's honesty and character was defended by him with full strength and legal support and ultimately he succeeded. This fact greatly enhanced his prestige in the masses for whom he lived and worked throughout his career.

Arrested Again

Curzon's reactionary rule, culminating into the Partition of Bengal, and the infructuous constitutionalism of the Congress had made the politically conscious youth and an important section of the press desperate. They wanted to do 'something', which meant violence. Two years after the Partition would coincide with the close of half a century after the first War of Indian Independence, the Revolt of 1857; this thought inspired the youth to make another attempt. The press appeared as a forerunner. Newspapers, pamphlets and handbills were distributed in large numbers, rousing the people to rise against the British.

But where were the arms to come from, and what form should the proposed violence take? The answer is to be found in the activities of Indian political abroad. In 1905, Shyamji Krishna Verma, inspired, as his biographer says, by Tilak's suffering, sacrifice and patriotism, went to England, and started the India Home Rule Society with himself as its president; its office was located in a building which was named the India House. Shyamji enrolled some revolutionary recruits, the most conspicuous among them being Vinayak Damodar Savarkar, then aged 22, who had been recommended by Tilak.

In India, Savarkar was associated with a revolutionary organisation, called the Abhinav Bharat Society. At one of its meetings, the Society had decided to depute Senapati Bapat and Hemchandra Das to study the art of manufacturing bombs.

They learnt it from a Russian revolutionary in Paris and bought a bomb manual from him. Then Bapat, Das and another man from U. P., Hotilal Verma, left for India with cyclostyled copies of the bomb manual. By now, the Deccan was "honeycombed with secret societies". The Abhinav Bharat had its own intelligence system, and some of its members had intercepted in Bombay a message from the British Government about Tilak's impending arrest.

In other parts of India also, many revolutionary organisations had sprung up; many young men had learnt the art of bomb-making. Liaison was established between these organisations and Indian revolutionaries abroad. The Government adopted a series of repressive measures.

The first was an ordinance issued on May 11, 1907, which made it obligatory for the organisers of public meetings to give the district magistrate seven days' notice. The magistrate could prohibit any meeting at his will. Those not prohibited were held under police surveillance. The ordinance was first applied to the Punjab and East Bengal. After six months, it was given legislative sanction and named the Prevention of Seditious Meetings Act. In 1908, the Explosive Substance Act was passed to deal with anarchists. Any one found in possession of explosives and implements and materials which could be used in the manufacture of bombs was punishable with transportation for fourteen years. Even an attempt or intention to cause explosion was made punishable with seven years imprisonment or 20 years transportation. Another law of 1908, the Newspapers (Incitement to Offences) Act, empowered the Government to confiscate the printing press of any paper which contained "any incitement to murder or any offence under the Explosive Substance Act or to any act of violence". The magistrates were empowered to order confiscation of printing presses even before the accused were produced before them for hearing. In cases which the magistrates considered emergent, they could order attachment before any legal formality was gone through. At the intervention of the Secretary of State, Morley, this sweeping measure was amended so as to include the right of appeal.

On April 30, 1908, the bomb made its first appearance with fatal results. Two Bengali young boys, Khudiram Bose and Prafulla Chaki, belonging to the revolutionary party of Manicktolla, threw a bomb at a carriage at Muzaffarpur which, they believed, belonged to the District Judge, Kingsford, who, as chief presidency magistrate of Calcutta, had awarded severe punishments to editors of several Bengal newspapers. He had also sentenced a revolutionary to whipping. But unfortunately the carriage was not Kingsford's, and the bomb killed the wife and daughter of a much respected and pro-Indian European, Pringle Kennedy. The two bomb-throwers were arrested. Chaki at once shot himself and fell dead; Bose was sentenced to death and hanged. He was hailed as a martyr.

His photographs had an immense sale, and by and by the young bloods of Bengal took to wearing dhotis with Khudiram Bose's name woven on them. On the date of his execution, the boys of several schools in the Province attended classes barefooted and without shirts on.

Tilak deplored the bomb outrage, but it appeared to him that the appearance of the bomb in India had changed the outlook of Indian politics. Week after week he asked Government, through the columns of the Kesari, to understand the implications of the new development, and act wisely. His advice was that the answer to the bomb was political reform, and not repression as had been advocated by the Anglo-Indian press. In his weekly comments he said: "Some people pay attention to the evil effects of a vice firmly established in the body, only when that vice begins to inflict trouble upon the body in the shape of a terrible abscess; and an effort is then made to remove the vice. The terrible murders that took place in Ireland spontaneously riveted England's attention to the grievances of that country and then Home Rule or Swarajya for Ireland began to be discussed. Such usefulness of one sort of these murders has been indirectly described by Lord Morley in one place. Will the terrible occurrence at Muzaffarpur rivet Lord Morley's attention to the grievance about the partition of Bengal?" Again, he wrote: "The evidence required for proving the loss which India is sustaining from the political, industrial, moral and material points of view, owing to the entire administration of India being carried on solely under the guidance of the white official class and in utter disregard of public opinion, is so very strong that none but the friends of the official class will have any doubt of the iniquitous character of the present administrative system. That such an administrative system should come to be disliked by the people is the effect of Western education itself."

The next week he published a long article answering the criticism of the Anglo-Indian press and of some prominent Englishmen: "Why do you, in the first place, drive the youths to the ditch of despair by repeatedly flogging their backs? It is human nature that one should try to drag down the precipice along with oneself the man who has flogged him to the ditch of despair, sorrow and exasperation. Mr. Rees, a Member of Parliament, advises Government—'if repression is to be practised, then press down forcibly without love or mercy, crush down the heads of all in one and the same fashion, let a level plain be made all round, and then the reverberation of your tyrannical acts will be heard nowhere. If Government leave all bounds, as suggested by Mr. Rees, then the consequence thereof shall never be beneficial to Government and to India.

Even bombs can be prepared with a little knowledge, at a small cost and with small effort. It is the opinion of Spencer that when a Government begins obstinately to practise oppression and persistently refuses to give proper respect to public opinion, then such a state of things is positively produced that changes in the administration are not brought about by means other than terrible means.."

In the following issues of the Kesari, he came out with more ardent pleas that the character of British rule in India was responsible for the appearance of the bomb.

These articles were causing a great deal of anxiety to the British authorities not only in the Bombay Presidency, but also in other provinces where the Kesari had a large circulation. The Governor of the Central Provinces repeatedly addressed private letters to Sir John Mackenzie, Home Member of the Government of Bombay "on the expediency of dealing with Tilak and the Puna and Satara newspapers which are entering my province in large numbers and preventing the whole of the Marathi-speaking people". The C. P. Governor indicated to the Bombay Governor that if the Bombay Government could not see their way to taking action he would be forced into the otherwise undesirable course of taking action myself in a province where the newspapers circulated instead of in the province where they were published. Later on, Sir John Mackenzie informed the C. P. Governor that the Government of Bombay were only "awaiting a good case against Tilak to take action"; and therefore, says the C. P. Governor, "I had to possess my soul in patience".

Some years later, he wrote in connection with Tilak's case against Sir Valentine Chirol of The Times: "I know how I should have welcomed it in the Central Provinces in the days when the Bombay Government had not made up their minds to grasp the nettle represented by Mr. Tilak in 1908".

Soon after the exchange of this correspondence, several editors were arrested and put on trial. Tilak's writings were being carefully examined to see which of them could secure his conviction. Tilak was the most popular leader in the country, and Government knew that repercussions of failure of prosecution would be terrible—it would considerably add to his stature, and ridicule the Government in the eyes of the people. In that wavering state of mind, the authorities picked out an article which appeared as the first leader in the Kesari of May 12, 1908. Success of the prosecution was still in some doubt and Tilak happened to make their victory certain by another article which he wrote on June 9. The prosecutors jumped with joy—this article would secure Tilak's conviction; that was certain, they said.

Bombay was chosen to be the venue of the trial; and on June 24, destiny took him to that city. The same day, at about 6 pm:.., he was arrested. Simultaneous action was taken in Puna; his house and press were locked up by the police, and the next day a search was conducted. The police took into their possession 63 documents, among which was a card containing names of two handbooks on modern explosives. This card played an important role in the trial.

The Article in Question

Country's Misfortune

The following is a summary of the leading article, entitled "The Country's Misfortune", which appeared in the Kesari, dated May 12, 1908, and in respect of which the Bombay Government ordered Tilak's prosecution:

"We never imagined that the high-handedness of the white bureaucracy in this country would so soon drive some of the youthful patriots of Bengal to such acts of violence as they have recently committed. Their statements before the police bear witness to the fact that these men were not at all inspired by self-interest in what they did, but it was out of sheer exasperation at the autocratic doings of the bureaucracy that they have chosen this path. It is further evident that the same circumstances that have given birth to the anarchist cult in Russia have come into existence in this country, and are producing the same result.

The British Government is, it is true, a mighty one, but all autocrats must bear in mind that there is after all a limit to human forbearance. All constitutional agitation for undoing the partition of Bengal having miserably failed, nothing could be more natural than that a few of the ardent spirits in Bengal should have lost their heads and resorted to excesses. It is true that long foreign domination has mostly quenched the spirit of the people, but it has not become altogether extinct. A knowledge of history and the rise of Japan has kindled in their minds a strong desire for Swarajya, and if there is no gradual fruition of that desire, some of them at all events will not hesitate to commit deeds of violence in a fit of exasperation and despair.

"We, along with other newspapers, have frankly told Government that if they resorted to Russian methods of repression, Indians too shall have to imitate the Russian revolutionaries in their defence. To exercise every sort of oppression on the subjects, and at the same time to expect them to bear everything with meekness is to exhibit an utter ignorance of ordinary human nature. Such ignorance has been disclosed by the Anglo-Indian Press, which conveniently overlooking the fact that the present undesirable situation is the outcome of the unrestricted exercise of autocratic power by the white bureaucrats, has been indulging in all sorts of wild vapouring.

Our rulers seem to desire that the indignation felt for their measures should never overstep certain prescribed bounds.

The Muzaffarpur outrage will teach a lesson to Government on the vanity of this desire. Government can, of course, suppress such outrages with a high hand, but that will not effect a radical cure of the disease. So long as its germs remain in the body politic, it will break out at some place or other.

"The remedies, therefore, must be prescribed with due foresight. The fact must be recognised by Government that these excesses on the part of an inconsiderate few are due to the refusal of the Government to give due consideration to the suggestions for reform in the administration which the people have begun to dislike. They must, therefore, with true statesmanship, try to avoid bringing matters to a crisis.

"We, on our part, do not think that our duty ends with condemning the Muzaffarpur outrage. We regret the occurrence, but we are of opinion that so long as the causes which gave rise to it are allowed to remain, it will be impossible to prevent its repetition. It lies entirely in the hands of the Government to prevent the growth of nihilism in India.

Reform in the administration is the only way to kill this new Upas tree, and if the powers that be are not disposed to resort to that remedy, nothing can be more unfortunate. If the authorities fail to read the signs of the times, what can we do?"

Court Case

On June 25, Tilak, as editor and publisher of the Kesari was produced before the Chief Presidency Magistrate, A. H. S. Aston. After Superintendent Sloane of the Bombay city police, who figured as complainant, had been sworn, and had identified the 'accused', Tilak's pleader asked that the case might be tried forthwith. But the Government pleader was not ready, and applied for an adjournment in order to call evidence. The hearing was postponed to June 29.

The Magistrate then took up Tilak's application for release on bail, and remarking that "the offence in question is not bailable", rejected it. He added: "I am of opinion that there are reasonable grounds for believing that the accused has committed the crime urging that if the 'accused' was not released on bail, he would not be able to instruct properly those whose help he wanted to secure for his defence.

Other grounds given by defence counsel Mr. Jinnah were: Tilak had a good defence; he had been suffering from diabetes for sometime past and was under medical treatment when he was arrested; the official translation of the articles used in the proceedings before the Magistrate were incorrect and misleading; the Counsel would not be able to make a proper defence unless the 'accused' had himself an opportunity of explaining the correct meaning and spirit thereof to his counsel.

Jinnah also invoked the judgement of Justice Tyabji, and emphasised that since there was no doubt whatsoever that Tilak would be forthcoming to stand his trial, justice demanded that he should be enlarged on bail.

The application was opposed by the Government counsel. In the written affidavit filed by the solicitor to Government, he made a reference to Tilak's imprisonment in 1897 and his conditional release, and said that he had been informed by Government that if the accused was released on bail, he would use his liberty to excite feelings of disaffection and hatred against Government and that it would be dangerous to release him.

The court was assured that the translation to be used at the trial of the case would be one made by the translator of the High Court itself.

After Jinnah had finished his arguments, the Advocate-General rose to argue the Government side of the case. But hardly had he uttered these two words, "I appear...", than Justice Davar, who was presiding over the session, intervened and said: "I will not trouble you, Mr. Advocate-General", and delivered his judgement without hearing him. He said that he did not agree with the statement "broadly made" that the only consideration, which ought to guide the court in deciding whether bail should or should not be granted, was the consideration that an accused would appear to take his trial. There were many circumstances that, in his opinion, should be weighed before coming to a conclusion. Unlike Tyabji, he thought that nothing should be said before the trial that would in any way prejudice either the case for the prosecution or for the accused. He, therefore, rejected the application and gave no reason for the rejection, for that, in his opinion, would prejudice the case one way or the other.

It would be interesting to recall that it was Davar who, as Tilak's counsel in 1897, four times argued the bail application and took his stand on the ground that the accused would not be able to instruct his counsel properly from inside the jail, and ultimately succeeded in securing his release. Then he had said: "I ask your

Lordship to exercise your discretion vested in you, and make an order which will show that the accused is not prejudged by the tribunals that administer justice and law". Now he said that the Judge of the High Court had no doubt unlimited discretion, unfettered by any condition, and could release an accused person on bail pending his trial. He argued that that was a judicial discretion, "a discretion that must be judiciously exercised, and exercised with care and caution", and therefore reached the conclusion that the bail application should be refused.

Meanwhile legal experts of the Government, both in Bombay and in Calcutta, who were assiduously preparing the prosecution, felt that the May 12 article might fail to secure conviction. A secretary of the Government of India suggested: "It is most important that the case against Tilak should be strengthened, for the present charge is a very weak one, and even if it end in conviction, which is improbable, we shall have an outcry from a large section of the radical party at home against a law under which an editor can be sent to jail for criticism which in England would be regarded as of quite a mild type. On the other hand, the incitement to the use of bombs which appears in the article of June 9 would excite no sympathy in England among any section of politicians whose opinions count. Now Tilak's prosecutors switched on their attention to that article which was entitled. "These Remedies Are Not Lasting", and which appeared in the Kesari, dated June 9.

The Viceroy, Lord Minto, agreed that no effort should be spared to secure Tilak's prosecution. "The present is not a time", he said, "to give a well-known agitator like Tilak the benefit of any leniency; and I certainly think we should call the serious attention of the Bombay Government to the possibility of proceeding against his press in respect to the article in the Kesari of the 9th June".

The exchange of official notes that followed the recording of his opinion by the Viceroy makes interesting reading. Everybody seemed anxious to imprison Tilak for a long period. The Bombay Government were in favour of taking action under the Newspaper (Incitement to Offences) Act, but they suggested two possible objections. The first was that the "offending article" was published only one day after the passing of that Act. The second possible objection was that action under the Newspaper Act would unfairly prejudice Tilak in his trial for sedition which is now pending before the High Court.

These objections, however, did not damp the enthusiasm of the officers at the Secretariat level, and the same secretary of the Government of India again said in his note: "I venture to think that it is most desirable that we should deal Tilak as shrewd a blow as we can. He is by far the ablest and most dangerous of the rebel party in this country, and his complete overthrow will stagger that party and show to all waverers the strength of the Government. It is not enough to imprison him when we can also suppress his newspaper. The Kesari has a circulation of 20,000 which is an enormous circulation for India.

This is no time for rose-water administration, and I am confident that the great mass of moderate men will be glad to see Tilak completely overthrown. He ruined the National Congress at Surat and his methods have given great offence to the Moderate Party".

But the Home Member of the Government of India brought about moderation in the official temper, and directed the Bombay Government to refrain from action under the Newspapers Act. "It is no doubt a desirable thing, he contended to suppress both Tilak and his newspaper, but we should be careful that zeal does not out-turn discretion in a matter which has to be laid before Parliament and which will attract worldwide attention".

The Bombay Government therefore took two vital decisions: first, to frame a second charge based on the article of June 9; and secondly, not to hazard prosecution under the Newspapers Act. But to depend wholly on Sections 124-A and 153-A of the Indian Penal Code, the following is a substantial summary of the article:

"The Government of India has again entered upon a career of repression from this week. This demon of repression periodically possesses the Government, and one of such periods has now recurred. As liberty of the press and liberty of speech give birth to a nation and nourish it, our bureaucrats had long wished to extinguish both in India, and the bomb outrage afforded them an opportunity to carry out their design. But the question is, will these repressive measures succeed in their object? The officials first of all wish to see the bomb driven out of India, and this desire is both natural and laudable. But the means they have adopted for this end being just the reverse of what should have been adopted, it is therefore plain that they have lost their senses. This mental aberration is a sign of impending ruin and one is grieved to think that worse days are in store both for the people and the authorities. The latter have raised the outcry that the cult of the bomb in Bengal is destructive of social order just like its prototype in Europe.

But there is a vast difference between the two cults. While the cult in Europe is the outcome of the hatred of the self-aggrandising wealthy classes, the Bengal cult has got at its root an excess of the patriotic sentiment. The Bengal bomb-thrower has got more in common with the Portuguese patriots, who assassinated Don Carlos for suppressing their Parliament, and with the hot-headed Russians who committed bomb outrages in desperation owing to the Tsar's refusal to convene the Duma than with anarchists pure and simple. The bomb in Portugal compelled the abandonment of the policy of repression in that country, while the mighty Tsar had to eat humble pie before the same engine of destruction. The cessation of the bomb outrages in the two aforesaid countries can never be ascribed to repressive measures. That consummation was due to the fact that the statesmen of both the countries recognised in the bomb new, rising aspirations of the people and made efforts to gratify these aspirations.

The condition of Indians is worse than that of a cage bird. For while the latter is supplied with delicacies with a view that it may not feel the misery of its captivity, the Indians have been ruthlessly deprived of arms in order that they might never dream of freeing themselves from their bondage. The English have evidently emasculated the whole nation and reduced it to a state of impotence simply to enable even the lowest of their officials to exercise their high-handed sway with impunity. The English possess neither the magnanimity nor the power of the Mughals who never disarmed the Indians, The Mughals were able to keep up their imperial status for over a century even after their forces had been annihilated during Aurangzeb's abortive campaigns in the Deccan. The British Government will not be able to outlive, even for a quarter of a century, a similar period of stress and strain.

The disarmed condition of the people combined with the military strength of the Government had so long made the English masters of the situation. But the bomb has changed all this.

Hitherto the Government had no means of knowing the degree of desperation to which some of their hot-headed subjects have been driven through exasperation at Government measures. The people only petitioned and their representations were regarded as mere froth worth no attention. They fretted and fumed in secret, but Government knew nothing about the matter. The bomb, however, has put a potent weapon into the hands of the people, and it has lessened the respect for the military prestige of the Government. England will not henceforward be able to carry on the administration of the country in a smooth manner unless Englishmen deign to take the people more into their confidence. Manufacture and possession of arms can be prevented by law and police supervision, but the same cannot be said about the bomb. It resembles more a magical charm than a visible object manufactured in a factory. The bomb required by hot-headed madcaps, bent on violence, does not require large quantities of materials for their manufacture, as was shown by the bomb factory unearthed at Calcutta.

It appears that Government have failed to learn a lesson from the discovery. No law possesses the power to keep the knowledge of the manufacture of bombs from those that are bent upon using them, for such knowledge is no longer regarded as a secret in Europe. It is still a secret in India, but if a policy of repression succeeds in adding to the number of hot-headed persons in the country, the knowledge will in no time spread to other parts of India from Bengal.

The manufacture of the bomb has become such an easy matter that the police can be easily evaded. It was not so easy when the Explosives Act was passed in England, but recently it has been vastly simplified in consequence of new scientific discoveries. How far can legislation restrict the operations of the scientific expert? Government have been trying their hand at achieving impossibilities, which are sure to prove disadvantageous both to themselves and to the people.

The new legislation will put a new weapon into the hands of the underlings of Government for the persecution of the innocent people. Government must act in such a way that no one should feel any necessity to have recourse to bombs. They must see that no keen disappointment is caused to those men of high ability who are seeking the rights of Swarajya.

But we fear that the new law about newspapers is likely to give a dangerous turn to the feeling of disappointment already prevailing in the country. The grant of, the important rights of Swarajya is the only means to get rid of the bomb in India".

The prosecution was now ready with its charges, which stated that "Tilak brought or attempted to bring into hatred or contempt or excited or attempted to excite feelings of disaffection towards the Government established by law in British India, and promoted or attempted to promote feelings of enmity or hatred between different classes of His Majesty's subjects by publishing the two articles". On the appointed date—June 29—the Chief Presidency Magistrate took up the Tilak case again, read the charges to the accused, recorded depositions, and committed Tilak to the Sessions.

July 13 was fixed for the hearing. In the meantime, the prosecution took a vital step to ensure conviction. On July 3, it applied for a special jury to be empanelled to try Tilak on the ground that the case was one of great importance and a special jury would be eminently fitted for it.

Tilak's counsel opposed the application. His argument was:

> "This is a prosecution instituted by the Government for a political offence under the special sanction of the Government. It, therefore, comes with a force and recommendation naturally calculated to overwhelm the defendant. A special jury means that the majority shall consist of Europeans, judging from the list of jurors. This list shows that there are 242 Europeans against 156 Indians. In all probability, therefore, the

> majority in the jury would be Europeans. That was the case in the last Tilak trial, and that was the case in all sedition trials in this court. Europeans would not make fit jurymen on the present occasion as they would be handicapped on account of their 'inability to understand the language of the alleged incriminating articles. Lastly, it is impossible to close one's eyes to the fact that these political offences and press prosecutions are really a struggle between the rulers and the ruled for political fights and privileges, which can be obtained from the rulers alone. Now Englishmen belong to the ruling class. There must exist some political and patriotic bias against Indian aspirations. Moreover, Englishmen at the present moment are rather inflamed on account of the assassinations in Muzaffarpur. There is, therefore, a real danger that Englishmen would be unconsciously biased against the accused to his great prejudice. But if the prosecution insists, we are willing to yield provided it consents that the majority on the special jury consists of Indians conversant with the language in which the indicted articles are written, viz., Marathi".

Davar, who presided over the sessions, rejected the defence arguments, and granted the prosecution application. Again, as in the case of the bail application, his reasons were hardly convincing. As he himself said at the outset, a special jury was necessarily summoned in all offences punishable with death; but the law—Section 276 of the Criminal Procedure Code gave power to a Judge of the High Court to call a special jury in any other case also. In the Tilak case, he said, a special jury was necessary: "There is no doubt whatever that the cases against Mr. Tilak are important cases from his own standpoint, and I feel in his own interest he should have the benefit of being tried by a jury selected from the citizens of Bombay, but from the higher class of citizens".

Answering the other points raised by Tilak's counsel, Davar said: "I hardly think that there is much substance in the arguments as to the knowledge of the language. Of course, if it comes to a conflict, then the court must necessarily accept the translations of its authorised translators. I am quite sure that any member of the special jury will come in and take his oath to administer justice and will leave out all prejudices if he has any and all extraneous circumstances entirely out of his consideration".

The 1897 trial was being repeated in every detail, and shrewd people began to forecast that Tilak would again be incarcerated for a long term.

Two Home Rule Leagues

Home Rule League elicited favourable reactions and I attracted notice in England A Home Rule for India League was established at 18, Tavistock Square, London, on June 7, 1916, It was agreed at the first meeting that the League should form an independent party willing to work with any party, but not definitely attached to any party. It was also agreed to form branches or centres with a small subscription of 6d. per head. The executive consisted of C. Jinarajadasa, Muriel '(Countess de la Warr), the Lady Emily Lutyens, George Sydney Arundale, (Miss) Esther Bright, John Scurr and George Lansbury. Major D, Graham Pole was appointed general secretary. It was decided to print 10,000 copies of a leaflet entitled "What India Wants". This was followed by several leaflets. Meetings were regularly held, and Home Rule propaganda was carried on.

The Times (June 19) made an embittered attack on the organisation. But Hyndman's Justice (June 22) welcomed it. The paper wrote: "We do not know who are members of the League, nor have we seen the leaflets. But so soon as peace is proclaimed, after the final defeat of the Germanic Powers, we shall be glad to cooperate in a movement for the emancipation of India. We do not see how Englishmen, who proclaim that they are fighting for national freedom in Europe, can honestly continue a system of foreign despotism over 315,000,000 people in Hindustan".

The paper challenged the Ex-Viceroy, Lord Hardinge's, speech made just about that time, in which he claimed marvellous beneficial results from our rule to India, and added:

> "It is simply not true. Moreover, so insecure is our tenure of this vast Empire that Lord Lansdowne and

> Sir Edward Grey have entered into treaties with Japan to hold India for us in case of need. In return Japan has been given a free hand in China. We may bear in mind, too, that Indian troops, on the strength of those Japanese treaties, have been fighting one our side in Europe as well as in Asia. Home Rule in India will greatly benefit both India and England".

Five or six weeks after the birth of the Home Rule League, Tilak with the assistance of Baptista, started work on a draft of a Bill for the Better Administration of India. His intention was to send the Bill, after it had been agreed upon by the people in different provinces to England, for being rendered into legal language by an English Barrister, and put before Parliament.

He made no secret of his plans. He told the district magistrate, Puna, who called him to explain the implications of a speech he made at Nagar early in June, that criticism of the Government was bound to be an important part of his speeches. Asked what his conception of Swaraj was, Tilak said that a Swaraj administration's first act would be to order compulsory free primary education, and its second would be to abolish all liquor shops. Therefore, he told people at Nagar that they would be better off under their own administration.

He made it clear that it was not his intention to produce a discontent that might result in trouble. But when the district magistrate made a report of his interview with Tilak to the Commissioner saying that he believed "Tilak to be in earnest in his disavowal of any intention to embarrass the Government", the Commissioner remarked that he did not trust Tilak's protestations and that his present activities are most undesirable.

While the Home Rule agitation had been going on, a movement was set afoot by Tilak's admirers to present him with a purse of a lakh of rupees on the occasion of his sixtieth birthday on July 23, 1916. Collections were started, Bombay alone raising Rs. 50,000 in about a week. Money came flowing from many parts of the country, and in a short time the purse was full on the birthday, a public meeting attended by 8,000 persons of all shades of opinion, was held. A large number of addresses and congratulatory messages were read at the meeting, where on a raised platform sat Tilak, heavily garlanded, amidst his friends and admirers. "Memories of storm and suffering", he said in a short speech, "rather than those of happiness rise before my mind's eye. Looking into the future, after completing sixty years, one's mind cannot but be filled with misgivings; and with declining strength, one is apt to feel less hopeful. But I devoutly hope that with your support, I may be granted life and strength to add to whatever work of public good I may have done".

About the purse, he said: "I do not know what to do with the money. I do not want it for my own use nor would it be proper for me to accept it for my family. I can only accept it in trust to spend it in a constitutional way for national work after adding my own quota to it".

Tilak's birthday celebrations gave impetus to the Home Rule agitation. With the fervour of a young man, he himself made hurricane tours, delivered speeches, and week after week wrote exhortative articles in his papers. Here is an extract from his articles:

"Even when war is going on in all its fierceness at a distance of a hundred miles, Home Rule for Ireland is being discussed in England. How are we to characterise the pretence of the officials that they are quite upset with the philosophical discussion of Home Rule which only breaks the deathlike silence of India? We think that Home Rule should be demanded all at once. It need not come into force immediately.

A time-limit may be laid down in a Parliament Bill accepting it. Do not ask for crumbs; ask for the whole bread. If there is any method to effect political reforms without riots and without the spread of discontent, it is this. All are demanding Swarajya".

The only other person who matched and sometimes excelled Tilak in carrying on Home Rule propaganda was Mrs. Besant.

Her promise at the Bombay Congress came in her way of being first with her League, but, as if to make good the loss, she greatly intensified her campaign against the bureaucracy and for Home Rule. Many eminent leaders of the Congress came forward to join her, among them being Motilal Nehru, Tej Bahadur Sapru, Ishwar Saran. They virtually came under her spell and decided to set her up for the Congress Presidentship of 1916 against A. C. Mazumdar. Lucknow was the venue of the Congress, and they believed they would be able to undo the nomination of Mazumdar. At a meeting of the reception committee, it was informally mentioned that the Raja of Mahmudabad would contribute one lakh of rupees towards the expenses of an Indian deputation to England in connection with the Home Rule movement, if Mrs. Besant was elected President. Their efforts, however, failed and Mazumdar presided at the Lucknow Congress.

Now, Mrs. Besant thought that the time was ripe for to start her own Home Rule League. The promised report of the All India Congress Committee on self-government not having been submitted by September 1, the date on which it was due, Mrs. Besant, in response to many urgent requests, decided to organise the League on a regular basis. Within a few days of her announcement, branches were formed at Bombay, Kanpur, Allahabad, Banaras, Madanpalli, Kumbakonam, Adyar, Madurai, Ahmednagar, Calicut, and Madras.

Now there were two Leagues in the field, and Mrs. Besant and Tilak came to an agreement about the sphere of action of the respective organisations. Tilak's League was to work in the Central Provinces and Bombay Presidency; Bombay city and the rest of India fell under Mrs. Besant's jurisdiction.

N. C. Kelkar, secretary of Tilak's League, proceeded to make arrangements to educate villagers on the objects of Home Rule agitation. Lecturers were appointed; they were given talking points and were asked to stick to a uniform pattern of propaganda. Only those who held a pass signed by the secretary could speak in the name of the League. The lecturers kept themselves within the limits of the law, the object being to use the law to spread the message of the League.

Tilak himself went on a tour of the Karnataka in November.

On the 20th, at Gadag, at an entertainment given him by the local people, he was served with an order prohibiting him from delivering a public speech in Gadag. He was also told to finish with the entertainment within five minutes. On his return journey to Puna, he halted for a day at Hubli. Here, he was conducted in a procession from the railway station to the house where he was to stay. A large crowd gathered to hear him; no restriction was placed on him here, and he spoke to eager admirers thus: "We do not want to trespass on the rights of any nation, we do not want supremacy over any people, we are only asking for what is our birthright". The occasion was utilised to establish a branch of the League at Hubli. He broke journey at several other places, making speeches and opening new branches.

In July, he became a member of the Puna Congress Committee, after a break of nine years, in order to qualify himself to become a delegate for the year's Congress. But he had already outpaced the Congress; the Home Rule League was now more popular.

Legal Proceedings

On the 22nd of July under the orders of Government the Deputy Inspector-General of Police, Criminal Investigation Department, laid an information under Section 108. Criminal Procedure Code, in the Court of the District Magistrate. Puna, against Tilak in respect of the Home Rule speech he delivered at Belgaum and the two speeches he delivered at Ahmednagar. The District Magistrate issued a notice returnable on the 28th idem ordering Tilak to show cause why he should not be bound over in a sum of Rs. 20,000, with two sureties for Rs. 10,000 each, to be of good behaviour for one year. On Tilak's application, the hearing of the case was first postponed to the 2nd of August and again to the 7th idem. The hearing lasted till the 10th of August, and on the 12th the District Magistrate ordered Tilak to sign a bond for Rs. 10,000 and furnish two sureties each in a sum of Rs. 10,000. Tilak signed the bond and tendered Trimbak Hari Avate and Ganpat Vithoba Morval as his sureties. They were accepted by the Magistrate.

Appeal to High Court

Tilak immediately preferred an appeal to the High Court which was admitted on the 1st August and came on for hearing on the 8th and 9th November before Justices Batchelor and Shah.

While admitting that there were passages in the speeches which were highly objectionable and seditious, the Judges were unable to agree that the natural and probable effect of the speeches taken as a whole on the minds of those who were addressed would be to bring into hatred or contempt, or to excite disaffection towards the Government established by law in British India. The order of the District Magistrate was accordingly reversed and the bond executed by Tilak and his two sureties cancelled.

The decision of the High Court was held on all sides as legitimatising agitation for Home Rule, but there was reason to believe that Tilak himself was not wholly satisfied with the judgement. Apart from the strictures passed on him, neither of the Judges was able to accept his contention that criticism directed against the Civil Service, generally described as "bureaucracy" in the speeches, could not in any circumstances be treated as criticism against the Government established by law in British India. As a result, the few speeches he was obliged to make during the remaining portion of the year were marked by unusual restraint and brevity.

A Purse Presented

Early in July a movement was set on foot by N. C. Kelkar and other admirers of Tilak to collect a purse of Rs. 1,00,000 for presentation to him on his 60th birthday. The birthday was celebrated in the Gaikwad Wada on July 24th. Between 5,000 and 6,000 persons were present, including, representatives from the Karnatic, Berars, Gujarat and Bombay City. Speeches were delivered by several prominent agitators present eulogising Tilak and his work for the Motherland.

Tilak was then garlanded and the amount subscribed was formally handed to him. Some persons presented him on the spot with clothes, pagris, rings, currency notes, etc. He was also tendered an address in a silver casket. In reply he said that he accepted the gifts in trust to spend in a constitutional way for national work. The birthday was also celebrated in Bombay and various other places.

Provincial Conference at Ahmedabad

Tilak attended the Provincial Conference held under the auspices of the Bombay Presidency Congress Committee at

Ahmedabad on the 21st, 22nd and 23rd October. It is said that he had from the commencement expressed his unwillingness to take any prominent part in the proceedings of the Conference, leaving it to N. C. Kelkar to do so in his behalf. His primary object in attending the Conference appears to have been to demonstrate the genuineness of the Belgaum Conference's decision regarding the compromise between the two parties, and his decision to take no part in the proceedings was due to a desire not to make himself too prominent and bring himself into collision with the Moderate leaders at that juncture, especially as he knew that some of them had a personal bias against him. In spite of Tilak's ostensible abstention, however, the conference witnessed the first trial of strength under the new conditions between the Extremists and Moderates, and on the only four points regarding which there was a difference of opinion the Extremists' view was carried.

At Bombay

On the 28th, he went to Bombay to attend the meeting of the Bombay Provincial Congress Committee to be held there on the 29th idem. He was elected a representative of the province of Bombay along with 14 others on the All India Congress Committee. He again visited Bombay on the 7th December. He had prepared a scheme for the better working of the Home Rule League which he placed before a private meeting of the Provincial Congress Committee held specially for the purpose on the 7th. The scheme required that the Congress should take executive work in hand, open a central office in Bombay for the purpose, appoint paid lecturers for the spread of the Home Rule propaganda and bring an amendment to the Government of India Act of 1858 so as to legalise agitation for Home Rule in India. The scheme was approved of by a majority of the members present and was to be placed for adoption before the ensuing Congress at Lucknow.

Sarvajanik Sabha and Congress

On the 10th December he returned to Puna and presided at a special meeting of the Sarvajanik Sabha when it was resolved to seek affiliation for the Sabha to the Congress organisation. The matter came up for consideration before the Provincial Congress

Committee on the 21st December, but recognition was refused on the ground that the Sabha had not satisfied requirements and that its main object was the attainment of "Independent Swaraj". Tilak was greatly incensed, and said he would appeal to the All India Congress Committee against the decision.

Defence of India Force

He attended a meeting held in the Kirloskar Theatre, Puna, on the same day to express satisfaction at the announcement made by the Viceroy regarding the intention of Government to enrol Indians in their units in the Defence of India Force for general military service in India for the duration of the war. In proposing the resolution he said that Government were making a move in the right direction in trusting Indians with the responsibility of defending their motherland. They would soon be asked to join the colours for the defence of their country and he hoped they would answer the call. Maharashtra should give at least 20,000, and if that number did not come forward, he would consider that they were unfit for Home Rule, and he himself would cease to be a Home Ruler. They would probably not get all the privileges they claimed at once, but a beginning had been made and the rest would follow. He offered the services of his own son.

On the 23rd a notice under the Defence of India Act issued by the Commissioner of Delhi, prohibiting Tilak from entering the Delhi Province was served on him.

Triumph for Home Rulers

Tilak did all he could to bring the Bombay delegates round to his views on the Home Rule question, and it was said that the Honourable Mr. Parekh and the Honourable Mr. Wacha had yielded to some extent. Many of the Bombay Moderates were said to be prepared to accept a large part of his programme, but fought she of the words "Home Rule". On the 27th December, the Bombay delegates met to elect their representatives for the Subjects Committee. The election was fought on the straight issue of Home Rule, and of the 15 delegates finally elected, 14 were pronounced Home Rulers.

The Subjects Committee held its sittings on the 27th, 28th and 29th. The draft of the Self-government resolution formed the subject of considerable discussion, especially to which Mrs. Besant, supported by Tilak, moved an amendment that Home Rule should be given to India after the war and of the resolution recommended a Royal Proclamation declaring Self-government to be the aim of British Rule in India and the grant after the war of the reforms set forth in the Congress-League scheme. The Moderates, therefore, rightly contended that the amendment to clashed with. The Extremists, however, stated that the amendment was necessary to prevent the Colonies exercising any control over Indian affairs through any scheme of Imperial Federation that might be introduced after the war. Mr. Jinnah, who reproached Tilak for not having given him previous intimation in regard to the amendment, moved an alternative amendment objecting to any arrangement which would place the Colonies in the position anticipated, and suggested that the Muslims were not ready to support any demand for the grant of Home Rule at an early date. His amendment was, however, lost and Mrs. Besant's when put to the vote was carried by a large majority. On the Moderates, however, threatening to oppose such a resolution in open Congress, Mrs. Besant and her party gave way and was modified so as to demand complete Self-government within a generation. Tilak spoke in support of the resolution in the Congress on the following day.

Tilak's scheme for the appointment of special Working Committees next came up for consideration, but greatly to the annoyance and discomfiture of himself and his followers, the President ruled it out of order.

Tilak was appointed one of the three trustees for the Bombay Presidency for the funds to be collected locally towards the three lakhs the Congress had recommended should be collected for a campaign in India and England.

Tilak attended the sessions of the All India Muslim League Conference held on the 30th and 31st December.

D. Healy,
Personal Assistant,
to the Deputy Inspector-General of Police,
Criminal Investigation Department.

Home Rule League Meeting

January 1917

On the 28th Tilak held a meeting of the Central Committee of the Indian Home Rule League in his own house, Gaikwad Wada. In summarising the work done by the League, he said that the Maharashtra and Madras Home Rule Leagues were instrumental in securing the Swaraj resolution at the Lucknow Congress, and in yetting the Home Rule movement stamped as lawful. That the whole Empire was now undergoing reconstruction, and that if they did not work now, as Ireland and the Colonies were doing, they would get nothing.

February

He attended a meeting in the Kirloskar Theatre, Puna on the 1st February to protest against the Indentured Labour System in the Fiji Islands. In seconding the resolution urging the abolition of the system, he said that the blame for allowing the system to continue was on the people of India, who had made no effort to put a stop to it. He called upon the young men of India to form themselves into societies, even at the expense of their college course, and go to the villages where the recruiting agents secured their victims and explain the iniquities of the system. If they did that, he declared that the System would not be heard of six months afterwards.

Information having been received that he intended to conduct a Home Rule campaign in the Punjab, a notice issued by the Government of the Punjab under the Defence of India (Consolidation) Rules, 1916, prohibiting him from entering the Punjab, was served on him on the 17th.

May

He attended the Provincial Conference held at Nasik on the 12th, 13th and 14th. In a speech at the Conference on the 12th on the Self-government resolution, he explained the necessity for having a separate political body, the Home Rule League, in addition to the National Congress. He said that but for the presence of the Home Rulers at the Lucknow Congress, it was doubtful whether the Congress would have passed the resolution on Self-government in its present form. The Congress and its committee had done nothing beyond assembling and talking, and on that account the League was started to do the work of the Congress. The League was loyal to the Congress. He did not wish a long life to the League, as he hoped they would attain their goal in two or three years.

In a speech on the 13th, he deplored that the Congress deputation has not yet left for England. He said that the angle of vision towards India in England had changed for the better and the British public was sure to listen to their legitimate demands. They did not want to get rid of the King and the bureaucrats, but desired that the latter should carry on the administration according to the wishes of the people. Home Rule was the panacea for all their ills.

July

Tilak's birthday on the 10th was celebrated throughout Maharashtra.

September

The Bombay Provincial Congress Committee met again on the 2nd in the Presidency Association rooms. Tilak was present. A resolution to the following effect on passive resistance, amended, to suit Tilak and his party was passed.

"Though the Bombay Provincial Congress Committee is of opinion that there is a strong feeling among the people to support the campaign of passive resistance on account of the coercive measures recently taken by the Government, it advises that, taking into consideration the fact that Mr. Montagu is coming on a visit to this country and that the reasons for his coming are well-known, the work of the consideration and giving opinion on the principles underlying passive resistance and the measures necessary to put them into effect, which has been entrusted to this Committee by the All India Congress Committee and the Council of the All India Muslim League, be for the present held in abeyance, and the meeting expresses the hope that the Government will take the necessary steps to allay the bitter feeling aroused among the people by the action of internments and other coercive measures taken by the authorities. This course will enable the Secretary of State to fulfil the work entrusted to him under normal conditions".

Before this proposal was agreed to, Tilak spoke strongly in support of passive resistance.

December

The Commissioner of Police, Calcutta, reported that on Tilak's arrival at Howrah on the 26th he was met by delegates and volunteers and given a most enthusiastic reception. His carriage was drawn by 50 Maratha and Marwari youths and the whole route to the Congress pandal was decorated with flags and festoons, and a halt was made at the headquarters of the Upper India "Seva Samiti", 191, Harrison Street. The procession was greeted with the blowing of conch-shells, the strewing of flowers and cries of *Vande Mataram* and *Tilak Maharaj ki jai.*

When Tilak entered the Congress pandal, the ovation he received exceeded that extended to the President-elect or any of the other delegates.

Tilak spent a very strenuous year in popularising the Home Rule League propaganda, and it may be safely said that his influence in the country is now greater than it ever has been.

D. HEALY,
Personal Assistant
to the Deputy Inspector-General of Police,
Criminal Investigation Department.

Comments on Trial

(*From Report on Native papers for the Week ending 25th July 1908*)

Dayan Prakash of 24th July 1908.

Every one has received an electric shock through the terrible decision in the Kesari Case.

Individual differences of opinion are of no account today. This is an occasion for greater sorrow than that felt for the death of Ranade. It is greatly to be lamented that we have lost the services of such a talented and heroic man at his age. We do not think that anybody will be able to fill his place.

Everybody could foresee clearly the end of the trial from the very beginning. This is the first occasion on which a Judge has allowed executive convenience to influence him; and Mr. Davar's concluding words create a doubt as to the purity of the Court. Government wanted to see Mr. Tilak out of the country in the present political situation and preferred to resort to the lawcourt to accomplish that end to deporting him outright. It is impossible for a community to do full justice to a man about whom it is prejudiced. Justice was surely blind in this case in as much as neither the prosecution nor the Judge had a word to say against the diatribes indulged in by the Anglo-Indian press which were placed before the court by Mr. Tilak in the course of his defence. Every one regretted the absence of the independent and outspoken Badruddin Tayebjee at this juncture. We do not know what Mr. Justice Davar meant when he addressed Mr. Tilak and talked about the country "you profess to love". We do not think he would have lost anything if he had resisted the temptation to use harsh language about a man whom he was on the point of ejecting from his mother country. He had no business to add insult to the enquiry. It does not lie in the mouth of Mr. Justice Davar to talk about Mr. Tilak's patriotism Mr. Tilak himself has suggested in his last pathetic remarks that the good of the country lies in pursuing the future course undaunted by difficulties.

Sentence, 1908

(From Reports on Native Papers for the Week ending 1st August 1908).

31st July 1908.

There is no sense in saying that Mr. Tilak was sentenced according to law. There was a mockery of justice, not justice. It is sheer madness to argue that there was a possibility of obtaining justice where everything was going on according to a prearranged plan. Every one knows what inferences to draw from the fact that Mr. Branson closed his speech all of a sudden and Mr. Davar tried his level best to end the matter the same night and read out a charge to the jury which had been already written out. It is a wonder that the Court that found Mr. Tilak guilty thought the Pioneer and the Civil and Military Gazette innocent. It is a consolation to think in this hour of sorrow that men of all shades of opinion without distinction have condemned Mr. Justice Davar's decision.

Government are playing a deeper game than is apparent to the casual observer. The present crusade undertaken by Government is very dangerous, and we should meet it in a becoming spirit.

Government are enraged at the Swadeshi and Boycott movement, but cannot oppose it publicly.

They want to kill the agitation by having recourse to subterfuges and by removing the renowned leaders of it from our midst. Do Government take us for idiots ? If we have any stuff in us, we will carry on the agitation with renewed vigour and bring Government to their senses.

It is the duty of every one of us to show that he is a Maratha in this hour of dire trial. Mr. Tilak was sent to Mandalay not because he caused any personal loss to the Governor, but apparently because the Swadeshi movement which he organised so successfully made the Manchester mills work half time. The same is the tale to be told about Chidambaram Pillay and Babu Aravind Ghose.

Our duty does not end with moaning for a day or two like women or closing our shops. If we have any manliness left in us or any sense of honour or any recollection of our best traditions, we can make the Government even now tremble with fear. When Bengal was partitioned, the Bengalis dealt a severe blow to British trade by fighting against it with the double-edged sword of Swadeshi and Boycott.

We should fight with the same weapons now and assist the Bengalis thus already engaged in the industrial war. We should spread Swadeshi and Boycott in every nook and corner of Maharashtra. We should follow unswervingly the vows of Swadeshi and Boycott, if our regret for Mr. Tilak is not a mere show. The history of Bengal teaches us what difficulties we will have to encounter in our undertaking. In this way lies our religion; to forsake it is the way to hell.

We will be faithless to our salt if we do not complete the work of Mr. Tilak. We would only then feel that we also did our little best in lightening the burden on our motherland in whose service our leaders sacrificed their very life, when we have carried out the vow in question.

Scholar and Unique Leader

The pursuit of knowledge was, for Lokamanya Tilak, a perennial source of joy. He would often say, "If I had been born in free India, I would have become a professor of mathematics and dedicated my life to research". This was not a casual observation made in a light-hearted manner; it was the expression of an inner urge. When studying in college, Tilak was never happy with those teachers who taught only from the viewpoint of examinations. Tilak appreciated the lectures of Prof. Chhatre who was keen on teaching the fundamentals of mathematics to his students. When Tilak started teaching in college, he adopted the same method and therefore his style of teaching was not very much appreciated by the average student. After resigning from the Fergusson College, Tilak jumped into the political fray which left him no time to devote to mathematics.

However, as editor of the Kesari, he was given to carefully studying the subject he proposed to write on in the next editorial. Facts were always sacred to him and as an educator of public opinion, he made it a point to explain the subject with the help of facts; he was a postmaster in marshalling his arguments in a logical manner. Owing to his training in mathematics, he believed in explaining concepts rather than on imparting the information. Despite his busy schedule, he always found time for reading scholarly books on indology and mathematics. Once, on a Diwali day, he was deeply absorbed in reading the latest issue of Indian Antiquary. His nephew asked him, "Dada, don't you enjoy yourself even during Diwali?" Tilak replied, "I am enjoying myself. You like playing cards and enjoy other games too. While reading this magazine and such other books, I get the same pleasure that you get from the games you play". Tilak not only read books but analysed them critically; he was never satisfied with mediocre books. He enjoyed books where original treatment was given to the subject. When he particularly liked a book, he would be seen deeply absorbed, in a contemplative mood. In such a state, he would be unaware of others' presence. His sharp intellect prods him to scale the highest peaks of knowledge. He had a peculiar fascination for the unknown and deep desire to come to grips with topics which had hitherto been uncharted. He considered the

Vedas in many respect a challenge to human intelligence. He was impressed by the antiquity of the Vedas and wanted to find out the exact date when they could have been written. He studied the Vedangjyotish — astronomy as expounded by the Vedas. He pursued the line of enquiry and arrived at a new thesis. He wrote the book Orion in 1892.

Tilak made a summary of this book and sent it to the Oriental Conference where scholars of international repute had gathered. In the conference only such research papers were accepted which were original works of high merit. Scholars scrutinised and read the essay written by Tilak and were impressed by its originality. The Oriental Conference later published the research papers and Tilak's Orion was included in the collection.

In 1893, the Orion was published in book form. Normally, in research a whole lot of information is collected on the basis of which a proposition is put forth. But there is another category of research scholars who sometimes falter and find a particular problem difficult to solve.

Undaunted, they take up the challenge and while searching for a solution, truth dawns on them in a flash. Tilak, while reading the Bhagavad Gita came across a verse which troubled his mind. He was not satisfied with the interpretation of this line as given by other scholars; he wanted to interpret the statement with the help of Vedangjyotish. After four years of research, he arrived at a conclusion and decided to write the Orion. He has mentioned this in his preface to the book.

The date and the time of the Vedas could not be pin-pointed even by eminent scholars of indology. Prof. Max Muller, an eminent German scholar, had done extensive research on the subject. His methodology was that of linguistics. He studied the changes in the Sanskrit language during the different periods of ancient history and deduced the period in which the Vedas could have been written. Max Muller divided the Vedic times into four periods — chhand kal, mantra kal, brahma kal and sutra kal. He put forth the thesis that each period comprises of two hundred years and therefore the complete Vedic period was of eight hundred years. Hence, the Vedas were written about five hundred years before the times of Gautam Buddha, i.e. about 1200 BC. Though Tilak had high regard for Prof. Max Muller's research ability, he found the linguistic method adopted by Muller rather vague and unacceptable.

Tilak used the Vedangjyotish in a highly original manner. Eminent scholars have summarised his thesis in the Orion as follows: The earth moves round itself and also round the sun. However, we feel that the sun changes its position and twice during a year man gets the illusion that the sun has moved over his head. The time when man feels that the sun is passing over his head to the north is called vasant sampat in the Vedangjyotish.

The time during which the sun moves over his head to the south is called sharad sampat.

The planets which are near the sun during the vasant sampat change their positions and in the Vedangjyotish, astronomers have calculated the time regarding the positions of the different planets in a very accurate and exact manner. Tilak pointed out that in the Rigveda it was mentioned that the vasant sampat took place in the Orion or the mrigashirsh nakshatra. He also drew the inference that as depicted in the Bhagavad Gita the vasant sampat took place during the mrigashirsh nakshatra (constellation). Tilak made mathematical calculations and drew the following conclusions: (i) Pre-Orion period — 6000 to 4000 BC (ii) The Orion period — 4000 to 2500 BC (iii) The Krittika period — 2500 to 1400 BC, (iv) The pre-Buddhist period — 1400 to 500 BC

Tilak's thesis was based mainly on the Vedangjyotish and he presented mythological evidence in support of his thesis. He found a striking resemblance between Greek mythology and Indian mythology. He stated that the other nomenclature given to mrigashirsh nakshtra was agrshayani which is akin to Orion in the Greek language.

Tilak's Orion was translated into Marathi by K.L. Ogale. Before writing the Orion, Tilak discussed his ideas about the antiquity of the Vedas with Shankar Balkrishna Dikshit, an eminent scholar and authority on Indian astronomy. Dr. Bloomfield, a renowned orientalist, wrote on the Orion: "I confess that the author of Orion convinced me on all essential points". He paid tributes to Tilak for his new perspective on the age of the Rigveda. Dr. R.N. Dandekar, an eminent indologist has, however, not agreed with the conclusion drawn by Tilak. He has pointed out that modern scholars have taken the help of anthropology and archaeology for deciding the time in which the Vedas were written.

But, he has paid tributes to Tilak's research because pursuit of truth is a long process in which generations of scholars contribute by adopting different modes of research. Tilak was instrumental in paving the way for research scholars who were to come after him.

In the concluding part of the preface to the Orion, Tilak wrote: "Owing to my other preoccupations it may not be possible for me to pursue this subject in the future".

However, in 1899, while undergoing imprisonment on the charge of sedition, Tilak had enough solitude to read books. Prof. Max Muller sent him a copy of the Rigveda — a copy he had edited. While reading it critically, Tilak did not agree with Max Muller's interpretation of the richa which said that many days passed before the sun rose on the horizon. While pondering over the probable meaning of this richa, it suddenly occurred to him that the richa must have been written at a place where for six months during winter there were long nights.

Hence, the statement that many days preceded the sunrise could only be made by those who lived near the North Pole. However, Tilak did not regard this brilliant idea as the final truth. On his release, he decided to study all that he could find on the subject. Making use of the geological evidence collected while studying geology, he arrived at the final thesis to write the Arctic Home of the Vedas.

Tilak went to Sinhgad during the summer of 1902 and dictated the entire voluminous text to Gogate, who accompanied him as a writer. There were thirteen chapters in the book containing a scientific description of the North Pole with evidence to support the statement that in ancient times the North Pole was inhabited by man. In the ninth chapter, Tilak gave a new interpretation to the mythological legend on the war between Indra and the demon Vritra. Tilak stated that the origin of this war was the continuous night which lasted for a long period and the day which followed it, also continued for a long period. Tilak then drew the inference that since such a phenomenon could only be seen on the North Pole, the legend must have been written somewhere in that region. In the thirteenth chapter, all evidence given in the earlier chapters was summarised and the conclusion drawn that the Aryans had their original home in the Arctic region.

Prof. Warren, an American scholar, expressed a favourable opinion on Tilak's thesis.

Of course, there were some scholars who did not agree with him. Narayanrao Pavgi of Puna wrote a book in which he refuted the thesis put forth by Tilak. After a few years, when research scholars studied the anthropological evidence, the thesis that the Aryans were the first to inhabit the Arctic Circle was not accepted. After considering the linguistic, anthropological, archaeological and cultural-historical evidence it was concluded that the North Kirgis Steppes between the Urals and the Altai was the home of the Indo-Europeans. Dr. Dandekar, on eminent authority on indology, has observed: "In spite of certain limitations, the Arctic Home of Lokamanya Tilak, contained many original views, and was a brilliant piece of research. It is to be appreciated for its rich possibilities rather than for the actual conclusions".

None can deny Tilak's enjoyment on reading the Vedas and other ancient literature and also in giving new interpretations to problems which baffled scholars. He did not base his study on preconceived notions. He was very proud of the ancient Indian culture which was a perennial source of inspiration for him. No doubt his sorrow was great on seeing India's degradation during his time for her noble heritage lay neglected by the world. He felt deeply hurt at the arrogant attitude of the British imperialists who claimed it the 'white man's burden' to civilize the backward eastern nations and lift them up from their downtrodden state. Tilak, while fighting for India's political rights, also wanted to restore India to its past glory and ancient cultural heritage and prove how misplaced British arrogance was. However, it needs to be clarified that he did not carry on his research to prove how great ancient Indian culture was; he simply regarded truth as sacred. Had he begun with the aim of establishing India's cultural supremacy, he would have supposed facts which would have gone against his proposition. He never distorted the truth and in his pursuit of truth, with the help of the Vedangjyotish and geology, he cited only that evidence which had stood the test of science. He made a comparative study of the mythological legends in the Vedas with those in the Avesta of the Parses or with those in the Greek mythology. He mentioned only those legends which were similar and he did not indulge in flights of imagination. He was conscious of the fact that his research was imperfect, as is evident when he spoke to Dr. Belwalkar, an eminent scholar:

> "I want to bring out the second edition, but it is necessary to study the latest books on Scandinavian mythology. If you agree to accompany me to Sinhgad for a month, we shall discuss the subject and make the necessary changes in the second edition of the Arctic Home".

Significant Writings

- The Hindu Philosophy of Life, Ethics and Religion.
- Vedic Chronology and Vedanga Jyotisha.
- Jedhe Shakawali (Edited)
- Letters of Lokamanya Tilak, edited by M. D. Vidwans.
- Selected Documents of Lokamanya Bal Gangadhar Tilak, edited by Ravindra Kumar.

New Research on Vedas

While undergoing imprisonment in 1893, he became concerned at a richa in the Rigveda, and in a brain-wave concluded that the richa must have been written near the North Pole which was the original homeland of the Aryans. This was not just a flight of the imagination but an original and brilliant idea to have struck a scholar of great erudition. Soon after his release from prison, he plunged into politics. However, he reserved a part of his time for reading books on geology and archaeology. From the evidence he had collected, he was confident of proving his thesis. He carefully sifted the data he had gathered and planned his book in a logical and methodical way. In the summer of 1902, he went to stay at Sinhgad fort where he found the necessary solitude and peace for writing the book. He took with him his writer Gopalrao Gogate, to whom he dictated his voluminous book, The Arctic Home of the Vedas. Gogate, in his reminiscences of Tilak, wrote: "Tilak dictated to me hectically for fourteen to fifteen hours a day. Sometimes, he would be so absorbed in contemplation of a new idea that I had to wait for hours before he would resume the work of dictation...He hardly spoke to anyone in the house,...the work continued till almost the last minute of our leaving Sinhgad...He was happy when the book was completed".

Gita Rahasya

The Bhagavad Gita was not merely a book to be studied, but it also influenced the work that he did in his life and the way in which he went about it. Tilak's philosophy of life had its roots in the Bhagavad Gita. In the preface to the Gita-Rahasya, he has cited when his association with the Gita began and how the relationship soon enveloped his entire being. He has written: "It is over forty-three years since I came in contact with the Bhagavad Gita for the first time. In 1872, my father was seriously ill and nearing his end. At that time, I had to read out to him the Bhashanivrutti — a commentary on the Bhagavad Gita, It was not possible for me to understand the meaning of the Gita because I was then only sixteen-years old. However, at that impressionable age, my interest in the Gita was aroused. Later on, when I studied English and Sanskrit, I read the Bhagavad Gita in Sanskrit and some commentaries in English too. I also read the writings of Marathi scholars who have given different interpretations of the Gita".

Understanding the meaning of a philosophical text like that of the Gita is possible with a certain amount of intellect; but a genuine comprehension of the Gita is possible only in the light of one's experiences in life. Tilak, after the age of thirty, threw himself headlong into the struggle against the British rule. He had to pass through many trying situations while striving to secure political rights for India. During this period, while reading the Bhagavad Gita, particularly the discourse given to Arjuna by Shri Krishna, Tilak received the inspiration to carry on his struggle against a mighty opponent. He had read and marvelled at Shankaracharya's intellect as displayed in the Shankar Bhashya. But he felt it necessary to delve deep into the meaning of the

Bhagavad Gita, as expounded by the Shankaracharya. He was not convinced by other commentaries or the Gita and therefore, set aside all the different interpretations, and read and reread it without any commentary on it. He pondered on it and analysed every verse to extract the essence of the message conveyed. He had lived the life of a kannayogi and was convinced that the message of the Gita was not sanyasa but karmayoga. It is difficult to say whether Tilak saw in the Bhagavad Gita reflection of the karmayoga as practised by him throughout his life or whether due to his deep study of the Gita he became a karmayogi.

One thing is certain that there was constant interaction between his life and the Bhagavad Gita. He derived inspiration from the Gita and had deep faith in the words 'action without expecting any fruit' as preached in the Gita. Lokamanya's life was an extraordinary blend of thought, contemplation and action. All the three processes were intermingled. The ideological basis of his political life placed his actions on a noble plane and his undaunted spirit chiselled his mind. This was possible because of his long association with the Bhagavad Gita since the young age of sixteen till when he was in prison at Mandalay.

Tilak says in the preface to the Gita-Rahasya: "All these years I was thinking on the message of the Bhagavad Gita. Contemplation on the subject gave me peace of mind, while preoccupation with the subject gave me a rare happiness. On completing the Gita-Rahasya, I felt as if my association with the Gita was over and it made me sad at heart". These touching words give expression to Tilak's attachment to the Bhagavad Gita, an attachment which continued till the end of his life. His outlook on life became positive and he took to a series of actions. He felt that most people around him were fatalists, resigned to their fate. He therefore wanted to reach out to them and communicate the message of the Gita so that their outlook on life could change. After thinking and contemplating for years, he was convinced that Lord Krishna after his discourse had asked Arjuna to follow him and fight against his foes because it was necessary for a person to act and not renounce life.

The Gita-Rahasya was expression of Tilak's mature mind wherein he expressed his philosophy of life. In the Orion and the

Arctic Home, Tilak's extraordinary intelligence found expression. Just as a poet has the irrepressible urge to convey his joy at beauty, an idealist who has pursued his ideals throughout his life, similarly feels the desire to convey the joy he experiences while pursuing his goal. Once the ideals crystallised in his mind, Tilak made earnest efforts at giving shape to them. Being a man of action, he wanted his countrymen to follow the path of action and strive for attainment of swarajya. He wrote the Gita-Rahasya because he wanted the people to become purusharthis and activists and join the freedom struggle.

In 1902, Tilak, in a talk to the students of Morris College at Nagpur, expounded on the central theme of the Gita-Rahasya. He explained the concept of action without expecting any fruit and exhorted them to practise the teachings of the Bhagavad Gita. In the Gita-Rahasya, Tilak discussed the different philosophic points of view and stated that action was different to self-aggrandisement because it was performed in a selfless manner. He supported Shankaracharya's views on mataphysics but differed from him as far as the ethics were concerned.

Shankaracharya considered ethics from the point of view of individual emancipation and therefore advocated sanyasa while Tilak viewed ethics in the context of social action and therefore advocated karmayoga. Tilak emphasised three aspects of the message conveyed by the Bhagavad Gita, viz. karmayoga, lokasangraha and bhakti. Tilak was known to the world as a practical politician, while Sarojini Naidu considered him "a born idealist perpetually seeking some unchanging reality in a world full of shifting disillusionment and despair". The Bhagavad Gita illumined Tilak's path in life and provided him with an incentive to work. In his life, private and public, he must have experienced doubts, agonies and even despair; but his belief in the Bhagavad Gita freed him from the bonds of his actions to acquire a philosophic peace in life.

The Gita-Rahasya was the finest chapter in Tilak life, which was a rare blend of perennial pursuit of knowledge and determined political action. It was neither a commentary nor an attempt at a novel interpretation; it was an expression of Tilak's faith and a quintessence of his experience.

He wrote the Orion and the Arctic Home in English. Had he written these two books in Marathi, his research on ancient Indian culture and the Vedas would not have reached scholars of indology in other countries. He was conscious of the originality of his research and was confident that eminent scholars would take note of it and express their reactions on it. Tilak wanted to be in the mainstream of research on indology. He was aware that some of his findings would even be refuted, but it was his earnest desire that in the process of discussion, new light should be thrown on the problems tackled by him. He also wanted to prove the superiority of ancient Indian culture over the modern materialist culture of the West.

Tilak wrote the Gita-Rahasya in Marathi. Had he been able to write it in Hindi he would have written the Gita-Rahasya in Hindi too. He was aware that Hindus had implicit faith in the Bhagavad Gita. He also knew that Shankaracharya's stress on sanyasa and Dhyaneshwar's on bhakti as constituted the central theme of the Bhagavad Gita had greatly influenced the minds of the people. Tilak had great regard for both these saints, but he did not agree with their interpretation of the Gita. He felt that as a result of these influences, people had resigned themselves to their lot which prevented them from facing the challenges of life. He believed that once the people accepted his interpretation that action without reward was the message of the Gita, a qualitative change could come about in their outlook on life and they would be prepared to fight against any injustice. Tilak, thus, addressed the people through the Gita-Rahasya and appealed to them to free themselves from the bonds of slavery. The Gita-Rahasya is a philosophic treatise written in a direct and lucid style. There is perfect harmony between the style and the content of the ideas. The discourse is nowhere obscure. It is a monumental work which has enriched Marathi literature and made a significant contribution to philosophical writings in Indian languages.

It is not easy to explain the content of the research work done by Lokamanya Tilak. In 1904, he gave a talk on 'Chaldean and Bharatiya Vedas'. In 1917, he wrote a long essay for the Dr. Bhandarkar Commemoration Volume pointing out the similarities between the contents of Chaldean literature and the Vedas.

Sankhya is an important darshan in Hindu philosophy. Ishwarkrishna wrote the Sankhya Karika, an important book interpreting the sankhya philosophy. According to him, his book contained seventy stanzas, while the Latin, French, German and English translations of the book carried only sixty-nine of them, Tilak meticulously studied the Sankhya Karika and pointed out that the sixty-second stanza was missing. He wrote a stanza and logically proved how it fitted into the pattern of the Sankhya Karika. The essay written by Lokamanya Tilak, 'A Missing Verse in Sankya Karika' is a highly original piece of research showing a critical study of the sankhya philosophy.

Shankar Balkrishna Dikshit, a renowned research scholar who explained in his book the concept of Vedangjyotish, failed to explain the meanings of certain twelve stanzas. Significant research work on the subject was done by Vyankatesh Bapuji Ketkar. Tilak studied the subject critically and threw new light on the Vedic calendar. His interest in astronomy made him conversant with the latest trends in the subject. He enjoyed explaining the intricacies of the Vedangjyotish.

Due to his hectic political life, Tilak could not find the time to write books on subjects like astronomy and Hindu dharmashastra in which he was deeply interested. When he was in England in 1918, he kept a busy schedule. All his time was devoted to the preparation of a memorandum to be given to the Peace Conference and collect relevant evidence to be submitted before the Joint Parliamentary Committee. As he was past sixty, the work he had undertaken was too strenuous. But he found time to go to the library of the India Office to read and transcribe the ancient brick inscriptions which throw light on Chaldean and Assyrian civilizations. His friend was Dr. Thomas, an authority on Assyrian civilization and with whom he discussed the subject for hours together. Dadasaheb Khaparde, a close friend of Tilak, once asked him, "After a day's strenuous work how you turn to such difficult subjects?"

Tilak replied, "The political work is strenuous and therefore to get over my fatigue, I read books I like and can discuss with scholars like Dr. Thomas. Conversation with him is a source of great relaxation". This remark throws light on the rare joy he got from subjects like mathematics and indology. Had Tilak been born in free India, he would have devoted his life to research in these subjects which, though difficult for others, satisfied the cravings of his extraordinary intellect. He did not like to go on an oft-trodden path. With his fascination for the unknown, he pursued his original method of enquiry so as to reach the unknown. And yet, despite his rare research talent, he suppressed his urge to explore truth on the many intricate problems present in indology because he chose to devote his energies to the struggle for India's freedom. He felt that so long as his motherland remained in bondage, he could not seek fulfilment in the field of knowledge.

Duty to his country came first. Just as Tilak was not interested in spiritual salvation or moksha for himself, he was also not interested in scaling the peaks of knowledge as an intellectual so long as India was not free. In fact he viewed intellectual gratification as being akin to the efforts of a sanyasi who seeks moksha (salvation) for himself. Pained and agonised at India's plight he regarded it his foremost duty to strive for emancipating India from the yoke of British rule. He, therefore, sacrificed his desire for research in order to plunge headlong into the freedom struggle.

In this respect, Tilak could be compared to an artist who gives up his pursuit of art to obey the call of some duty in life. This was the noblest act of his life; the highest kind of sacrifice.

Conflict must have been there regarding the choice between knowledge and action, dhyan and karma, but Tilak chose to give priority to a life of action for liberating India; but he did not renounce the pursuit of knowledge. His leisure hours in the midst of hectic political activity and those during his days in jail were devoted to pursuit of knowledge.

Though he was a man of action, he was never intoxicated by action for its own sake. He first thought about the problem he faced, then studied its different aspects, read almost everything available on the subject, carefully considered the probable consequences of his decision and finally took a firm step of action. Tilak's actions marked the synthesis, of his two urges: one to pursue knowledge and the other, to lead a life of action. This was not an easy decision, but he took it and acted upon it.

He displayed scholarly learning while speaking and through his writings. He gave a number of speeches in order to make people politically conscious. He criticised and, when necessary, condemned the British government. But while doing this, he never distorted the truth. He was not a demagogue and nor did he get carried away by sentiments. He stated facts on which he based his conclusions. His editorials read like lessons given by a conscientious teacher. As editor of the Kesari, his writings educated the people, provided them information and taught them to think. His editorials had a fine pattern — a beginning, a middle and an ending. He first stated the facts about the problem, then presented his arguments in a logical manner before coming to the conclusion, which was always presented convincingly. He did not dictate his editorials till his thoughts and ideas were clear. He regarded journalism as a noble profession and religiously followed the ethics of journalism.

In his efforts to enlighten his readers, he introduced some books and summarised them in such a manner as to create in the readers a desire to read the book. He wrote a comprehensive article on Dadabhai Naoroji's Poverty and British Rule in India and the introduction to William Digby's Prosperous British India. C.V. Vaidya, an eminent writer and scholar in Marathi, had written the voluminous book Sartha, Sateep Mahabharata.

Tilak wrote seven articles on this book and discussed and analysed the various problems depicted in the Mahabharata. These articles showed Tilak's erudite scholarship and critical study of the epic. While reviewing Vaidya's book, he threw new light on it by giving an original interpretation of the different aspects of the Mahabharata. When writing on a topical subject, Tilak transcended the limitations of topicality to state his views which held perennial significance. His editorial, 'Constitutional or Legal' shows his capacity to raise a topical issue to the level of ideas.

The purpose of the article was to criticise Gopal Krishna Gokhale who, after the Calcutta session of the Congress in 1906, made a fervent plea to adopt constitutional methods for carrying on the political struggle. Tilak in his editorial, while refuting Gokhale's arguments, wrote that constitutional methods could be adopted only in those countries where there was a Constitution and where people enjoyed political rights as stipulated in the Constitution. Tilak pointed out that India, under British rule, had no Constitution and hence no constitutional methods. He further wrote that the only question was whether our methods were legal or illegal. He added that in many respects laws by an alien government tended to be tyrannical. He summed up the editorial by saying: "When law is divorced from morality, we should abide by morality, break the law if necessary and bravely accept the punishment for breaking the law". This observation of his raised the discussion to a philosophical level. Later, when Gandhiji launched the satyagraha movement, he openly appealed to the people to break the law because it was unethical.

Tilak lived in the present but was way ahead in his ideas and put forth his ideas which would be significant for all times to come. Addison, the great English essayist has said:

"Literature that does not last is journalism; journalism that lasts is literature". This holds true for Tilak as many of his editorials have stood the test of time and the ideas expressed in them are significant to this day.

The tributes which Tilak paid to his adversaries in the Kesari were also quite remarkable. In the article written on Justice Ranade, Agarkar and Gokhale following their deaths Tilak analysed the significance of their contribution to life in general.

Without getting sentimental he showed his deep respect for contemporary thinkers and leaders and his understanding of their noble motives while serving the society. On Max Muller's and Herbert Spencer's deaths too, he paid excellent tributes to these eminent scholars and thinkers for their work in the field of knowledge. These articles have been appropriately described as "appreciation of eminent scholars by another great scholar".

Tilak's mind was enriched through wide reading, deep thinking and varied experiences. His writings were rich in content and never tended to be verbose. As a student of mathematics, he liked precision in the delineation of ideas. His style was lucid and direct. His method was first to impart information and then state his point of view emphatically. Tilak while trying to persuade the readers also made an effort to stimulate their thought process. As he dictated his editorials, these could never get bookish. They had the flavour of his public speeches, and incisiveness of style essentially aimed at influencing the audience. As he was serious by temperament, he never indulged in humorous writing. However, he had the bluntness which is a characteristic of the people of Konkan region in Maharashtra and therefore, some of his remarks evoked a smile.

Sometimes Tilak was sarcastic in his ridicule of his opponents. The headings of his editorials were always appropriate and conveyed the thrust of his argument in an effective manner. On Rand's assassination when the government resorted to ruthless repression, Tilak wrote the editorial under the heading, "Is the Government in its Senses?"

Tilak chose brevity and never was the one to waste his words. There was a dignity of style as particularly seen in the Gita-Rahasya. His style expressed his personality; forthright, outspoken, assertive, sometimes aggressive but keen on establishing a bond with the people with a view to involving them in the struggle for swarajya.

Swarajya was his goal and a multiplicity of means was the strategy he adopted for achieving it. However, it is necessary to understand his strategy. Among his contemporaries were the liberal leaders like Gopal Krishna Gokhale, Pherozeshah Mehta, Surendranath Banerjee and others. They believed in moderate methods and insisted on constitutional means. They submitted important memoranda before the commissions appointed by the government and gave expression to the political aspirations of the people. Their arguments were always supported by facts.

Gokhale played a prominent role in the Central legislature by criticising the shortcomings of government policies and suggested ways through which justice could be ensured. Through his speeches and writings he made an effort to influence public opinion in England. The moderate leaders had a constructive approach but their faith in the justice of the British rulers was misplaced. Tilak did not overrule the means and methods of the moderates. He was aware that during the initial phase of the struggle for freedom, work done through moderate methods had proved useful and so he was full of praise for Gokhale for the work he had done in England. However, Tilak believed that the politics of petition and prayers could never succeed/ and that political demands must be backed by political sanction created through joint action by the people. When Morley became the Secretary of State for India, Gokhale heartily welcomed the appointment because he hoped that a liberal thinker like Morley would be favourably inclined towards the Indians. But in his editorial in the Kesari under the title, 'Philosopher or a Diplomat?'

Tilak pointed out that Morley was a liberal in England but an imperialist vis-a-vis the Indians. And his words proved to be so true! Tilak was a shrewd politician who insisted on using means appropriate to the situation. After 1916, he thought that while consolidating the political forces in India, he should adopt liberal methods in order to influence the British rulers and the public opinion in England. The work he did in England by giving evidence before the Parliamentary Committee, submitting a memorandum to the Peace Conference at Paris, distributing copies of the pamphlet entitled, Self-Determination — all this was on the lines followed by Gokhale. The difference between the two leaders was that while Tilak knew when to agitate, when to launch a political movement, when to pressurise the government and when to adopt moderate methods, Gokhale preferred to use moderate methods consistently, convinced as he was of British justice.

The moderates were on one end and the revolutionaries on another end of the political spectrum in India. The revolutionaries were young men who were determined to win swarajya, even if it meant armed revolt. Tilak had immense faith in the patriotism and courage of the revolutionaries, but was equally aware that the masses could not be expected to display the same courage as the revolutionaries. During the 1896 famine in Maharashtra, Tilak organised the peasants and succeeded in getting redressal of some of their grievances. He worked within the framework of law while strengthening the political base. He knew fully well that for building up a mass movement, he would have to keep away from those persons who advocated violence. It may be quite possible that Tilak knew about the group of revolutionaries led by Damodar Chapekar, but he neither encouraged nor advised them in any way. Tilak's belief was that one had the right to serve his motherland according to his own conscience. On his release from prison in 1901, Tilak offered all help to those who wanted to participate in the armed struggle. In 1904, he developed close contacts with Aurobindo Ghosh as he held him in high esteem.

However, he was conscious that as a leader it was his responsibility to see that the young revolutionaries did not sacrifice their lives by acting in a rash manner. He helped them prepare for the revolution but warned them to keep away from insurrectionary or terrorist acitivities. His advice to revolutionaries was, "Keep your powder dry". When Aurobindo and his colleagues broke off with the moderate leaders, after the split in the Congress at Surat, Tilak decided not to desert the revolutionaries for he did not want them to be isolated.

On his release in 1914, he emerged as a popular leader. When the revolutionaries sought his advice on the future course of action, he sternly told them that the time was not yet ripe for revolutionary action. Acknowledged as 'Lokamanya' by the people, he exercised his authority firmly. He did not rule out the possibility of using arms for winning swarajya but approved of preparing for a revolution but, not an armed revolt.

During the last phase of Tilak's life, Gandhiji emerged on the Indian political scene.

Gandhiji had used the weapon of satyagraha in South Africa and he wanted to use the same means in India's struggle for swarajya. He was appreciative of Gandhiji's sentiments. He was in England when Gandhiji went on a satyagraha to protest against the Rowlatt Act. Tilak had condemned the Rowlatt Act in one of his public speeches in England. On his return to India, he said in an interview, "I regret that I was not in India to participate in the satyagraha launched by Gandhi". Later when Gandhiji pleaded for adoption of satyagraha as the method for fighting the British, some moderate leaders opposed him on the ground that it was unconstitutional. But Tilak, in his editorial in the Kesari, wrote: "A time there was when there existed a difference of opinion about the goal of the Congress. Dadabhai Naoroji as president of the Congress declared that swarajya was our goal and it was accepted by all. Now some people doubt whether satyagraha can be accepted as a means. But this problem would have to be resolved and means appropriate to the goal of swarajya would have to be accepted by all. Satyagraha is a powerful weapon". However, Tilak did not agree that satyagraha was the only means to be used. While speaking to Kaka Kalelkar, a disciple of Gandhi, Tilak observed that though he supported satyagraha, he was not sure whether in the struggle for swarajya, satyagraha could prove useful.

He considered the people's movement as the most effective means in the struggle for swarajya. No wonder that Tilak was called "the apostle of civil revolt".

Tilak was not just a man of action; his political actions were firmly rooted on sound ideas. He was influenced by the thoughts voiced by Mill and Spencer during the early period of his political life. On observing the society around him, Tilak was convinced that though the social structure of the Hindu society had certain faults, it somehow had an inner vitality. While accepting concepts like democracy, he felt that it would be improper to reject outright the traditional mode of life. He criticised those who borrowed ideas from the West and tried to transplant them in India. He wanted new ideas to be grafted on the traditional way of life. In one of his speeches, he pleaded that nationalism should be grafted on the Indian's inherent love for his motherland. Tilak thus wanted to blend the old with the new. He was conscious of the conservative nature of the Indian society and was confident that the people would accept new ideas provided those fitted into their pattern of life. He admitted that it was not an easy task to create a feeling of unity in India, because people belonged to different religions and to different castes, spoke different languages and had different lifestyles. And yet, despite this diversity, there were some ties which held them together. Tilak wanted to bridge the gulf between the different groups so as to achieve unity in the midst of diversity. He candidly stated that under British rule, people were developing the consciousness that they were one as a nation. He regarded the Indian National Congress as a national unity platform which helped to promote unity amongst people belonging to different social groups.

He was the first to point out that the British followed the 'divide and rule' policy in order to perpetuate their domination over India. In his editorial on Hindu-Muslim riots, he wrote: "Every right-minded person knows that it is not possible to analyse the Hindu-Muslim problem without considering the three parties — Hindus, Muslims and the government. If we have to stop Hindu-Muslim riots, it is necessary that people of both the religions are allowed to celebrate their festivals without interferences or obstructions. If Muslims slaughter cows in a Hindu locality, they must be punished. Similarly, if a Hindu enters the house of a khatik (person who slaughters animals) and by using force takes away the cow from his house, and then the Hindu should be punished".

Tilak made a plea for peaceful co-existence between the Hindus and the Muslims and wanted them to follow the example set by America where people of different religions lived in harmony with each other.

The movement for swarajya could not be expected to gather momentum unless the Hindus and Muslims united. It was entirely due to his efforts that in 1916, at the Lucknow session of the Indian National Congress, a pact was made between the Hindus and the Muslims. The pact came to be known as the Lucknow pact.

In the political field Tilak wanted to achieve national unity. He knew that language is one of the main factors which shape people's lives in a particular manner and he wanted different linguistic groups to preserve their identity. He believed that administration of the country should be done through the mother tongue of the people and not through English. He, therefore, supported Dr. Pattabhi's suggestion seeking formation of linguistic provinces.

By swarajya, Tilak meant a government of the people. He said, "It is true that we understand the aspirations and the needs of our people far better than the British. But we must ensure that the expectations and the grievances of the people are expressed by the people themselves". He observed, "We would deserve our political rights only if we succeed in achieving unity, first in every village, then in every district, then in provinces and finally at the national level in the Indian National Congress". Prof. G. D. Parikh, an eminent thinker in Maharashtra, rightly described Tilak as "the architect of Indian nationalism".

He said that nationalism meant power of the people. He expounded this idea in his editorial entitled, 'Self-government and Good Government'. Tilak wrote: "With the spread of education, the aspirations of the people will also grow. They would not be satisfied merely by self-government; they would then say that self-government cannot be a reality unless the country becomes a republic. At this stage, self-government will be a good government". His trust in the common man made him plead for a republic over which sharp differences arose between Gokhale and Tilak. Gokhale said that we should not release the forces over which we had no control for he feared that the people could become unruly and unmanageable in their resistance to British rule. Tilak, on the other hand, felt that once people developed self-respect, they would automatically become disciplined and direct their energies in the right direction.

Tilak's confidence resulted not due to his faith in the Western concept of democracy, but his unstinted faith in man's conscience or atma, which helps one to distinguish between good and evil, truth and falsehood. Tilak thought that if, like the conscience of the individual, the conscience of the society was awakened, and political movement can not take a wrong direction.

Tilak's faith in the democratic idea had a spiritual basis. Though many respected him, few understood him. In that sense Tilak was a lonely person. N. C. Kelkar, a close associate of Tilak, wondered why Tilak, in spite of his ideological differences, loved Aurobindo Ghosh. Some others were surprised at how a radical leader like Tilak could have faith in N. C. Kelkar who was a moderate, both in thought and action.

Dadasaheb Khaparde failed to understand why Tilak, in spite of his ideological differences with Gandhi, praised Gandhi and acknowledged his greatness. Tilak did not offer any explanation for his actions. During the later phase of his career Tilak began regarding himself as a person chosen by destiny to lead the struggle for swarajya. He was not a self-centred person, but was conscious of his immense strength to strive towards his goal.

Owing to his philosophic approach to life, the popularity that he enjoyed did not affect him; he remained a simple and unassuming man. He wanted the message of Swarajya to reach the people of distant villages of India and take its roots in their hearts. He wanted to teach the people the dignity of life, and promote in them a sense of patriotism and work towards Swarajya. He passed through many trials and tribulations and emerged not only unscathed but, a more noble and heroic person than ever before.

Tilak's intense love for his motherland, his sacrifice and suffering and the values which he stood for, all became a perennial source of inspiration to his countrymen. The method for political work adopted by Tilak in the later phase of his life holds a special significance for the post-Independence period. Tilak described his method as 'responsive co-operation' and explained that he would accept the rights given by the people, use them for their benefit and continue to work for securing greater rights for them. In the free India of today, the same method can be adopted during the process of development.

People have to participate in the process of development, earn the rewards and continue to work for securing for the poor all the benefits of integrated development. A positive approach, from the Parliament to the Gram Panchayat, would benefit the society all the more in India, where democracy has taken its roots. Some leaders are victims of circumstances and though for some time they earn a measure of success and popularity, gradually they fade into oblivion. A few leaders, however, rise to the occasion to confront all kinds of circumstances and help shape the destiny of the nation.

Such leaders continue to live in the life of a nation long after they are no more. Tilak was a leader who belonged to the latter category and his life is a message for generations to come. He is like a mountain peak which continues to give dignity to our nation, even when fast and far-reaching changes are taking place. He has left his footprints on the sands of time, never to be effaced.

4

Leader of Congress

The public meeting held by Congress at Bombay was historic and significant. In that meeting Tilak was elected at a public meeting as a delegate to the Bombay Congress. The following entry appears in the Congress register:

> Delegate number—401; Presidency or Government—Bombay; Congress circle—Deccan; Electoral Division—Puna; Name in full with honorary titles, scholastic degree, etc.—Mr. Bal Gangadhar Tilak, B.A., L.L.B.; Race, religious denomination and caste, if any—Hindu, Brahmin; Occupation and address—Professor, Fergusson College and journalist; How and When elected—By public meeting at Puna, 15th December, 1889.

It was a memorable session. Future leaders of India Tilak, Gokhale and Lajpat Rai appeared on the Congress platform for the first time. The trio of Lal, Bal and Pal (Bal G. Tilak, Lala Lajpat Rai and B. C. Pal), popularly known in the first two decades of the twentieth century as the extremist leaders of India, saw one another little knowing that at no distant future they would join hands in a big undertaking. Pal was their senior then, having been associated with the Congress since 1886.

The first day of the Congress was almost wholly occupied with the long addresses of the President and the Chairman of the Reception Committee. On the second day December 27, the proceedings began with the resolution on the expansion and reform of Legislative Councils to which Tilak moved an amendment in a maiden speech.

The President, opening the proceedings, said: "Gentlemen, the first business and it is a very important one that will be brought before you today will be the scheme for the reform of the Legislative Councils. As you are aware, a Draft Bill has been prepared by Mr. Bradlaugh and has been circulated throughout the whole of India". The scheme proposed:

- Hie Imperial and Provincial Legislative Councils to consist respectively of members, not less than one-half of whom are to be elected, not more than one-fourth to be ex-officio and the rest to be nominated by Government.
- Revenue districts to constitute ordinarily territorial units for electoral purposes.
- Voters in each district to elect representatives to one or more electoral bodies, according to local circumstances at the rate of twelve per million of the total population of the district, such representatives to possess certain qualifications, and not to be subject to certain disqualifications, both of which will be settled later.
- All the representatives thus elected by all the districts, included in the jurisdiction of each electoral body, to elect members to the Imperial Legislature at the rate of one per every five million of the total population of the electoral jurisdiction, and to their own provincial Legislature at the rate of one per million of the said total population, in such wise that whenever the Parsees, Christians, Muslims or Hindus are in a minority, the total numbers of Parsees, Christians, Muslims or Hindus, as the case may be elected to the Provincial Legislature, shall not, so far as may be possible, bear a less proportion to the total number of members elected thereto, than the total number of Parsees, Christians, Hindus or Muslims, as the case may be, in such electoral jurisdiction, bears to its total proportion.

Members of both Legislatures to possess certain qualifications and not to be subject to certain disqualifications, both of which will be settled later.

The amendments moved by several delegates from distant parts of the country, though not accepted, are interesting and worthy of notice, representing as they do the sentiments of the age. Hume wanted the 'minority clause' to be deleted. His argument was: "Indians are Indians. Why should there be majority or minority?" But many did not support him. Hidayat Rasul, of Oudh, proposed that, "although the Hindu population was a majority, the number of Hindu and Muslim members in the Central Council should be equal". His own co-religionist, Hamid Ali Khan of Lucknow, opposed him, arguing that "no such question as Hindu or Muslim should be raised". Another Muslim delegate, Wajid Ali Biwaji said, in an excited tone of voice, that "the number of Muslim members in the Council should be thrice that of Hindus".

A fourth Muslim delegate, opposing these suggestions, said:

"We have assembled here for one common object. On such an occasion the Muslims cannot call themselves Muslims; nor Hindus, but rather, forgetting all differences of creed, caste and colour, we should call ourselves Indians". And when Hidayat Rasul's amendment was put to vote, even the Muslim delegates voted against it.

Tilak did not take part in the Hindu-Muslim controversy but moved a basic amendment to the scheme. He said:

"I beg to propose, as an amendment, that instead of asking the different electoral bodies to elect members to the Imperial Legislature, the elected members of the Provincial Legislative Council should constitute the body to elect members to the Imperial Council. As I have moved this amendment more from a sense of duty to my province than from any confidence in my own oratorical powers, I shall not trouble you with any platitudes about this National Congress. What I have to do is to place before you the reasons that induce us to come forward with this amendment, although we know there is very little chance of its being accepted by other provinces.

The Supreme Legislative Council must have on it representatives from the different Presidencies and not from districts or divisions, and I think it will be more in accordance with this principle to allow representations to a Presidency than to a subdivision of it. It is not each division that has to elect a representative to the Imperial Council, but it is each Presidency that has to do it.

Then, you have adopted indirect representations; that is the members of the Council are not to be directly sent by the voters, but through the medium of electoral bodies. Therefore, the natural sequence is that the Provincial Councils should elect the Imperial Council.

You have been told that municipalities and local bodies are not allowed representation direct because they have not the best of your men. But you have the best men in your Provincial Councils, and, if you entrust them with the task of selecting men for the Imperial Council, I am sure you will not be placing the power in the wrong hands.

The last objection I have to urge to the proposed system is that it is cumbrous every time to ask an electoral division to send members to the Provincial Council and also to the Imperial Council.

If you will consider the logical sequence of the proposal and the local circumstances of the several Presidencies, especially that of Bombay, where there will be several electoral bodies, if you will consider that it is the provincial interest that you have to represent and not the divisional interest in the Imperial Council, you will find that the amendment is at least more in conformity with the view you have already adopted than is the resolution as it now stands. With these few words I propose the amendment, which will run thus: 'That elections to the Imperial Legislature shall be made by the elected members of the Provincial Councils'".

The amendment was ably supported by G. K. Gokhale. This was incidentally the first and the last occasion on which the two Maharashtrian leaders agreed with each other. The amendment was, however, rejected.

The Father of Indian Unrest, as Tilak was later called by British historians, gave absolutely no hint of his bitterness against the British rule at the annual meeting of the national assembly. Perhaps he had no bitterness yet. But his future collaborators in the extremist party, Bipin Chandra Pal and Lajpat Rai, broadly indicated that the British exploitation had made India poor.

Lajpat Rai's speech was interrupted by Pherozeshah Mehta, who rising on a point of order said that the speaker ought to confine himself to the proposition before the Congress.

And the President asked the speaker to keep to the question of the resolution that had been placed before the meeting.

Now that the history of the activities of these leaders is common knowledge, Mehta's interruption appears to be very significant. We had in him a strictly constitutional politician, and while Pal and Lal steadily gravitated towards extremism, he became a confirmed moderate.

In several provinces, the local authorities behaved very shabbily, and a feeling of bitterness against the British was bound to grow. For example, Ajudhia Nath, a delegate from the North-West Provinces, brought to the notice of the Congress that he had been shadowed from Allahabad by a head constable who was moving about in the compound and making close enquiries about the persons from the North-West Provinces, especially the Government officials. After Ajudhia Nath had narrated his story, Eardley Norton of Madras (who had moved the resolution on the reform of Councils), told the Congress that Colonel Weldon, the Madras Commissioner of Police, "is here in charge of all the delegates from Madras". There was uproarious laughter, followed by cries of 'shame'.

The Congress was an innocuous body, but several provincial administrations frowned on those participating in it and, for that matter, in any political organisation. The barest criticism that was offered at the annual sessions was enough to offend them.

In the Bombay Presidency, as in other provinces, there were imposed several new taxes which hit the poor hard.

These were the salt tax, excise duty, forest laws, etc. against which the Congress ceremoniously adopted resolutions and the press protested every now and then. Government's indifference to protests exacerbated men like Bal, Lal and Pal, and with the passage of time, their opposition to the British rule grew. With most Congress leaders being satisfied with the annual Congress show, the pace of men like Tilak was bound to be slow. But he seized every opportunity that came his way to arouse feelings of national self-respect in the people which was another way of telling them that they were under the domination of a foreign power and that they should be prepared to fight for their political rights.

Indian National Congress

In the Abstracts of 1889, Tilak is alluded to as one of the Secretaries of the Deccan Branch of the National Congress in which capacity he appears to have been chiefly used to draft circulars, letters, etc. explaining the objects of the Congress and soliciting contributions for the one which was to assemble in Bombay that year. At the end of the year, he and Mahadev Ballal Namjoshi were, at the request of the Sarvajanik Sabha sent to Bombay to arrange for the reception of the delegates.

Reform of Legislative Councils

In the early part of this year the Mahratta informed its readers that the Secretary of the Deccan Congress Committee would shortly circulate for signatures copies of a petition to Parliament asking for certain reforms in the Legislative Councils.

Tilak is reported to have been the draughtsman of this memorial.

Social Reforms

In August Tilak with 13 others, amongst whom was Mr. (afterwards Justice) Ranade, signed a circular letter advocating the following reforms:

- that not more than half a year's income should be expended on the marriage ceremonies of a son;
- that not more than a year's income should be expended on the marriage ceremonies of a daughter;
- that boys should not marry before the ages of 16, 18 or 20;
- that daughters should not be married before the ages of 10, 12 or 14;

- that polygamy should be prohibited;
- that no one should marry after the age of 50;
- that liquor should be taken medicinally only;
- that every possible endeavour should be made to promote female education.

This seems to have been the only occasion on which Tilak advocated social reform, for not very long after, in an article in the *Mahratta,* he condemned Mr. Malabari's suggestions for the reform of the Indian Marriage Laws and objected to social reform being forced on the people by law, as such was an interference with the religious practices and beliefs of the Hindus. Again at a large meeting in Puna, called for the purpose of adopting a petition to Government asking them not to interfere with the long established habits and customs of the Brahmins by legislation, he publicly denounced Mr. Malbari's suggestions as absurd and as involving an interference with the Hindu religion.

Hindu - Muslim Riots

In connection with these riots Tilak's personality asserted itself and he stood forth not only as an opponent of the measures of Government but also of the " Moderate " party of the community. In September, he convened a meeting with the intention of publicity condemning the action of Government and the Muslims and expressing sympathy with the Hindus, which caused no little anxiety to the leaders of the Hindu community; and it is reported that a letter signed by a number of influential Hindu gentlemen in Bombay, among whom were Justice Telang and Ranade and Dr. Bhalchandra Krishna Bhatawdekar, was received in Puna appealing to him to refrain from the course he contemplated owing to the consequences which must ensue, and that he was also approached by some of the local Hindu leaders. To all entreaties to desist he turned a deaf ear and posed as the champion of the Hindus. But at the last moment discretion prevailed and he got the meeting to pass resolutions:

- expressing its sense of gratitude to Her Majesty the Queen empress for her message of sympathy in connection with the recent disturbances in Bombay;

- regretting the breach of amicable relations between the Hindus and Muslims in Bombay and thanking Lord Harris for insisting on toleration and charity as the best means for maintaining mutual relations;
- stating that the meeting firmly believes that the movement for the due protection of cows had not led, and cannot lead to any estrangement of feelings between Hindus and Muslims; that in its opinion the regrettable riots that have of late unfortunately become so frequent are traceable to the absence of any authoritative exposition of policy for the guidance of Government Officials in such matters to the want of authoritative records for reference, of existing religious and social rights and privileges and to mistaken notions, calculated to set one race against another about the equal and impartial protection of law guaranteed to all Her Majesty's subjects by the Queen's Proclamation of 1858; and praying that Government may be pleased to institute an independent enquiry into the causes of these riots generally, with a view to provide machinery for the amicable settlement of any disputes that might hereafter arise between the two brother communities that had lived without any such breach for several centuries;
- authorising the President (Sardar Balwant Ramchandra Natu) to embody the above resolutions in the form of a memorial and submit the same for the consideration of Government.

At this time, he is also reported to have inculcated the doctrine of force by representing that Government sided with the Muslims because they resorted to force and implying that if the Hindus wished to obtain a respectful hearing, they would have to adopt similar tactics and, as if to give point to his preachings, he advised all Hindus to go in for physical exercise and to acquire familiarity with the use of weapons. The outcome was that physical drill was introduced into the curriculum of many of the Native schools and many private gymnasiums were opened.

The following paragraph from Setlur and Deshpande's report on the Tilak case shows how his friends construed his attitude at this period:

> "The deplorable riots between Hindus and Muslims and the many new questions suggested by them brought about a great change in our political atmosphere, and Mr. Tilak was again to the front. Never before did he place himself in such direct antagonism with the apparent policy of some Anglo-Indian Officials and never before did those Officials realise so well his influence over the masses. Mr. Tilak's attitude with respect to this riot question, whether right or wrong, was clear and unmistakable. He attributed those manifestations of racial prejudice mainly to the secret instigation of some short-sighted Anglo-Indian Officers. The policy of divide and rule initiated by Lord Dufferin, was according to him, at the bottom of all the mischief, and the only effective way he contended to check these riots was for Government Officials to observe strict neutrality between Hindus and Muslims".

Music Question

There is reason to believe that the music question was raised by Tilak to qualify the privilege enjoyed by Muslims of music being stopped when passing mosques and masjids and to hamper the action of Government in regard to the Hindu-Muslim disputes. It was also used to discredit the management of the Sarvajanik Sabha which was then guided by the "Reform" or "Moderate" party under Mr. Justice Ranade by compelling it to a line of action which pleased neither the Hindus nor the Muslims. The outcome was the withdrawal of the Muslim members of the Sabha and the displacement of the " Moderate " party in its Councils.

Ganpati Celebrations

As another method of widening the breach between the Hindus and Muslims, Tilak encouraged if he did not instigate the holding of Ganpati celebrations on a much larger scale than in previous years. The original idea was to make them as distasteful as possible to Muslims by having them as much like the Muharram as possible and by withdrawing the Hindu interest from it. Tilak and his party worked hard to secure this object and then conduct caused no little anxiety to the "Moderate" section of their community, the head of which called on the District Magistrate and suggested the advisability of convening a meeting and settling a programme for the Ganpati processions, and in the course of conversation this gentleman dropped some remarks to the effect that the possibility of overthrowing the British Government was not an uncommon subject of discussion among the Tilak faction in Puna. As Ganpati day approached, the results of the organisation became apparent. Gangs of Hindus paraded the streets of the Puna City singing verses which tended to intensify the strained relations between the two communities, and on " Nag Panchmi" day a procession attempted to dispute an order directing all music to cease playing in front of mosques and when it was compelled to conform to it. It endeavoured to obstruct the road by throwing the image of the " Nag" off the cart on to the road. Tilak, though not present on the occasion, exhibited his interest and sympathy by convening a meeting to collect subscriptions for the defence of the persons concerned in the incident. The late Mr. Brewin in reporting on the incident wrote as follows:

> "The tension between the Hindus and Muslims everywhere continued and the fears entertained by Ranade and Co., consequent on Tilak's new doctrine, were soon to be realised. Tilak had openly advocated the use of force, and knowing that without unity nothing could be accomplished, he set to work to inaugurate the Sarvajanik Ganpatis. His ideas in this respect soon caught fire among the people and the Hindus gathered in such numbers as must have pleased even Tilak. He advocated each Ganpati having a mela and each mela being composed of as many gymnasts as possible. All *melawallhas* were to acquire familiarity in the use of weapons. In this movement, Tilak had the assistance of Namjoshi, Bhau Laxman Jaola alias, Bhau Rangari, Balasaheb Natu, Tatiasaheb Natu, Wassudeo Ganesh Joshi, Dagdu Halwai and a number of malcontents. With a view to inculcating the necessity of unity at Puna and all places where

the Ganpati movement had been established Tilak's emissaries produced and distributed among the people shloks (verses) which set forth the advantages of unity".

When the festival came round Ganpatis were publicly exposed in *mandups,* in the way tabuts usually are, and the processions imitated similar processions during the Muharram.

The music rules which had been framed did not meet with the approval of Tilak and his party who determined to ignore them and to play music while passing mosques. The result was the fatal riot on the morning of the 13th September 1894. After quiet had been restored Tilak's party thought the Muslims might lay violent hands on him and for sometime he was always accompanied by a band of Hindu youths who acted as a sort of bodyguard.

'Moderate' and 'Extreme' Parties

At a meeting of the members of the Sarvajanik Sabha to elect a Managing Committee, the "Extreme" or Tilak faction mustered strong and voted for the infusion of fresh or radical blood into the Committee, while the "Moderates" were for a continuance of the old Committee. The discussion was heated and terminated in an unseemly squabble and the interference of the Police. The "Extremists" ultimately carried the day and from that time Tilak has been recognised as the leader of the Sabha.

Another bone of contention between the parties was the holding of the Social Conference at the National Congress Venue. Tilak took a prominent part and on behalf of the " Extremists" urged that the principles of the social reformers, who mostly belong to the " Moderate" party, are antagonistic to the teachings of the Hindu religion and not acceptable to the masses; and if the Conference is allowed to be held in the Congress *Mandup* the idea will get abroad that National Congress, which represents the claims of the people of India of all castes and creeds, approves of the Conference and that this may be used as an argument in support of legislation interfering with the social customs of the people on the lines advocated by the Social Reformers. Opposition to these views resulted in Tilak's resigning his post as a Secretary of the National Congress Reception Committee and organising an agitation against the Social Reform; party feeling ran so high that numerous assaults were committed on members of the Reform Party.

Shivaji Celebrations

A movement professedly to collect funds for the maintenance of Shivaji's, tomb at Raigadh was started and Tilak undertook to plead the cause in his papers and to receive subscriptions for the purpose. The object of these celebrations is to sow the seeds of patriotism in the rising generation and to incite Hindus to emulate the deeds of Shivaji.

Tilak conceived the idea of turning the movement into a medium through which he could preach sedition under the cloak of extolling the life and deeds of Shivaji and inducing all Natives to combine for the common good against the foreigner (Government). He presided at the commemoration ceremony at Raigadh and made two speeches in both of which he advocated combination and loyalty to leaders. In referring to the celebration, he said it was the first of its kind and its object to bring together all Marathas and to foster a feeling of regard and confidence which would conduce to the maintenance of their religion and institutions. It was not, he said, as some supposed, convened by the Brahmins to subvert the existing Government, but on the contrary, they were helping Government by educating the masses and engendering amongst them a feeling of unity, loyalty to their leaders and love and reverence to their National institutions.

The Central Provinces Police report the receipt of a letter from Tilak suggesting that instructions in the use of the gun and sword should be freely given in the Shivaji schools in Nagpur, weapons made of wood being used.

At the Shivaji celebrations in Puna, the usual disloyal sentiments were inculcated in the shape of lectures and purans which were regularly attended by Tilak and his party. Tilak spoke once and then said Shivaji was greater than all European heroes from Caesar downwards in as much as his object was not usurpation but the redemption of his religion and co-religionists and the deliverance of Brahmins and cattle from molestation at the hands of the Muslims. The narrow-minded view held of Shivaji by educated natives of the present day, he attributed to sentiments imbibed from Western authors and observed that the popularity of the present celebrations was a sufficient contradiction and a satisfactory sign of the times, notwithstanding the fact that a few Government officials were still against them.

During a visit to Kolhapur, Tilak is reported to have said that there was much difference between Shivaji and the present period, patriots like Shivaji being rare now-a-days, and that subjects of Native States were better able to attend to the affairs of their country than inhabitants of a conquered country, the former having the privilege of self-government which the latter have not.

At the Shivaji Celebrations, Tilak spoke on the third day on "Imperialism". He said *inter alia* that Great Britain in her desire to acquire dominion over Africa had encountered the Boers who, though numerically weak, had fought bravely and secured favourable terms of peace; that their system of warfare was that which Shivaji had adopted against the Muslims; and that the lesson to be learnt from the war was that it was not impracticable or impossible for any other people to do the same if all acted together and cautiously. He concluded with saying that celebrations such as they were commemorating were a good sign of the times and that the thoughts they awakened should not be allowed to slumber from year to year, but should induce men to emulate the past.

Famine

The distress in several parts of the Presidency owing to the failure of the monsoons was seized by Tilak as an opportunity to pose as a friend of the people and to thereby strengthen his hold of the masses. He addressed the students assembled in Puna for the University Examination and told them of the existence of a Famine Insurance Fund and advised them on their return to their villages to instigate villagers to agitate to have it expended. He made a tour in the Puna and Sholapur Districts during which he advised ryots, weavers and others of the poorer classes to go in bodies to the District Authorities and clamour for relief measures, fodder for their cattle, etc. At the same time, representatives of the Sarvajanik Sabha held large meetings in the Thana, Kolaba and Ratnagiri Districts at which they advised the people to claim remissions of land revenue and to withhold the payment of taxes. Other means were also adopted to create popular discontent. In one instance, an agent was prosecuted to conviction and in another the Sabha was asked whether it held itself responsible for the utterances and notices distributed by one of its reputed agents. After considerable delay, the agent was acknowledged but his notices and utterances were repudiated on which Government intimated to the Sabha that it must cease to recognise it as a body having any claims to address Government on questions of public policy. When the poorer classes threatened to loot the grain shops in the city and cantonment of Puna, Tilak intervened and with the help of some friends established cheap grain shops which broke the ring formed by the grain dealers.

Plague Measures

On the first appearance of plague in Puna in 1896-1897, Tilak remained in the City and took an active part in the fight against the disease. He established a Hindu Plague Hospital and opened a free kitchen in the segregation camp for the use of the poor and worked as a volunteer with the search parties. In his papers, he strongly supported the various measures adopted by Government for the suppression of the pestilence, but appears to have disagreed in regard to the powers of the search parties for on the 20th March, he convened a meeting at which resolutions were adopted suggesting the restriction of the powers of the search parties, and thereafter articles appeared in his papers which savoured of disaffection and sedition for which he was subsequently tried and on conviction sentenced to 18 months rigorous imprisonment.

Arrest and Trial

Tilak's arrest was reported to have been universally disapproved of in the upper circles of Hindu society while the lower classes viewed it with indifference and the Muslims with gratification.

His trial was closely followed all over the country and caused a large circulation of his own and other vernacular papers.

Defence Fund

His popularity was so great that as soon as it became known that he was arrested and proposals for raising subscriptions for his defence were mooted in all parts of the Presidency and when he, through the columns of the *Kesari*, asked for assistance for his defence on the grounds that what he had done had been in the interests of the public, subscriptions which aggregated some Rs. 40,000 poured in.

Imprisonment and Release

After Tilak's conviction efforts were made in England and India to obtain a remission of his sentence, and on the anniversary of Her Majesty the Queen Empress' birthday many of his friends drove out to the Yeravda Prison in the expectation of his release on that day. He was eventually released on the 6th September, 1898, the unexpired portion of his sentence having been conditionally remitted. The news of his release was wired to all parts of the country and spread rapidly through the Puna City, where throughout the night and the whole of next day thousands of Hindus of all classes flocked to his house to congratulate him and many of the vernacular newspapers issued special supplements for the purpose of publishing the intelligence. In all parts of Maharashtra and Baroda, the release was celebrated with prayers of thanks-giving, illuminations and the distribution of sweetmeats. Congratulatory telegrams were sent to him from many places, his photo was exhibited at all meetings and in some places carried round the town in procession.

Tour to Burma

From the Congress meeting at Lucknow, Tilak proceeded to Calcutta, Rangoon and Mandalay and returned to Puna via Banaras and Jabalpur.

In lecturing on his travels in Puna, a few months later he drew invidious distinction between the French and British Governments in India. In Burma, he said, there was no caste distinctions and the women enjoyed full liberty, yet Burma had fallen, so how could any one accept the Social Reform argument that India's calamities were attributable to caste distinctions and the want of liberty and education to women. He allowed that reform was needed, but it was political reform and that Social Reform would follow as a matter of course.

Prosecution of Globe Newspaper for Libel

Tilak instituted proceedings against the editor and publisher of the Globe newspaper for libel.

The Times of India which reproduced the article apologised for doing so, and the proprietors of the *Globe* in addition to publishing an apology undertook to defray Tilak's expenses in connection with the proceedings and to make a donation to the Indian Famine Fund.

Trial in Tai Maharaj Case

The District Magistrate, Puna, writes: "Tilak seems to be a popular hero throughout this district and his present trial is being watched with interest by all classes who care at all about anything outside their own immediate surroundings. Tilak's paper is now very widely read, its circulation having been greatly increased through the advertisement afforded by his former trial".

The almost universal hope appears to be that he will emerge successfully from the present proceedings.

The Brahmins of the Sadashiv Peth performed the " Swahakar" (offerings thrown into a fire) ceremony for the removal of difficulties, present and anticipated, from the inhabitants of Puna and Bal Gangadhar Tilak in particular. Tilak was present on all five days. In a lecture on the fourth day, a hope was expressed that the ceremony would relieve Tilak of his difficulties in the criminal prosecution.

Festival in Honour

A pupil in the Government High School, Satara, issued invitations to a meeting to celebrate what he termed the festival of the patriot, Bal Gangadhar Tilak. At the meeting, Tilak's picture was exhibited and garlanded and speeches made in which Tilak's history was briefly narrated, his merits praised and all recommended to serve their country as he does.

Dissemination of Disaffection

A public meeting was held in Puna on the 4th June under the presidency of Tilak to congratulate the Japanese on their successes by land and sea at which Tilak referred specially to the effect the war had and would have on affairs in the Far East and to the fact that it exploded the idea of European supremacy over Asiatics.

At a party given to Tilak at Bhusawal on the 17th August, in returning thanks for some present made to him, he said that the misunderstanding between himself and some of the higher officials of Government was due to their considering his representations on behalf of the people as disloyal, whereas he claimed that in ventilating the grievances of the poor he was doing Government a service; and further he was unable to desist from portraying, pictures of some of the miseries from which the people suffered. Tilak presided at a lecture given by Bhaskar Balwant Bhoptkar on the political, social and religious condition of the Indians in which the speaker urged his countrymen to work for their national regeneration.

During the month of September, Tilak presided at several lectures in which the sentiments expressed were distinctly disloyal and the trend of all was the political regeneration of India.

Swadeshi Movement

A meeting of some 3,000 native students, convened by printed hand-bills freely circulated, was held in Puna on the 22nd August under the presidency of Tilak at which speeches were made advocating the boycott of articles of British manufacture and expressing sympathy with the Bengalis in the partition question.

In September, Tilak visited Bombay for the purpose of getting Mr. Dinshaw Edulji. Wacha to influence Bombay Mill-owners to assist the *swadeshi* movement by supplying dhotis manufactured in Bombay at moderate rates. The appeal is said to have been placed before some of the millionaire at a private meeting who decided that they could not be supplied except at market rates.

On the 11th September, Tilak presided at a lecture in Puna on Swadeshi, which was anti-British in tone.

In September, the District Magistrate, Belgaum reported that the movement was filling a large space in some of the local papers than it did in real life and that it was being engineered entirely from Puna under the direction of Tilak.

On the 15th October, Tilak presided at a large meeting in Bombay at which the following resolutions were passed:

- to encourage as far as possible the use of country-made goods;
- to request the mill-owners of Bombay to stop increasing the price of locally manufactured clothes;
- never to use foreign-made articles, especially English.

Tilak's speech summing up the proceedings bristled with political suggestions and in it he made a violent attack on the *Times of India* newspaper which he described as selfish and onesided.

On the 4th October, a private meeting was held in the New Preparatory School, Puna, to discuss the action to be taken in regard to the disposal of European made clothes, etc. After such articles as were voluntarily offered were collected the students marched in procession to a spot outside the City, placed them in a heap and burnt them. Tilak was present and exhorted his audience to cherish and support the movement.

On the 22nd October, Tilak presided at another largely attended meeting in Bombay when he again attacked the *Times of India* and intimated that through his exertions a Co-operative Stores for the sale of country-made goods would be opened in Bombay on the next Hindu New Year's day.

In the same month, Tilak preached *swadeshi* at a well attended meeting at Lanowli.

On the 25th October, Tilak was again on the platform in Bombay when he spoke on:

- the necessity of holding meetings in different parts of the city to keep the public alive to the advantages of boycotting;

- the legal aspect of boycotting English goods. Sedition, he said, consisted in creating disaffection against the Government and not against goods produced in England, and he could find nothing in Section 124A of the Indian Penal Code which could bring the present movement within its purview;
- the recent action of the Bengal Government in rusticating students taking part in the boycott movement.

On the 4th November, he spoke at a meeting in Puna justifying the action of students taking an active part in the *swadeshi* movement and condemning parents and men like Professor Selby for prohibiting boys from attending such meetings. He urged his audience to continue agitating until they obtained Home Rule.

During this month, he visited Miraj and Kolhapur where he preached *swadeshism*. It was also reported that he has an extensive organisation for preaching the movement from village to village and at all fairs.

In December, he was at Yeola in the Nasik District on the same mission. His speeches were reported to be temperate.

On the 10th December, he was present and spoke at a large meeting in Puna convened to congratulate the Honourable Mr. Gopal Krishna Gokhale and Lala Lajpat Rai on the success in their recent mission to England.

On the 9th September at a meeting of the Swadeshi Wastu Pracharini Sabha, Bombay, he exhorted his hearers to do all in their power to further the cause of *swadeshism* and expressed sympathy with the Postal strike and deprecated the action of those Bombay gentlemen who induced the peons to resume work before they had derived any benefit from their action. On the 7th October, he presided at a meeting of the same Sabha and in the course of his address commented on the awakening of Persia, China and Afghanistan and its effects on the swadeshi movement in India. He deprecated the extension of Railways with British capital on the score of its facilitating the export trade and advocated the Anti-Free Trade policy for which, he said, there were no hopes as long as the Government supported the Free Trade policy. Reverting to *swadeshism,* he said that the partial support now being extended to it by officials was due to the hold the movement had acquired among natives and contended that *swadeshism* and boycotting were inseparable. He again presided at a large meeting convened by the Sabha to present an appreciatory address to Seth Khemraj Shri Krishnadas, part proprietor of the Venkatesh Samachar Printing Press, Bombay, for the practical work he had done in the *swadeshi* cause. At the commencement of the meeting, a shout was raised demanding the expulsion of one Venkatesh Abaji Marathe, who was seated beside Tilak, denouncing him as a traitor and paid agent of Government on account of his having induced the postmen to resume work during the recent strike. An accident to the platform on which Tilak and Marathe were seated necessitated the latter moving to a less prominent seat and this terminated the uproar.

In presenting the address, Tilak referred to the practical work performed by the recipient in the *swadeshi* cause and said that on a recent pilgrimage he had induced many native confectioners to give up the use of foreign-made sugar and that he had repaid to many of them the losses they had sustained by the destruction of their stocks of foreign sugar. Referring to the opposition of the Anglo-Indian Press towards the *swadeshi* movement, he compared it to the opposition shown to Galileo when he asserted that the world rotated and was not stationary.

In regard to the denouncement of Mr. Marathe he said in the absence of better proof he did not believe he was a paid agent of Government and, even if he was, it was no reason for expelling him from a *swadeshi* platform or meeting; but apart from that, in his opinion, Mr. Marathe had in the particular instance acted rightly and that whatever blame there was not with him but with the public who had not yet come to fully realise the advantages of combination.

At a meeting of the Sabha on the 21st October, which was attended by the Bhattia and Bania merchants of Bombay, Tilak said that the essence of *swadeshism* did not lie so much in boycotting foreign articles as in making an effort to reduce the imports and increase the exports of India and he appealed to the merchants of Bombay to seriously consider the question in this light and to encourage the movement without fear and religious scruples. He also advised all native merchants to transact business direct and not through foreigners.

Tilak is reported to have interviewed the Russian Consul ostensibly to obtain letters of introduction to firms in Russia with a view to purchasing goods, machinery, etc. in furtherance of the *swadeshi* movement. He was advised not to try Russia at present, and given a letter of introduction to the German Consul, whom he subsequently interviewed. He also saw the Austrian Consul and obtained letters of introduction to firms in Austria.

Press Prosecutions

It is reported that Tilak, as principal trustee of the balance of the Fund, raised in 1897 for his defence, set apart Rs. 5,000 for a Tress Prosecution Fund, out of which a sum of Rs. 3,000 was contributed towards the expenses for the defence of B. B. Bhopatkar in the *Bhala* case and that the fine of Rs. 1,000 was paid from the same fund.

Tilak is reported to have been present and to have taken a keen interest in a meeting of the Industrial Association in Puna on the 15th and 16th May when the following suggestions were unanimously approved:

- to depute a commission of experts to Japan, England, Germany, Switzerland and other foreign countries;
- to appoint district committees for furthering the cause of industrial reform and affiliate them to a central association to be located at Bombay or Puna;
- to send qualified students to foreign countries for industrial and commercial education;
- to establish banking firms and credit societies on the principles of co-operation;
- to start an industrial and commercial periodical and to publish a directory annually;
- to hold, if possible, an Industrial Conference along with the Provincial Conference in June 1906.

On the 1st March, the first annual gathering of the Maharashtra Boarding House was held in the Maharashtra Vidyalaya when Tilak gave an address in which he advised his audience to work for the welfare of the institution and to prefer education in a school which was conducted without a grant-in-aid, as it was therefore unlikely to be subservient to the Government.

Tilak visited Calcutta in June to discuss with the Bengali leaders, it is said, the following points in connection with the establishment of a National University:

- ways and means to collect funds for such an ambitious scheme;
- centres at which to establish branches;
- the number of colleges to be opened at the start;
- the curriculum of studies.

A notice signed by M. G. Deshmukh, Tilak, D. A. Khare, and V. G. Vijapurkar has been published in the Kesari and other newspapers inviting pecuniary assistance for the establishment of national schools all over Maharashtra for the purpose of training and educating youths who are prepared to dedicate themselves to the welfare of their country. The signatories to the notice undertake the management of the institution under the title of the Board of Maharashtra Educationists on the understanding that subscribers will have no voice in the Government.

Influence and Popularity

In a so-styled national song which was being distributed in the Puna City in the form of a hand-bill, Tilak is invoked as a demi-good.

In May, the Political Agent, Kolhapur and Southern Maratha Country reported that Tilak was reported to be the secret adviser of the Chief of Miraj (Senior).

Tilak is reported to have declined to assist W. S. Khare or to have anything to do with Nasik until its present methods of agitation are abandoned.

Shivaji Celebrations: From Bombay, Tilak and his party proceeded to Raigadh where the anniversary of Shivaji's birthday was celebrated with unusual pomp and ceremony. The District Magistrate, Kolaba, wrote that he did not consider the Raigadh celebration was intended to be altogether harmless, as from a report received from the District Deputy Collector, it appeared that very disloyal songs were sung by schoolboys trained for the occasion. This officer also drew attention to the fact that it is customary to celebrate only the death days of saints and heroes and considered that some significance should be attached to the fact that on this occasion it was the birthday that was celebrated.

Ganpati Celebrations: During the celebrations in Puna, Tilak urged the necessity for having unions and organisations throughout the country similar to those in England, America and Russia to represent the grievances of the public, and observed that the recent strike of Postal peons in Bombay proved futile for want of a union. The leaders of the country, he said, had succeeded in making the present state of affairs, known to all and it was now their duty to stimulate matters by putting forward suggestions for the formation of unions with a view to approach Government in a more systematic way.

Dussehra Celebrations

On 27th September, Tilak spoke at an assembly of some 3,000 persons convened by the Arya Mitra Mela, Bombay, to celebrate the Dussehra festival. After the meeting a procession of gymnasts and *melas* was formed and headed by Tilak proceeded to the Laxmi Narayan Temple where a gymnastic display was given and prizes awarded. Tilak in addressing them said that the Dussehra holiday, which he named "Vijaya Dashami", which means the 10th day of conquest, is maintained as a political, social and industrial festival, as in the days of the Mahrattas it was considered an auspicious day on which to embark on warlike expeditions, and though in these days such expeditions are not practicable, the day was one on which they may start plans and resolutions such as not to be idle, not to join in internal dissensions, to remain faithful to one's caste and creed, to work in such a way as to ensure the prosperity of one's country, etc. And that it was the duty of the Indians to start on such expeditions as were admissible in the times and if they worked wholeheartedly God would grant them success.

Dissemination of Disaffection

Tilak was in Kolhapur in March, and in a speech recommending the resuscitation of the Lok Sabha or Local Congress pointed out that the Mysore Government had sanctioned the holding of such Congress but that was a poor end to agitation; in Kolhapur the people should aim at forcing the Darbar to grant something more, and he suggested their claiming a share in the Government of the State whereby they may limit the power of the ruler and allow him to retain merely his patronage and ostentation. If they succeeded, the British Government could be shamed into granting similar rights in British territory.

Tilak is reported to have had an interview with the Honourable Mr. Gopal Krishna Gokhale on his return from his tour in Northern India to discuss the lines on which agitation should be run. Tilak is alleged to have advocated the adoption of extreme measures and Gokhale to have considered the time not yet ripe for them.

Meeting at Nasik

Tilak presided at a meeting in Nasik on the 31st May convened to protest against the recent circular of the Government of India prohibiting students from taking part in politics. He said the proposed protest described the circular as " oppressive, annoying and Russian" and explained how it was so. He then discoursed on Russian methods of agitation and said that in that country the people, students and lawyers united to strive for liberty and in the strife many have been deported and many impaled; newspapers have been suppressed and editors silenced; but with what success ? After a long struggle the Government have granted the people half their demands.

In India, it is the same; the people are struggling for *swarajya* not for sovereignty; their present condition is even worse than that of the Russians and however much the Government may trample them down they will ultimately accomplish their ends. True it will take time and not be easy of accomplishment; the desire for liberty, however, does not die, but goes on increasing. The methods of Government are not worthy of them nor are they congenial to the people, and under such circumstances the people cannot do better than learn from Russia what to do.

J. A. Guider
Personal Assistant
to the Deputy Inspector-General of Police
for Railways and Criminal Investigation

Puna, 14th October 1907.

Industrial Conference at Pandharpur

Tilak was one of the Delegates for the Maharashtra Industrial Conference held at Pandharpur in the Sholapur District on the 15th of November. In a speech made by him on that occasion, he bemoaned the fact that industries in India were no longer what they used to be. He attributed this to the lack of Government support. Government was indifferent to the industrial needs of India; the cry of the people received no consideration; the people had not sufficient to eat, not because there was no enough corn, but because the people had no money, all India's wealth having been carried away to a foreign country. He concluded by advising his hearers not to rely on Government, but to strike out for themselves.

Congress Meeting

On December 11th at a meeting was held in Puna, Tilak proposed that certain subjects should be discussed at the ensuing sessions of the Congress: they were:

- *Swadeshi* and *Swaraj*.
- National Education considered purely from a National point of view.
- Boycott.
- Criticism of Mr. Morley's Reform Bill, newly introduced.
- Criticism of the Bill for the prohibition of Seditious Meetings.
- The question of the stopping of the annual sum of 30,000 rupees sent to London to maintain the British Congress committee.

- To consider the letter sent by the Indians living in the Transvaal to the Congress Reception Committee.

Split in Congress

It was over some of these points that very shortly afterwards split occurred amongst some of the leaders of the National Congress. Those in favour of "boycott" called themselves the Nationalist Party and decided to hold a Congress of their own at Surat before the actual Indian National Congress held its sitting. B. G. Tilak was one of this party.

At the end of December, the delegates of the 23rd Indian National Congress assembled at Surat from all parts of India.

On the 24th December, the Nationalists held their 1st Conference with Babu Arvind Ghose of Calcutta as President, and G. S. Khaparde of Amraoti as Chairman. Tilak was called upon to state in detail the object of the Conference. Tilak in his speech said that their object was not to secede from the Indian National Congress, but to try and make all members of the Congress Nationalists.

The difference between the Congress and the Nationalists was this, viz., the Congress wanted self-government on Colonial lines, but the Nationalists wanted Independence. The Nationalists expressed their ideal freely and were prepared to suffer for it. If they were forced to transgress the law, the fault would not be theirs.

As regards Education, they did not want the Education which was in the hands of bureaucracy but National Education.

The thing was to force the Nationalists views on the Congress, or at any rate to see that it did not slide back. After Tilak's speech, it was decided to request the Congress to move Resolutions on Swaraj, Boycott and National Education.

Surat Session

On the 26th, the first sitting of the 23rd Indian National Congress began, and the proceedings were very soon brought to an end in confusion owing to the disagreement about the election of the President, Dr. Rash Bihari Ghose.

On the next day, the 27th, the meeting was resumed, and the proceedings got so far as the election of the President of the

Congress, when Tilak got up on the platform and said he wanted to speak and refused to be moved. Tilak apparently wanted to move an amendment, as he said that the election of the President has not been unanimous. He was asked to sit down, but refused.

Uproar in the Congress was the result, and the meeting of the Congress came to an end in confusion.

On the 28th December, in the evening a meeting of the Nationalists only was held at Surat.

Amongst those taking a prominent part was Tilak. At this meeting Arvind Ghose presided, and Tilak in his speech explained how the quarrel at the meeting of the Congress had taken place because he was not allowed to put forward certain arguments. He proposed the formation of a Committee of 50 persons representing the various Provinces of India. This proposition was carried.

At the end of this meeting, Tilak presented Ajit Singh (the man deported along with Lala Lajpat Rai) with an embroidered velvet cap.

On the 29th of December, another meeting of the Nationalists was held in Surat, at which he proposed that each province should give the names of its delegates for the Committee he had proposed the previous day. It was also resolved to open schools in each province for the teaching of the Nationalists' propaganda, and how to teach them without transgressing the limits of the Penal Code. A Nationalists' Fund was also opened.

1908: In February, it was reported that a National Volunteer Club had been started in Puna of which B. G. Tilak was one of the principal members. The chief rule of the club laid down that its members should strictly adhere to the principles of Swadeshi, efforts for *Swaraj,* National Education and Boycott.

Public Meetings

On the 28th of February, B. G. Tilak took part in a meeting held at Puna in honour of the anniversary of Ramdas. In his speech on the occasion Tilak said that Religion and Politics went hand in hand, and that the religious festivals would best be celebrated if political preachers would go about the country and teach the people what their rights were.

On the 21st and 22nd of May, Tilak attended meetings of the Extremists to discuss the situation caused by the discovery of the anarchist plot in Calcutta. One of the resolutions passed at these meetings was to the effect that subscriptions should be raised for the defence of the Calcutta Anarchists. The meeting also passed a resolution that " the regrettable occurrences were in their opinion due to the persistent disregard of public opinion and continued policy of repression on the part of Government".

Conviction and Sentence

On June 24th, B. G. Tilak was arrested in Bombay on a charge under Section 124A and 153A of the Indian Penal Code in respect of an article headed "The Country's misfortune" which appeared in the issue of the *Kesari* of the 12th of May 1908.

He was placed before the Chief Presidency Magistrate, Bombay, on the 25th June and remanded to Jail till the 29th idem.

On the 27th June he was again placed before the Chief Presidency Magistrate for a similar offence in respect of an article headed "These remedies are not lasting", which appeared in the issue of the Kesari of the 9th June 1908. Tilak was convicted and sentenced by the Sessions Court to six years transportation and to pay a fine of Rs. 1,000 on the 22nd July 1908. The same day he was taken to the Ahmedabad Central Prison, Sabarmati.

F. M. Gandey,
Personal Assistant
to the Deputy Inspector-General of Police, for
Railways and Criminal Investigation.

Transfer to Mandalay

Tilak was, under the orders of Government, removed from the Ahmedabad Central Prison to the Mandalay Jail. He sailed for Rangoon in the R. I. M. S. Hardinge which left Bombay on the morning of the 14th September, 1908.

The sentence of transportation for six years passed on him by the High Court was commuted as an act of clemency by

Government into one of simple imprisonment for a like term and the fine of Rs. 1,000 remitted.

F. C. Griffith,
Personal Assistant
to the Deputy Inspector-General of Police,
for Railways and Criminal Investigation.

After Release from Mandalay

After the Madras Congress (December, 1914), negotiations for a compromise continued. The attitude of the late Mr. Gokhale was described as conciliatory and it is said that the late Sir Pherozeshah Mehta gave him a personal assurance that he was prepared to consider every reasonable amendment in the Constitution that would bring back the seceders to the Congress. Mr. Gokhale was prepared to concede that all associations should have the right to send delegates, provided some limit was placed on the number each district was to send, a safeguard which was considered essential to prevent the platform from being swamped by irresponsible persons coming in large numbers from some localities and forcing their opinions on the general body. It was not certain whether such representation was to be based on the number and strength of existing bodies in each district or on the population of the district. In any case, the introduction of such a proviso would have exposed the strong as well as the weak points of the Congress propaganda, as many districts would probably remain unrepresented on account of their apathy.

The result of these negotiations made it clear that both parties were afraid that any reform in the Congress Constitution on the lines proposed might expose the fact that the Congress had no real backing in the country.

Difference in Methods Only

The whole question was to have been discussed at a meeting at the Servants of India Hall, Puna, on the 7th February 1915, where many mofussil Congressmen were to meet Mr. Samarth of Bombay. Meanwhile, however, Mrs. Besant had not been inactive. She was anxious to obtain a clear statement in writing from

Mr. Tilak as to the intentions of the Nationalist Party once they re-entered the Congress. It will be remembered that in the course of his statement to Mr. Subba Rao at Puna on the 8th December 1914, Tilak is alleged also to have said that though the aim of both the Moderates and Nationalists was the same, namely, the attainment of self-government within the Empire by constitutional means, there was a difference between the methods of the two schools and that if the Nationalist Party were enabled to rejoin the Congress they would seek to obtain "recognition of their methods by educating public opinion and working for and securing a majority in the Congress, if possible".

Mrs. Besant's Statement

It was this, according to Mrs. Besant, which had alarmed certain Congress leaders, including Mr. Gokhale who up till then had been in favour of the proposed amendment to Article XX of the Congress Constitution and led to its being referred to a Committee. They had urged that it opened up an indefinite vista of conflicts in which the Congress, instead of working to obtain its objects, was to spend its time in fighting over methods, the fighting to continue until some methods, not those of the Congress at present, should be substituted for these by a majority vote and that therefore before anything could be done it at least would be necessary to clear the matter up. To that end Mrs. Besant prepared a review of the various stages of the negotiations leading up to the proposed amendment at the Madras Sessions to Article XX of the Congress Constitution and, after emphasising the part of Tilak's statement to Mr. Subba Rao referred to above had played in the shelving of the amendment, she added the following "friendly request to Mr. Tilak":

> "For myself, I ask Mr. Tilak in all friendliness to make his meaning clear; to tell us what these methods are, and to assure us that he does not come into the Congress to work for any radical change in its methods, or any wrecking of its organisation, explaining the phrase used which has caused such natural alarm as to its intentions. If I have been mistaken in my belief that the difference of methods

> is merely the introduction of a little added vigour and insistence, and not a demand for a fundamental change, then I must regretfully give up any further effort to bring about a union which would not invigorate but would destroy the Congress, which is India's only representative institution, commit it to a period of strife when harmonious efforts are necessary, and radically change the methods of work which have done so much for India".

After some editing by Mr. Gokhale, Mrs. Besant sent this statement to Mr. Tilak on the 20th January 1915 and in reply she received on the 30th idem a copy of the Maharatta of the 10th January containing its answer to a similar request from Professor Kale, and a letter from Tilak suggesting that she might publish that answer as a reply to her statement, but he asked her to postpone publication till the completion of certain negotiations then in progress.

The answer to Professor Kale in the Mahratta was particularly the same as Tilak's statement to Mr. Subba Rao and left the matter as nebulous as before. Mrs. Besant found it left her no option but to give up her attempt at uniting the two parties and she regretted that she was unable to delay publication of the correspondence. She accordingly reproduced it in *New India* of the 2nd February 1915, the full text of which appeared in the local Puna and Bombay papers on the 6th idem.

This must have affected the meeting at the Servants of India Hall on the 7th, but no details regarding it have transpired. Mr. Gokhale followed Mrs. Besant's statement up with a letter to the Press on the 9th February, to which and Mrs. Besant's statement Tilak replied on the 11th. It was said that Mr. Gokhale was glad of the opportunity afforded by Mrs. Besant's statement to the Press of vindicating himself. Considerable resentment had been fostered in a large section of the public, particularly in Puna, owing to his failure to publish his letter to Bhupendranath Basu regarding Tilak, which it was alleged contained statements amounting to a libel in law and for which, it was reported, Tilak contemplated proceeding against him. As Gokhale and Tilak's letters to the Press throw some light on the situation, they are reproduced below.

Another Move for Unity

The next move towards a compromise came during the Provincial Conference organised by the Extremists of Puna early in May when Mr. Joseph Baptista in his presidential address pleaded for unity, and a resolution appointing a committee, consisting of the Honourable Mr. Belvi, Mr. Baptista and Tilak, and empowering them to take the necessary steps to bring about a united Congress, was unanimously carried. In spite of this, it was clear that Tilak had no intention of going into the Congress except on his own terms. There was no evidence to show that this committee took any action to effect a compromise. When R. B. Phatak of Satara and other delegates broached the subject of compromise in the Subjects Committee of the Moderates Provincial Conference held in Puna in July and expressed the intention of bringing forward a resolution appointing a committee to consider how it could be attained, it was decided after much discussion to approach Tilak and ask him to explain what he wanted. Tilak said he was prepared to join the Congress under its Constitution, but refused to give a guarantee for himself and others that when once in the Congress they would not bring up such subjects as the " Boycott" and " National Education " before the Congress. He maintained that the majority should always decide what line was to be taken and that everyone should be free to induce his colleagues to his side. He was not prepared to surrender any of these rights simply for the advantage of being in the Congress. Ultimately when it was found that no immediate compromise was possible, it was decided to leave the subject open.

Clause Amending Congress Constitution

Tilak, however, made one last effort to get into the Congress. At the beginning of December, he sent N. C. Kelkar to Calcutta, and Upper India to interview the political leaders there and so pave the way for a compromise. He was to represent that the Extremists did not now preach "Boycott" or "Passive Resistance", in fact that their programme did not differ in essential from the general programme of the Moderates. It was on this basis that the attempt was to be made to win over or at least soften the Moderate leaders in those parts in order to bring about a compromise which would have allowed the Extremists to enter the Congress honourably.

The Bombay Congress Committee were willing to admit Tilak as a delegate if he signed the convention, but were not willing to hold a public meeting at which he might be elected. It appeared, however, from a telegram from him to Babu Motilal Ghose that he expected the Provincial Congress Committee to authorise the holding of such meetings all over the Presidency at which "as many Nationalists as we want may be elected to carry through any amendments to the Constitution that we require". It this arrangement had been carried through it is very evident that there would have been a large body of Extremists in the Congress, and, though they had signed the Convention in order to gain admittance, would have put forward embarrassing proposals for the amendment of the Constitution and that the Bombay Moderates would have bad some difficulty in restraining their young adherents as information to hand showed that the Moderate leaders had already experienced some difficulty in controlling the younger members of their party. Some Puna Moderates, it is said, did actually approach the Bombay leaders with a view to electing Tilak as a delegate at a meeting of the District Congress Committee though he did not belong to it. But this move proved futile as was also, apparently, the attempt which it is said, was to be made at the meeting on the 25th December of the Committee appointed at Madras to report on Mrs. Besant's amendments to settle finally in an indirect fashion Tilak's admission to the Congress. It, however, resulted in the following draft amendment to the Congress Constitution which was carried a few days later at the Congress Sessions.

That any public association of two years standing having accepted the Congress Creed, and made the acceptance of the Creed a condition precedent to membership, and having notified such accéptance of the Creed to the Congress Committee of the Province in which that Association is situated, will have the power to hold public meetings for the election of delegates to the Congress, the number of delegates thus elected being 15.

"That the All India Congress Committee will have the power of disqualifying any such Association to elect delegates when they think that these Associations are acting in a way contrary to the first Article of the Constitution".

Mrs. Besant's Home Rule League

Mrs. Besant, having failed also to carry her suggestion that the 1915 Congress make a formal demand for Home Rule, inauguranted the Home Rule League, to the presidentship of which she managed to inveigle Mr. Dadabhai Naoroji. She approached Tilak, who of course promised her hearty support seeing that this presented a means whereby he could return to active public life with dignity and ostentation.

Mrs. Besant's idea, though not definitely opposed, was not taken up by the Bombay Moderates enthusiastically. They considered that it was the Congress who should organise such a League if it was at all necessary.

Mrs. Besant soon realised that the admission of Tilak to the League, while the Bombay Moderates were still hesitating, would prejudice her chances of success, and the League not receiving a very encouraging response from the Bengal leaders, Mrs. Besant notified that there would be no admission to the League until the political leaders of the Congress and the Muslim League, whom she had invited, met on a day previous to the Congress to discuss her proposals and frame rules for submission for the approval of Dadabhai Naoroji and Sir Subramaniam Iyer.

This action naturally excluded Tilak and the Extremists for at least a year from taking any active part in the management of the League, a great disappointment to the Extremists to whom the League would have been of the utmost value. It was affirmed that Mrs. Annie Besant sincerely believed that the League would enable her to preserve the enthusiasm of the Extremists, a factor which the present Congress party considerably lacked, as well as strike out the unconstitutional and dangerous element.

It was said that as far back as February, Tilak had contemplated starting a Home Rule League, but had refrained from doing so on Mr. Gokhale informing him that it would at once be suppressed by Government.

Personal Activities

Now to turn to Tilak's personal activities during 1915.

He was present at the entertainment given in Puna in honour of Mr. Gandhi by the Sarvajanik Sabha on the 12th July and by the citizens of Puna in the Kirloskar Theatre on the 13th idem. On the latter occasion he arrived a little late and was given a great ovation.

Early in March news was received from D. A. Khare that Tilak's appeal to the Privy Council with regard to the Tai Maharaj Adoption case had ended in his favour. This decision of the Privy Council caused great jubilation among his friends and followers as a vindication of his character and as a blow to Government's endeavours to dub him as a common criminal and cheat.

On the 13th March, he was in Bombay to attend a private meeting of the Swadeshi Cooperative Stores, when it was decided to open a branch of the concern in Puna, which was subsequently done.

Provincial Conference at Puna

On the 20th April, a meeting was held in Sarvajanik Sabha Hall to appoint a Chairman and Reception Committee for the Provincial Conference to be held in Puna on the 8th, 9th and 10th May. Tilak was elected a member of the Reception Committee and in proposing a vote of thanks to the chair urged upon the assembly the necessity of realising the importance of the object for which they had assembled. All had a right, he said, to put their views before the assembly, but when the questions had been fully discussed they should abide by the decision of the majority. The Moderate Congress party refused to recognise the Puna Provincial Conference, regarding it as having been called without complying with the Rules and Regulations of the Congress organisation. On the other hand Tilak, Kelkar and other notables of the Extremist party left no stone unturned in their efforts to make it a success, and they succeeded so far in their efforts that some 2,000 persons assembled on the day fixed. Mr. Joseph Baptista, the President-elect, arrived in Puna on the 7th May and was given a great reception. Tilak himself, Patwardhan, chairman of the Reception

Committee and R. P. Karandikar drove with him from the station to the bungalow in which he lodged. The proceedings of the Conference were carried out in a spirit of moderation, compatible, it is apparent, with a realisation of the difficulties that faced Government at the time.

The speeches were all fairly moderate in tone. In fact a few of the delegates held the view that they were going too far in their moderation, but their opinions were overruled by the majority who were animated by a conciliatory spirit. The whole affair was a triumph of organisation for Tilak, who dominated the whole proceedings, Baptista, the President, playing but a small part. After the conclusion of the Conference on the 10th May, Tilak delivered a speech in the Kirloskar Theatre, the venue of the Conference. Having promised that the views he was going to propound had no connection with the programme of the Conference, but were his own thoughts, he went on to discuss the past and present state of the country.

The present system of Government, which had been gradually evolved since the overthrow of the Peshwa, was not suited to India's needs and a change in the administrative system was needed. India needed British rule but not bureaucracy. The goal of their ambition should be Home Rule. The British wanted to rule India and derive as much benefit as they could from it and there was no use trying to prevent them. However, whatever concessions were given should be accepted and they should not cease asking for further concessions.

The Conference had formed no definite opinion on the form of Home Rule that we required and had not, therefore, discussed the matter. Their leaders should, therefore, come together to discuss and formulate their demands, as the proper time for moving for a change of policy was approaching. The questions would come before Parliament after the war and they should then be prepared with one demand which would meet all their wants. To that end, the leaders should move about the districts and explain to the people what was wanted. Nothing should be done to embarrass the Government while the war was in progress, but they should raise their voice after the war and let Government see that the country was united in its demand.

Bharat Itihas Sanshodak Mandali

On the 9th May, he presided at the meeting of the " Bharat Itihas Sanshodak Mandali". The "Mandali", he said, had come into being while he was absent, but on hearing of it on his return, he had at once joined it as he considered that a knowledge of the previous history of a nation was essential for its prosperity.

Government might be approached for help, but he advised the members to run the "Mandali" themselves.

The Mandali is a purely harmless institution and enquiries show that the promoters are not likely to be influenced by Tilak.

Compromise between Extremists and Moderates

The National Congress held in December 1915 passed an amendment to Article XX of the Congress Constitution, which afforded the Nationalists an opportunity of entering the Congress under its provisions, should they choose to do so. The amendment granted automatic affiliation to all political bodies of two years standing on the 31st December 1915, but limited the number of delegates from such bodies to 15. Though the Nationalists resented this limit of 15, they were to a great extent disposed to recognise that a concession to their susceptibilities had been made. Tilak said that before taking up any definite attitude he would first have to consult the members of his party, and to this end a meeting of prominent Nationalists of the Deccan, Central Provinces and Berars was held in Puna on the 16th January 1916, at which it was decided that the question should be deferred for final settlement at their Provincial Conference at Belgaum in the coming April.

The question as to whether it should be a United Conference was discussed, but it was finally decided to leave it to the Moderates to come and join if they liked, or to hold a separate conference as they had done the previous year or not hold any at all. As regards the compromise, Tilak expressed himself fairly satisfied with it, but added that he did not wish to influence the opinion of others in any way. The Belgaum Conference opened on the 29th April and ended on the 1st May. All the leading Nationalists of the Presidency attended and also a few leaders from the Central Provinces and Berars. After a lengthy discussion on the compromise question, following final draft was prepared and adopted by the Subjects Committee:

> "That this Conference adopts the reports of Messrs. Belvi, Baptista and Tilak, and as in the interest of our Motherland under the present circumstances it is desirable to unite, resolves to accept the Constitution of the Congress as amended at its last sessions, though the amendment is highly unsatisfactory, and appoints a committee composed of the following gentlemen, to do further work from within: G. S. Khaparde, J. Baptista, D. V. Belvi, B. G. Tilak and N. C. Kelkar (Secretary)".

Even after the final adoption of the resolution in the subjects Committee, Paranjpe and others argued that there was a strong feeling among the delegates against the resolution. Tilak stoutly opposed them and in the end challenged Paranjpe to bring in an amendment before the Conference if he wanted. Tilak's firm attitude carried the day. The resolution which was proposed by Tilak, seconded by Belvi and supported by Gandhi, R. P. Karandikar, S. M. Paranjpe, Dr. Munje and others, was eventually carried unanimously.

War and Loyalty

Tilak was called upon to support the first resolution of the Conference " War and Loyalty". He said that in the resolution they asked for certain concessions whereby they could attain the full status of British Citizens, not as a recompense for the services they had rendered to the Empire, but on the grounds of justice and equity. These concessions they had been asking for the past 25 years, but they were always met with the argument that if they were conceded it meant the extinction of British power in India. The war had, however, brought about a crisis, and in that crisis the British Government had found the whole of the Indian nation loyal. Indians wished to support the British Empire and had no desire for another foreign power to rule over them, and were, therefore, willing to sacrifice their lives and their money for the retention, the strength, and ultimate success of the British

Government. Persons had cast a slur on their loyalty in order to prevent their obtaining the rights of British citizenship, but the experience of the war had demonstrated their loyalty and proved that any concessions made to them would not be abused by them.

Tilak's Home Rule League

On the 24th of December 1915, there was a meeting at Tilak's house at Puna of several Nationalists at which it was resolved that a Home Rule League for Maharashtra should be established in the near future. The assembly of a large number of Nationalists at Belgaum for the Provincial Conference was seized on as a fitting occasion to launch this scheme. Accordingly on the 23th April, a meeting was held to consider the question. At this meeting, it was decided that a League should be established with a view to educating and organising public opinion throughout the country to agitate for Home Rule. Provincial office-bearers were appointed. Baptista was nominated President, N. C. Kelkar, Secretary and D. V. Gokhale, Assistant Secretary. Tilak appeared as one of the member of a Committee of 17 persons nominated to carry on the work of propagating the Home Rule doctrine, enlist members and organise branches. He opened the compaign by delivering a lengthy oration on Home Rule at Belgaum on the 1st at the conclusion of the meeting held there under the auspices of the Historical Research Association.

United Congress

After a spell of nine years, the Extremists under the leadership of Tilak returned to the Congress in 1916 at the Lucknow session. They were yet in a minority, but unlike in 1907, it was an effective minority, and already the Congress was showing positive signs of being converted to their programme. Even during the period of their absence from the stage, they continued to have an invisible hold on people, and it manifested itself when they decided to re-enter politics actively. In 1914, after the negotiations with Congress leaders broke down, Tilak convened a meeting of the Bombay Provincial Conference. The call was responded to only by Extremists of whom a thousand attended the conference. Two months later, the Moderates called a similar gathering, but the poor attendance confirmed that, as before Tilak's incarceration, Extremists still had a far greater hold on the Presidency. And in 1916, when they reappeared in the Congress pandal, they largely outnumbered the Moderates. An interesting anecdote has made the fact of their majority memorable.

Delegates, province-wise, were electing members for the subjects committee. Gandhi too was one of the delegates from Bombay, and when someone proposed him for membership of the committee, an Extremist proposed the name of a colleague.

Gandhi was defeated. Tilak at once stood up and said that Gandhi had been elected. It was the Master's wish, and up went so many Extremist voices, "Yes, Gandhi is elected".

The Lucknow Congress is a landmark in the political history of India. A new chapter was written. The separation of Muslims from the political agitation of the Congress, brought about by Principal Beck, was completely undone in 1916. Both the Congress and the Muslim League held their annual sessions simultaneously at Lucknow, and produced an agreed scheme of reforms. The President of the Congress, Ambika Charan Mazumdar, proudly declared in his presidential address: "The Hindu-Muslim question has been settled, and both the communities have agreed to make a united demand for self-government".

The main proposals of the scheme of reforms that were evolved by joint deliberations are known as the Lucknow Pact. The scheme may be divided into two parts: The first dealt with the Muslim question, and the other with constitutional reforms. Seats were proposed to be reserved for Muslims in the provincial legislatures in the following proportions: the Punjab—one-half of the elected Indian members; the United Provinces—30 per cent of the elected Indian members; Bengal—40 per cent of the elected Indian members; Bihar—25 per cent of the elected Indian members; Central Provinces—15 per cent of the elected Indian members; Madras — 15 per cent of the elected Indian members; and Bombay — one-third of the elected Indian members. The proposal provided for their election by separate electorate.

The second part of the scheme proposed that in the reconstruction of the Empire, India should be raised from the status of a dependency to that of an equal partner in the Empire as a self-governing dominion; the provincial legislative councils should consist of four-fifths of elected and one-fifth of nominated members, elections being held on as broad a franchise as possible. The provincial Governor and members of his executive council should not ordinarily belong to the Indian Civil Service. The provinces should be perfectly autonomous.

All the local bodies should have elected chairmen of their own. The strength of the Imperial Legislative Council should be 150, of which four-fifths should be elected, one-third of the elected members to be Muslims elected by separate Muslim electorate. The Council of the Secretary of State for India should be abolished. The franchise for the Imperial Legislative Council should be widened. India should have a national militia to which all the races should be eligible.

In recommending the scheme to the British Government, the Congress resolution said that "His Majesty, the King Emperor, should be pleased to issue a proclamation announcing that it is the aim and intention of the British policy to confer self-government on India at an early date".

Tilak generally agreed with the scheme, but differed on one point. He emphasised that it was necessary that the succeeding instalments of self-government should be definitely determined and announced together with the time-limit for complete realisation of all our aspirations. He tried his best to press the inclusion of this limit in the resolution, but the Moderate leaders, conscious of their majority, did not agree.

In the interest of unity, Tilak dropped the proposal and gave his unreserved support to the scheme. The Moderate leaders seemed equally anxious to work with the Extremists and to preserve unity in the Congress. Congress President Mazumdar, in his address, voiced their sentiments at some length. He said: "Gentlemen, even the darkest cloud is said to have its silver lining, and in this vale of sorrow, there is hardly any misfortune which has not both a positive and a negative side.

If the united Congress was buried in the debris of the old French Garden at Surat, it is reborn today in the Kaisar Bagh of Lucknow, the garden of the gorgeous King Wajid Ali Shah.

After nearly ten years of painful separation and wanderings through the wilderness of misunderstandings and the mazes of unpleasant controversies, each widening the breach and lengthening the chain of separation, both the wings of the Indian Nationalist party have come to realise the fact that united they stand and divided they fall. Brothers have at last met brothers and embraced each other with the gush and ardour peculiar to a reconciliation after a long separation Blessed are the peacemakers.

Then, fixing his eyes upon Tilak, he said: "Most cordially, I welcome Mr. Bal Gangadhar Tilak, Mr. Motilal Ghose and other brave comrades, who separated from us at Surat and have been happily restored to us at Lucknow. I rejoice to find that they are after all of us and with us—and let us hope—never, never to part again".

As usual, the Congress adopted a number of resolutions, but Tilak was interested only in one resolution, and that was on self-government, and he spoke only once. He believed that the various demands which the Congress had been putting forward from year to year had become out of date in view of the demand for early establishment of self-government.

There were prolonged applause and cheers when he rose to support the resolution on self-government. He said: "The resolution which I wish to support... is the resolution of self-government. It is that for which we have been fighting, for which the Congress has been fighting for the last thirty years. The first note of it was heard ten years ago on the banks of the Hooghly, and it was sounded by the Grand Old Man of India, that Parsee patriot of Bombay, Dadabhai Naoroji. Since the note was sounded differences of opinion arose. Some said that the note ought to be carried on and ought to be followed by a detailed scheme at once, that it should be taken up and made to resound all over India as soon as possible. There was another party amongst us, that said that it could not be done so soon, and the tune of that note required to be a little lowered, and that was the cause of dissension ten years ago, and I am glad to say that I have lived these ten years to see that we are reunited in this Congress and we are going to put our voices and shoulders together to push on this scheme of self-government; and not only have we lived to see these differences closed, but to see the differences of Hindus and Muslims closed as well.

So, we have now united in every way in the United Provinces, and we have found that luck in Lucknow, There was an uproar of laughter.

Then he spoke on the resolution; he was the greatest leader of India in his times, and uttered words which added to his greatness:

> "There are only one or two points on which I wish to address you. It has been said by some that we Hindus have yielded too much to our Muslim brethren, I am sure I represent the sense of the Hindu community all over India when I say that we could not have, yielded too much. I would not care if the rights of self-government are granted to the Muslim community only. [Hear, hear] I would not care if they are granted to Rajputs; I would not care if they are granted the lowest classes of the Hindu population, provided the British Government consider them more fit than the educated classes of India, for exercising those rights I would not care if these rights are granted to any section of the Indian community. Then the fight will be between them and other sections of the community and not as at present a triangular fight. Remember, we have to gain these rights from a powerful bureaucracy, an unwilling bureaucracy, naturally unwilling because the bureaucracy now feels these rights, these privileges, this authority will pass out of their hands".

The resolution was not meant only to be formally passed and then slept over, and he exhorted the audience to carry on the agitation. "We cannot now afford to spend our energies on all the resolutions on the Public Services, the Arms Act, and sundry others. All is comprehended and included in this one resolution. I would ask every one of you to try to carry out this one resolution with all your effort, might and enthusiasm. I do not care if the sessions of the Congress are held no longer; I believe it has done its work as a deliberative body. These are the days of work and incessant labour, and I hope that by the help of Providence, you will find that energy and those resources which are required for carrying out that scheme within the next two years to come, and if not by the end of 1917, when I expect the war will be closed, and then I hope we shall meet at some place in India where we shall be able to raise up the banner of self-rule". (Loud Applause).

The resolution was carried unanimously.

Tilak's acceptance of communal electorates was based on the hope that the system would not last and would only be temporary and that the Muslims themselves would soon give it up. His hope was shared by Jinnah, as would appear from the following extract of his evidence before the Parliamentary Select Committee in 1919.

Examined by Major Ormsby-Gore, Jinnah was asked:

Q. "You said you spoke from the point of view of India? You speak really as an Indian nationalist?"

A. "I do".

Q. "That is to say that at the earliest possible moment you wish to do away in political life with any distinction between Muslims and Hindu?"

A. "Yes; nothing will please me more [than] when that day comes".

In the changed political atmosphere, the Congress had adopted a resolution on self-government, but many delegates were not serious about it. It was with great difficulty that Tilak was able to persuade the Congress to pass another resolution calling upon the Home Rule League and other public associations to carry on continuously a vigorous propaganda. The Moderates were reluctant. Even Jinnah and Malaviya voted against it. He put forward another proposal, i.e., the Congress should have a small and compact executive so that the work during the year might be carried on more efficiently. He said it would be like a war-cabinet But the Moderates thought that they had already yielded enough, and declined to give their support to the proposal, and Tilak, being not prepared for a showdown, withdrew it.

The Congress, however, passed a resolution, authorising the All India Congress Committee to arrange that a deputation consisting, as far as possible, of representatives from different provinces, should proceed to England immediately after the war to press Indian claims on the attention of the Government and people of England.

At the Congress, Tilak's party was in minority. But among the people, an overwhelming majority was with him.

At Lucknow, no Congress leader was given so great an ovation and such a rapturous reception as Tilak. When he arrived at the Lucknow railway station after 12 noon on December 25, he was surrounded by a large crowd, shouting, "Tilak Maharaj ki Jai!" The reception committee had arranged for a car to take him and his party to the place of their stay in the city. But the people gathered to receive him insisted that he should be taken in a procession. They had brought for him a tastefully decorated carriage. The reception committee men asserted their right, and put him into the waiting car.

This the young men would not allow, and they punctured the tyres of the car with their knives. Some of them had stood before the car obstructing it. Ultimately, they succeeded in their efforts and drew the carriage themselves, with Tilak seated in it, heavily garlanded, and carried him to the Chhedilal Dharamshala over a circuitous route. After the Congress session was over, Tilak was taken round the city which was richly decorated. At many places, his car was stopped to enable people to offer Aarti and Flowers. He addressed several meetings in the city, the biggest being the public meeting which was attended by 20,000 people. Never had so much enthusiasm been shown to a public leader, and never had so many people gathered together for a political meeting where Home Rule was to be dilated upon. A number of organisations entertained him, and everywhere he spoke on the same subject—Home Rule for India; it was his message which inspired the people more than the Congress resolutions.

Home Rule Propaganda

After the close of the Congress session, both Mrs. Besant and Tilak toured the country and explained the implications of the

Congress-League scheme at largely attended public meetings. The Government of Madras in order to put a stop to this propaganda interned Mrs. Besant and two of her associates at Ooty. Public feelings grew acute, and there was great agitation all over India. Many prominent leaders of public opinion joined the Home Rule League, and the situation grew very tense. Montagu in his Diary narrates a story and draws a lesson: "I particularly like Shiva who cut his wife into 52 pieces only to discover that he had 52 wives", and he adds: "This is really what happened to the Government of India when it interned Mrs. Besant".

There was a move to start a passive resistance movement to get Mrs. Besant released, but in the meantime Chamberlain resigned and Montagu succeeded him at the early age of 36. The ban on Mrs. Besant was lifted.

But the Government of India and local Governments were seriously perturbed. "For good, or for evil, Tilak and Mrs. Besant have had a triumph over the Moderates", wrote the Home Member of the Government of India to the Viceroy, "and we can only hope that this triumph will prove to be short-lived, and ultimately disastrous to their leadership. The purity of the intentions of Mrs. Besant and of Tilak has been certified by two Higja Courts, though everybody knows that the former is influenced by the passionate desire of a vain old lady to be a leader of movements, and knows too the venom and hatred of the latter against everything British.

These two may cover their language under the cloak of loyalty to the Crown, and the affected desire that India shall continue within the Empire, but if you read the speeches and articles, it is impossible to discover why a continuance of the British connection is desired at all, or what India has to gain from it, if all the rest of the assertions made are true.

Proposals were made to the Viceroy to order some action against the two Extremist leaders. He replied that he was prepared to consent to summary action being taken against Tilak, Mrs. Besant and such like, if a clear case is made. But as things stand, it seems to me impossible on paper to draw a distinction between the self-government which we advocate as the ultimate goal of British rule in India, and Home Rule as advocated by Tilak and

Mrs. Besant, though we know in fact that the two policies are as poles apart". (February 1, 1917).

But when the Punjab Government came to know that Tilak was meditating a visit to the Punjab, it came out with an order (February 1917) prohibiting his entry into that province. Sir Michael O'Dwyer was then the Governor of the Punjab. He had become known for his anti-Indian attitude, and then, he had to deal with people who had gone some time ago to America and other countries and were now returning full of revolutionary ideas given them by leaders of what was known as the Ghadar Party. While passing the prohibitory order he expressed his view in these words: "As the Ghadar movement, with some phases of which we are still dealing, shows how ignorant or half-educated Punjabis practically interpret the Home Rule propaganda, it is considered that in present conditions of the Punjab the visit of Tilak to this province in support of the propaganda would be fraught with considerable danger to the public tranquillity."

In March, the Bombay Government too made a complaint against Tilak to Delhi. In its letter (March 22), it said:

"The effect of the judgement of the High Court has been most unfortunate. The violence of the speeches and writings in connection with Home Rule and kindred movements has increased in volume. The Government of Bombay have been watching the developments of this movement with growing anxiety. The Governor-in-Council regards Tilak as a man whose political activities are fraught with public danger, and while their last attempt to cure him ended in failure, they feel that the time has now come for some further measure to be taken in that direction. Again, however, they hesitate to act because of the official recognition given to him by the presence of His Honour the Lieutenant Governor of the United Provinces on the same platform at Lucknow last Christmas".

The letter then suggested that "all agitation aiming at Home Rule must be regarded as seditious because it is calculated to stir up disaffection not only against the Government as at present constituted, but against any form of government that was likely to be established within any reasonable time that can be foreseen.

The absence of such a declaration makes it difficult for the Government of Bombay to take effective action against persons, Indian or European, who are fanning the flame, and leads to desultory and inconsistent action in the different provinces",

In March, 1917, the Government of India issued a circular to local Governments outlining the policy to be pursued with regard to the Home Rule agitation. In cases where law had been transgressed, prosecutions were to be launched without any hesitation. Students were prohibited from attending meetings where Home Rule was likely to be discussed. The letter, in brief, said: "It is scarcely necessary to state that neither the reforms recommended by the Government of India, nor any reforms which His Majesty's Government are likely to approve, can bear resemblance to the extravagant demands for the grant of early Home Rule to India, which the agitators present to their deluded audiences. It is evident therefore, that the wilder the hopes that are excited by the Home Rule organisations, the greater will be the disappointment and the more violent the protests when the actual reforms that may be approved by His Majesty's Government come in due course to be promulgated.

And here is what the letter required the local Governments to do. "In these circumstances, it is most important that the several Local Governments should take steps to check these extravagant expectations which have been engendered by the Home Rule agitators. It seems desirable that the Local Governments should, through their experienced officers, point out to all Indians who are likely to listen to reason that any thought of early Home Rule should be put entirely out of mind. They should warn all men of light and leading and all those who have hereditary influence over the people at large to dissociate themselves from the Home Rule campaign as it is at present being conducted".

In its turn the Bombay Government was being pesterepl by district magistrates who asked that a more decisive action be taken against the agitation.

The Bombay Governor, Lord Willingdon, now suggested to the Viceroy that a conference of representatives of various provinces should be held in Bombay on April 7, to consider the desirability of dealing with the Home Rule agitation on common lines throughout India. In his zeal, he sent out invitations to the provinces direct, a step which the Government of India resented, and asked that the invitation should be cancelled. Bombay carried out the order explaining that:

> "the idea of the conference was not inspired by any hostility to the Government of India".

The Bombay Government again pressed the suggestion, but modified it by proposing that the Government of India should invite an informal conference. The Government of India, as a first step, invited the views of the local Governments on how the Home Rule agitation should be dealt with. The replies confirmed its earlier belief, and it informed the Bombay Government that "the disadvantages of such a conference on the whole outweigh the advantages".

Then the Bombay Government came out with a specific suggestion, that it should be a common policy of all provincial governments to prohibit organisers of any meeting from in-deluding in their agenda of business the subject of Home Rule.

Again it was discouraged by the Government of India saying that "such a general prohibition could not legitimately be issued, because by this course, the difficulties of the provincial Governments would only be increased".

But the Viceroy, apprising the Secretary of State for India of the situation, suggested to him that some public declaration in regard to the constitutional and administrative changes proposed after the war, was desirable. The statement should also deal with Government's attitude towards the agitation.

Mrs. Besant, Tilak and others, said the Viceroy, "are fomenting with great vigour the agitation for immediate Home Rule, and in the absence of any definite announcement by Government of India as to their policy in the matter, it is attracting many of those who hitherto have held less advanced views. The agitation is having a mischievous effect on public feeling throughout the country. Consistent and malicious attacks on the system and method of present administration are aggravating the danger".

The Home Rule League itself, without any knowledge of what was passing between the local Governments and the Indian Government, and between the latter and London, also demanded a similar declaration. The first annual conference of Tilak's League was held at Nasik on May 17 and 18, under the presidentship of Joseph Baptista. A private meeting at which about 50 leading members were present was held in the morning of the first day. The principal subject discussed was the attitude of officials towards the League. It was suggested by several persons that, until Government made a definite expression of its policy, opposition from local officials was inevitable, and that particulars of cases of obstruction to the movement should be collected as a preliminary to getting a question asked in the Legislative Council with a view to eliciting an expression of Government policy.

It was at first intended that the Conference, which was held in the afternoon, should also be private, but at the last moment, it was decided to admit non-members on payment of one rupee each. The attendance was about 1,500. The proceedings began with the reading of the reports of the League and its branches. The League had now 14,000 members, its income had been nearly Rs. 16,000, and its expenditure about Rs. 2,800; twenty-five lectures on Home Rule had been delivered during the year, and three pamphlets had been published in English, Marathi and Gujarati.

One of the resolutions passed by the conference was to the effect that the executive committee of the League should make arrangements to carry on propaganda work in England.

At the close of the conference, Tilak delivered a winding-up speech, in which he explained the difference between the functions of the Congress and those of the League. The former, he said, was a deliberative body, which passed resolutions on a multitude of subjects, but did very little in the way of propaganda. The League devoted all its energies to the one question of Home Rule, and was meant to work zealously throughout the year. He concluded by saying that some people had wished the League long life. He did not think that was an auspicious wish and he would be much better pleased if the League attained its objects in a short time, say, two years, and were then dissolved.

After the conference, Tilak's lieutenants went into the countryside on a lecture tour. They gathered together villagers, and told them what Home Rule was and why they should have it without further loss of time. Villagers were asked to sign the roll of the League, and became fearless in the hope that soon British rule would end and Home Rule would be established.

About these visits, the district authorities were very apprehensive. The district magistrate of Satara reported to the Government that he had been informed by some villagers that the visitors had advised them not to subscribe to the war loan because Government was deceiving them and they would lose their money, and had told them that they had much better give the money to Tilak, who was going to England to ask for Home Rule.

But the higher authorities were cautious, having learnt from the past experience that repression only added to the tempo of a political movement. And the movement did receive incentive from certain utterances in England of men like Lord Pentland who ridiculed India's claim for Home Rule. Tilak and his colleagues took the Pentland speech as a challenge, and they advised the Congress committees all over the country to enter protests and arrange to get up a monster petition on the subject of Home Rule addressed to the Secretary of State for India. They also stressed that Government orders prohibiting participation of students in political agitation should be resisted as they were directed against the Home Rule movement. They were in favour of a movement for passive resistance in this connection. Talk of passive resistance was already in the air over the internment of Mrs. Besant, and Tilak naturally suggested that if a passive resistance movement was to come, it could be broad-based.

In this tense atmosphere, a joint meeting of the All India Congress Committee and the Council of the Muslim League was convened in July. The meeting decided to ask the opinion of the provincial Congress committees and the Muslim League units on the question of passive resistance. The meeting demanded an authoritative pronouncement pledging the Imperial Government in unequal terms to the policy of making India a self-governing member of the British Empire; immediate steps to sanction the scheme of reforms conjointly framed by the two bodies;

the publication of official proposals; and reversal of the repressive policy.

Meetings were now held in provinces to consider what attitude to take in respect of passive resistance. Some considered the step inadvisable, but the Madras and Bihar Provincial Congress committees strongly expressed themselves in its favour. The Bihar committee even demanded that a date must be fixed within which to release all Home Rule internees as well as Khilafat prisoners. In the city of Madras, a pledge was drafted for carrying on the constitutional agitation. The first man to sign it was Sir Subrahmaniam Iyer, a retired Judge of the Madras High Court and President of Mrs. Besant's Home Rule League. He renounced his knighthood.

The Government reporters were busy collecting political information, and one of their reports said: "The only people who have a well-conceived plan of passive resistance are the friends and followers of Tilak who are of opinion that Indians should refuse to co-operate with Government in the various spheres of life and public activity, viz. educational, industrial, moral, commercial, political and administrative".

There was a more interesting report. Dr. Moonje, the leader of extremists in the Central Provinces, told the Director of Criminal Intelligence, who had sought an interview with him:

> "Mrs. Besant had done her best for Home Rule but, as a matter of fact, she had been used throughout as a tool by the real Home Rule Statesman, who was Tilak. Mrs. Besant was really a mere agent of Tilak, although she did not know it herself".

While Madras and a few other provinces were preparing for passive resistance, the political situation underwent a sudden change, and the movement did not come off. On August 22, the Secretary of State for India made two pronouncements in Parliament. The one said that "the policy of His Majesty's Government is that of the increasing association of Indians in every branch of the administration and the gradual development of self-governing institutions with a view to the progressive realisation of responsible government in India as an integral part of the British Empire".

The pronouncement added "that progress in this policy can only be achieved by successive stages". The Secretary of State also stated that he would be going to India to discuss these matters with the Government of India and the leaders of public opinion. The other pronouncement said that the British Government had decided to admit nine Indians to commissioned ranks in the army. Montagu's policy had an assuaging effect on Indian politics. Internment orders were withdrawn.

Tilak, however, did not slacken his propaganda. His League was getting ever more popular, and prominent Muslims were also joining it, among them being Jinnah and the family of Maulana Muhammad Ali.

To the chagrin of the Government in India and the Secretary of State in England, Tilak's steam-roller of agitation was going ahead ever more vigorously. Their hope that the August pronouncement would calm down Tilak was belied. The pronouncement was the result of constant agitation which had compelled British statesmen to recognise India's claim to self-government, though at an unforeseeable distant date.

It was, therefore, obvious that withdrawal or relaxation of agitation would be undoing two years hard work. It was he, who had put life into India's dead politics.

A report to the Government described Tilak's activities after the pronouncement thus: "The capture of the Congress organisation by Mrs. Besant and Tilak is complete. The Moderate party in the Congress is extinguished. The Congress is completely identified with Home Rule. The only effect of all this will be that the Congress will alienate the sympathies of many loyal Indians".

In October, another joint meeting of the All India Congress Committee and the Council of the Muslim League was held at Allahabad, and it was decided to send an all India deputation to the Viceroy and the Secretary of State, Montagu (who had since arrived in India) with a representation in support of the Congress-League scheme. On November 26, the deputation, which consisted of among others Tilak, Gandhi, Jinnah, Tej Bahadur Sapru, Motilal

Nehru, waited on Viceroy Chelmsford and Montagu. They had their say.

An immediate answer, however, was not expected. Again on November 27, Tilak had another interview with Montagu.

This time, most of the talking was done by Montagu, who made great efforts to secure Tilak's support to the impending reforms, which fell far short of Tilak's expectations. Montagu failed. Montagu knew, as he noted in his diary, that Tilak "is at the moment probably the most powerful leader in India, and he has it in his power, if he chooses to help materially in the war effort. His procession to Delhi to see me was a veritable triumphant one. He was really the author of the Congress-League school".

There is an interesting episode associated with Tilak's visit to Delhi with the Congress-League deputation. Like the Punjab Government, the Chief Commissioner of Delhi had also prohibited Tilak's entry into Delhi. He cancelled the order on hearing that Tilak was one of the delegation, but the Punjab Government was not prepared to withdraw its order. The map was consulted and it was discovered that by whatever route Tilak approached Delhi, he would have to traverse a portion of the Punjab. The Government of India, therefore, sought the permission of the Punjab Government by telegram, and the permission was given on the condition that, while passing through Punjab territory, Tilak would not take advantage of the permission and address meetings or receive deputations. This decision was communicated to Tilak, and he agreed to the condition.

In November, he resumed his propaganda work which had been disturbed for over a month. Towards the end of the month, the Gujarat Political Conference was held at Godhra under the presidentship of Gandhi. The commencement of the proceedings had to be slightly delayed until the arrival of Tilak. Gandhi spoke a few apologetic words for the delay for which, he said, he was not responsible, and humorously added that they were asking for Home Rule, and it should not matter to them if they got it forty minutes late. He would not spare even Tilak for unpunctuality.

The year's campaign had virtually finished the Moderates, They made up their mind not to attend the year's Congress.

They feared that the overwhelming majority of the followers of Tilak and Besant would outshine them in the subjects committee.

During the year, the message of Swaraj had been delivered at every door. This was the common subject of talk in the country. Tilak had told the Indian people what was meant by Swaraj or Home Rule, and his arguments were repeated from mouth to mouth like textbook lessons. "What is Swaraj? It is replacement of bureaucracy by the people themselves....., Ten years ago to talk of Home Rule was sedition, and people were afraid. But now it is conceded both by the judiciary and the executive. Let there be a Viceroy and let him act according to the advice of the people.

Let our money be spent upon us and with our consent. Let public servants be really servants of the public and not their masters as they at present are. Our opponents say: Ask for your Home Rule as much as, you like, but you must not criticise the bureaucracy; that creates discontent. This is asking us to achieve an impossibility. It is as if you ask a man to eat a fruit without biting it".

Tilak invoked the scriptures to bring home his exhortation: "Swaraj is the natural consequence of diligent performance of duty. The Karma-yogi strives for Swaraj, and the Gnanin or spiritualist yearns for it. God does not help the indolent. You must be up and doing. Action alone must be our guiding principle, action disinterested and well-thought-out. It is your birthright to govern your own house; nobody else can claim to do it".

Inaian Home Rule League Conference

The second Conference of the Indian (Mr. Tilak's) Home Rule League was held at night on Tuesday, in a specially erected 'Shamiana' at the Chaupati end foot of the French Bridge under the presidency of Mr. B.G. Tilak. The proceedings commenced a little after ten o'clock and lasted up to 2.30 a.m. The 'Shamiana' was filled 'to the brim' with an enthusiastic audience consisting of not small number of ladies. Members of different Class Volunteers Corps were drawn of in an attractive manner in different parts of the hall, the most noticeable among them being the tiny 'soldiers' hailing from the Depressed Class Volunteer Corps.

'Distinguished gentlemen' began to pour in from 9:45, the first of the gentry to arrive being Mr. S.R. Bomanji accompanied by Mr. Jatnnadas Dwarkadas. Then came the Hon. Mr. Belvi (Belgaum), the Hon. Mr. Manmohandas Ramji (Bombay), Messrs. N.C. Kelkar (Puna) and R.P. Karandikar (Satara) arriving at five minutes past ten. At 10:15 the air was suddenly rent with cries of Vande Mataram by the thousands of people that had ensconced themselves on the French Bridge roadway and the parapet wall announcing the arrival of Messers. K.P. Khadilkar, followed a few seconds afterwards by Mr. Tilak. Cheers after cheers rang in the 'Shamiana', the enthusiasm of the audience being further kindled by the encouraging words emanating from the lips of some of the more energetic members of the audience. As soon as Mr. Tilak's turban was seen through the crevices of people's necks, the whole assembly rose to its feet and gave him a very cordial welcome. Bowing and bowing and bowing, he ascended the 'dais', and that was the signal for Mr. Paluskar, proprietor of the Gandharva Mahavidyalaya, to strike up the note of 'Bharat hamara desh hai', The singing over, Mr. Tilak asked the Hon. Mr. Manmohandas Ramji, Chairman of the Reception Committee of the Conference, to deliver his opening speech. Mr. Manmohandas rose amid cheers and said as follows:

Chairman's Speech

I have great pleasure in welcoming you all on behalf of the second Indian Home Rule League Conference. The first Conference, as you know, met at Nasik last year and was presided over by Mr. Joseph Baptista, who is now have to undergo a great deal of expense and so wherever he has gone, he has been given something and so we, the millhands of Bombay also intend to give him something that lies in our power. Every one of us has given something willingly. No one has been forced to give anything.

Mr. Tilak who was received with cries of Vande Mataram and Tilak Maharaj ki Jai, said:

> Mr. Chairman and gentlemen, a representation is going to England on behalf of the Home Rule League and I am one of that representation. I will first of all tell you why this representation is going to England,

> what is their duty, what is the relationship between you and that representation, how we all will be benefited by home rule and what this representation is going to do there. Some people who are not our friends but who are our enemies and your enemies also say that we are cheating the marwaries and treadsmen and millhands. They say that the people of India and especially the masses should hear what Government tells them and that they should not hear what the Khatpati Brahmins like us tell them. They say that we should all obey without any complaint the Collector and the Police Commissioner and all other Government officials. They say that we should not even dispute their unjust actions and that we should not criticise their actions. We have no right to say whether their actions are just or unjust. They say that we should allow the Government officials to manage the people just as a shepherd manages his flock of sheep. They say that we are not fit for Home rule and that we are only fit to be ruled by them. Lord Sydenham (cries of shame, shame) the late Governor of Bombay is saying all these things in England at present. His regime is well known to all of you. He used to do anything he liked when he was here. He was at that time called the wise Governor of Bombay and he is now using his wisdom in England and telling the English people that we are not fit for home rule, that the masses of India do not want Home rule and that if Home rule is given to India the masses will be trodden down by Brahmins. Now when that is the case is it not better that there should be some one there in England to refute all his arguments.

Last time when I spoke to you I told you what is Home rule. Our opponents say that the millhands and the masses of India do not want Home rule. And the object of today's meeting is that when we go to England we must be able to tell the English labour class that the millhands of Bombay are on our side, that such a vast gathering of millhands is behind us, that they are helping us and that we are not only the representatives of the educated India but of the masses of India. (Applause). Today's gathering is the vivid proof of the fact that so many people know what is Home rule and that they know why we the representatives of the Home rule league are going to England. I am very glad to find that you also participate with us in this great cause. You have not gathered together here today for me and I have not come here for you. But we all have gathered together here today to help in the cause of Home rule. You must not think that you have come here for me. I have come here for some work sacred to my heart and I am going to England for the work which is as much yours as mine.

The first essential thing that you ought to remember is that Home rule is not the rule of Brahmins as our opponents, the bureaucracy is telling you. When we have Home rule whoever are elected will be the members of the Cabinet. What we want is that we must have the power of electing the officers who are to administer the law. Now some of us say there ought to be community election. I do not agree with them; that is a wrong idea. We have now got the bureaucracy, namely the Collectors and the Commissioners, etc. who are appointed by the Governors, and the Governors and Governor-Generals who are appointed by the King. There is one Act called the Government of India Act and that Act says that the Secretary of State is the minister of the King and that he ought to appoint the other officers of the bureaucracy and that they should administer the laws in this country. At present, the people of India have no right to say that such and a man should be the Collector or the Police Commissioner of Bombay. It is the bureaucracy who makes the laws and it is the bureaucracy who administers them according to their discretion. We have got legislative Councils but they are in name only. Suppose a certain community says "We do not want a liquor shop in our vicinity" they have got no power to dictate to the officers.

If the officers desire that the shop should be there the community are helpless. What kind of administration is this ? Under the present administration even time may come tomorrow when the bureaucracy may tell us that we must eat only a circular or a triangular bread and if such things happen we are nothing better than beasts. That is the way how India is being administered at present. We are not heard at all. We have to abide by the wishes of the bureaucracy. The will of the bureaucracy is the law. And this is the state of affairs not only of Brahmins but of all creeds and classes in India at present. This morning we had a depressed classes mission Conference. It is not only the Antayjar who are depressed but the whole of India is at present depressed. All the classes and creeds in India are being treated by the bureaucracy as depressed (Antyajas). The present state of affairs is troubling not only Brahmins but it is troublesome to all castes and creeds in India. And to remedy this evil we went home rule.

Now if they do not give us home rule we are not going to have a revolt against them. We are not going to break railways or burn mills. Railways and mills are the means of increasing our wealth and we do want them. We only want that the administration of the country should be carried on in such a way that it should be beneficial to us, the people of India, suppose tomorrow the bureaucracy want to tax the mills. It is not in your power or even in the hands of your millionaire to prohibit them from doing that. No doubt there are our legislative councils where there are our representatives. But these legislative councils, as I told you, are a mere farce. I say they are a farce because not withstanding our representatives being there, when the time of voting for a measure which we disapprove comes, we find that the white hands outnumber the black hands. Even if our elected members raise both their hands they cannot outnumber the white hands (Laughter). The Acts under which India is administered at present are passed in the legislative council in this manner and we all have to suffer from the effects of those Acts.

No doubt the bureaucracy is opening its eyes only now a days. Of course, the King does not know all these things. And we do not blame him and we are not against the King and the King is not against us. It is the bureaucracy who is against us and it is the bureaucracy against whom we are complaining. It is the bureaucratic administration from the Secretary of State down to the police that we are complaining against. Formerly, there was the East India Company who was administering India and under the administration of the East India Company we were not being treated properly and so the present bureaucratic administration was created. Now if we show to the Parliament and the Kings that this bureaucracy is not administrating India properly, the King and the Parliament will appoint some other body to administer India. Once we prove that the present bureaucratic administration is bad we can ask the Parliament for whatever kind of administration we want. Take the example of your mills. If your mill-owner finds that his officers do not carry on the management of the mill properly he dismisses them and appoints other officers. In the same manner if the King and the Parliament find out that under the present bureaucratic administration India is not being governed properly they will give us some other administration. When the administration of the East India Company was taken over by the present bureaucratic administration it was declared that this present administration was appointed for the comelioralion of the condition of the Indian people. And we must therefore see whether the present administration has in any way benefited us and is benefiting us.

Now workmen in England know all these things about administration which knowledge you all lack. Mr. Lyod Gorge once asked a workman in England whether he was satisfied with his administration and the workman told him of course he was but that if he had not been satisfied he would have through his representative outvoted him from the Cabinet. Now is here any chance of any one of you and the Governor to speak like this ? Can any one of you say to the Governor that if you did not like his administration you would outvote him and ask for another Governor ? Hardly any one of you know that the bureaucracy that is administering India is being paid by us.

Some years ago there was one Viceroy by name Lord Curzon who was ruling over us and be then said that it was impossible to administer India according to the Queen's Proclamation, Why? Because it did not suit his way of administering India.

Now by having home rule we do not want this bureaucracy to go away from India. We do want collectors and commissioners but we want collectors and commissioners who we will hear us to the way in which they should work and not there who will tell us that it is they who will impose their will upon us. We want our own laws made by our own legislative councils of our own representatives who should be in majority therein. We shall only be in good condition on the day on which we shall have our own legislative councils with a majority of our own elected representatives.

Now as regards representation the question of communities has nothing to do with it. If you want communal representation, tomorrow even our Bhikshuks (Brahmin priests) will ask for having their own representative in the legislative councils. This is the question of administration. You all must remember that communal representation is destructive to ourselves. The question of caste should not come in home rule. Every one who has the good of his country at heart should have the right to vote. Once we are given the right of voting we shall elect the men of our own choice. That should be the spirit. You must not fight for such things as communal representation at such a time. It is nothing but treason to think of such things at such a time.

Now I turn to the question as to why our representation is going to England. As I said before the bureaucracy has opened its eyes. The British Parliament is also now of opinion that the present bureaucratic administration is not administering India properly, and they are thinking of effecting some change in that administration. But there are some self-styled well-wishers of India like Lord Sydenham (cries of shame, shame) who have eaten the slat of India, who are misrepresenting facts in England. From there he is also fostering trouble among the various classes here.

This Lord Sydenham and Co. are telling the British people that the masses of India are quite satisfied with the present administration and that it is only the Brahmins who want home rule. Now this Lord Sydenham and Lord Harris were the cruelest Governors of Bombay as you all well know. While here they tried to tyranise over us as much as they could when they were Governors of Bombay, and now in England in their old age, they are trying their best against us. I will tell you the story of a magistrate. There was once a gentleman who during all his service was a magistrate and was accustomed to pass sentences of imprisonment and fine. After he retired he was unable to pass his time as he had no opportunity to pass sentences of imprisonment and fine. He then tried through some of his friends to get himself appointed an honorary magistrate and when as such he began to pass sentences upon people he felt at case. The same is the case with these two gentlemen, Lord Sydenham and Lord Harris. While in India as Governors, they were accustomed to tyrannise over us and now in their retirement they are unable to pass their time without doing some tyrannical act to India and therefore they are trying to put their spokes in the wheel of Indians getting something better in the form of home rule. And so at such a time it is necessary that our representation should go to England and should counteract their efforts.

Owing to this great war, the English people have opened their eyes. They now sympathise with you. The ti me has now come when they have lost their faith in the bureaucracy. We have been complaining against the administration of the bureaucracy for the last forty years in our journals but upto now the British people did not believe us. Upto now they believed in the bureaucracy. But now owing to this great war, they are feeling the want of manpower. Germany has got 50 lakhs of army while the English people have got only 5 lakhs. So now they want to increase their army. Upto now they did not take us into their confidence. Had they done that their army would have been double of that of Germany. Now although their eyes are opened they are not opened fully. There is still want of confidence in us. Some months ago I gave a lecture in Bombay on recruiting and 8000 people came forward to enlist themselves. But none of them were taken. Some of them were not taken because they were homerulers. Some did not get replies to their applications at all. Some were given some other reasons and in fact none were taken. We are ready to fight for the Empire, Hindus, Musalmans, Parsee, Brahmins and all castes and creeds. But they would not take us, the people of India, into their confidence. They do not want that we should rise higher. They want to keep us pressed.

But now the times are changed. The eyes of the British administrators are opening. They are Boding out that we are not being treated properly. They now feel that they have committed a mistake in not allowing the Indian people that place in the Empire which would have made them think themselves as a part and parcel of the Empire. They are feeling now that had they taken these thirty crores of people into their confidence, they would have been able to defy Germany in point of the numerical strength of their army. They now feel why they are not getting recruits readily of course no one would like to endanger his life for Rs. 11. You millhands get more than Rs. 11 in your mills. Had the Indian people been accustomed to think that they were being treated as part and parcel of the Empire they would certainly have thought it their duty to endanger their life for the Empire. But they say, why should they fight, and for whom they should fight. They say that if we are to remain depressed as we are it is better to die of plague than to die in war. When people will have confidence in the administration and when people will get home rule they will surely feel that they are a part and parcel of the Empire and then they will certainly fight for the Empire and will be ready to die for the Empire. The British Parliament and ministers have now recognised this.

Ten years ago, the state of affairs in England was such that even an author and a minister like Lord Morley had expressed his opinion that India will not get home rule any time. He said to in the face of the late Mr. Gokhale. But now see how times are changed. The thing which Lord Morley even never dreamt of has now found expansion in the speech of Mr. Montagu. Mr. Montagu wants to give us something.

To the days gone by these British Ministers were deaf to our cry but the shots of German guns have opened their ears now. Guns generally make people deaf but the German guns have opened the ears of the British ministers. Now even Lloyd George is for home rule for India. The Country like America who has faught for its liberty is also saying that India must have home rule. We say that not only that we are fit for home rule but that if we are given home rule we are fit to kill the German Imperialism such is the time. The King and his ministers and the British people are thinking of giving us home rule. If Lord Sydenham and his party have thought there was no possibility of our getting home rule now, they would never have commenced their campaign against home rule in England. But now they are sure that India is about to get home rule and so they are working against us. I would ask you to imagine that our suit is before the Court of the British people. We Indians are the plaintiffs, and Lord Sydenham and his party are the defendants. Tradesmen in England are helping Lord Sydenham's party. But the working class which is styled as labour party fall with us. The labour party is not helping Lord Sydenham and his party in their campaign. This is the state of affairs at present in England. The labour party is full of hope that the labour ministry which is likely to come into power hereafter will surely give us home rule.

Home rule will not only do good to the educated people but it will do good to all and when we get home rule your own status, that is the status of the millhands and the working people will also be changed. In England on the election day, even a labourer thinks that he himself is the King that day because he has the right to vote and the different candidates come to him seeking his vote. When we get home rule you will also have such a day when you will think yourself to be the King that day. When you get the power of voting these big people will send their carriages for you to come and vote for them. This is how your status will be changed if we get home rule. When the whole of the working class will get the right of vote it will create inspiration in you. And when you get the right of voting on the election day you will consider yourself to be the King. There is the benefit of born rule. Perhaps instead of working in the mills some of you will get places in the army.

Owing to having been depressed by the bureaucracy, we have lost our Kshatra Tej (warrior's spirit) and we have become of feminate. When we get home rule there will be no depression by the bureaucracy and with the inspiration that home rule will instill in us our Kshatra Tej will return among us.

You must remember that you are the means of the riches of Bombay. It is by means of your labour that your mill-owners become rich. And it is in your hands to settle what rights you should have and what is for your own good. When we are given home rule you must try to elect good men.

So our representation is now going to England to tell the British people the real state of affairs, and it is with the greatest glory that I will describe to them the occasion of today's gathering. We will prove to the British people that what Lord Sydenham is telling them is not true about India. I can tell them many things against him now because I know that now he cannot imprison me although I am sure that had he been the Governor of Bombay now he would surely have imprisoned me. (Laughter). At present Lord Sydenham is like a bird without feathers. He had feathers when he was Governor of Bombay but now those borrowed feathers have been removed and he is now a bird without feathers.

Now I am telling you in plain words that this work for which we are going to England is the work of all of you. If we get home rule each one of you will get the right of voting so each one of you will be King at least on the day of voting. Do you prefer that or do you prefer to remain labourers for the whole of your life? I do not think that there is any one amongst you who would like to remain a labourer the whole of his life. If we are asked in England whether the working classes of India are on our side, we must be able to say yes, I have seen them, thousands and thousands of workmen attended a meeting to wish me god-speed and that they have expressed their consent to our demand of home rule for India. I must be able to reply like that and that is the reason why this monster meeting is called today.

I do not wish to have any money from you. The rich are giving money. This is the question of demanding our birth-right and all castes and creeds in India, Hindus, Musalmans, Parsee all are unanimous in thinking that we must try and do away with the yoke of the bureaucratic administration under which we are bending down.

Justice is on our side, the time has arrived when the British people are willing to hear us. It is only the party of Lord Sydenham (cries of shame, shame) that is trying to spoil our pot of home rule which we have boiled and made ready for us.

Now some people say: Tilak is going to England in his old days. Welt I am sorry it is so. Now that the time has come for work I must go. I must not take back because I am old. God is always willing to help us. There are signs which are showing that the time has come for our good days. Even astrologers of this nation are telling us that time has come when India will see good days. This is not the question of caste or creed. The whole nation will be benefited if it gets home rule.

Try therefore to help those who are trying and exerting for home rule and help in the evolution of the Indian Nation.

With these word I beg your leave. (Deafening cries of Vande Mataram and Tilak Maharaj ki Jai and Tilak Raj ki Jai).

Representatives of about ten mills then presented purses and garlands to Mr. Tilak.

Mr. Cangadharrao Deshpande, the chairman said:

> I need not remind you all what happened to Lokamanya in the regime of Lord Sydenham and how you showed your disapproval of his action that time. Lord Sydenham has still some feathers and with them he is working against us in England and it is to counteract that work that we are sending Lokamanya and others to England.

Now there is every likelihood of Lord Sydenham and his party creating difficulties in the way of the work that Lokamanya is going to do in England and it is to be.

On Sunday the 24th March 1918 in the morning, Mr. Tilak immediately after his arrival in Bombay, was present at the Depressed Classes Mission Conference held in the Mundap near the French Bridge.

In moving the resolution about allowing the representatives of the depressed classes to be present at the meetings of the national congress, industrial conference, social conference, etc. Mr. Tilak said:

> Mr. President and gentlemen, the question of the depressed classes and of the untouchables is very important and from the political and social point of view it must be solved scorer or later and it is quite possible to do so. What are the depressed classes and the untouchables ? Is there any authority in the shastras to call any class of the community depressed or untouchable ? There is none.

The question whether the depressed classes and the untouchables should have the right of communal representation is, in my opinion, a different one. The question of communal representation has nothing to do with the question of the untouchables. The untouchables must mix with all of us. Political and social work is the work of the whole country and the question of untouchables does not come in there. We do want the untouchables to join us in our national work.

During the times of the Peshwas, Brahmin sepoys in the army used to drink water from the Pakhals brought by untouchables. You find instances in the Peshwa's Daftar that the Peshwas themselves used to drink water from the Pakhals. The very fact that socially we are treating the depressed classes as untouchables and are keeping them apart from us shows that we are losing our nationality.

Only consider what is happening at present. In India in the eyes of a white man, a black man is untouchable. But what is happening on the front at present? There as well as in Mesopotamia while fighting the whites and the blacks have to fight shoulder to shoulder and they forget there the difference between the while and the black. It is stated in the Shastras that before the King, in great Darbars and at the time of fighting the question.

Let me tell you how I myself treat these untouchables. I do not observe this difference between touchables and untouchables at my place. (Loud applause). Some Mahars of the Chokhamela creed had come to me for some business once. I did not make them stand outside my house but I allowed them to come and sit with me in my sitting room. So what I want to tell you is this that although have not taken this work in my band I fully sympathise with it. If the main work which I have taken in hand is done I will consider that I have fulfilled my mission of life. When that main work is done the question of touchables and untouchables will be solved by itself. As we sympathise with the question of the untouchables, they must also sympathise with the work that we have taken in hand. Let me tell you plainly that I am not at all against the untouchables. I am strongly of opinion that the word untouchable must disappear from amongst us. It is only a custom or traditional usage which must disappear.

Just as the bureaucracy has at present created the untouchableness of a sort, the Brahmins had done the same many years ago. This question of untouchableness is a kind of disease which is eating a way the society. And is the bounden duty of every one of us to do away with this disease. And I am full of hope that this disease will soon disappear.

A public meeting of the Marwari merchants of Bombay was held in the hall of the Marwari Vidyalaya on Sunday the 24th March 1918 at 3 pm in honour of Mr. Tilak. The hall was tastefully decorated. Most of the leading members of the Marwari community and some Brahmins were present. The hall was overcrowded and a large number of people were standing in the compound.

Mr. Tilak, Khaparde and Belvi arrived at three o'clock when all got up. Mr. Govindlal Shivlal Motilal who presided on the occasion explained the object of that day's gathering. He said Tilak and other members of the deputation were going to England to place before the British Democracy their case for home rule for India and that it was their duty to honour them and to help them.

Another Marwari gentleman declared that they intended that day to present Rs. 15000 to Mr. Tilak. They had already collected Rs. 12000 and he hoped they would be able to collect Rs. 3000 more the e on the spot.

There was some commotion among the audience for some time and after about twenty five minutes the Chairman declared that he was glad to announce that they were able to complete the sum of Rs. 15000. A purse of Rs. 15000 was then presented to Mr. Tilak by the Chairman on behalf of the Marwari community of Bombay for being used in the cause of home rule.

Mr. Tilak then rose to speak and he spoke in Hindustani for about ten minutes. He said:

> Mr. President and gentlemen, it is really a matter of great delight to find so many merchants coming together to help us in the cause of home rule. Why have all of you gathered together in this hall on this occasion ? Why have I come here today 7 Our chairman said just now that you have been called here today to do me honour. I disagree with him. You have come here today not do me or the deputation honour. You have come here to show your appreciation of the

> work that some of us are doing in connection with the cause of home rule. I have not come here to do you any honour. I have also come here to show my appreciation for the very keen interest you all, business men, take in the cause of home rule.

What does this home rule mean? It does not mean, as our opponents have been telling you, the rule of Brahmins. The question of caste or creed or profession does not come in home rule.

Suppose tomorrow Government want to impose a certain tax on a certain kind of commodity in which some of you are trading. It is not in your power to prevent Government from imposing that tax. No doubt we have got our legislative councils in which all such measures are discussed. But at present our representatives there are in minority and the resolutions of the legislative councils are not binding upon Government. By the congress-league scheme, we have asked for a substantial instalment of home rule, and if we are granted that substantial instalment of home rule, it is not the Brahmins and educated people only who will be benefited but even you businessmen will also derive a benefit.

Our opponents, Lord Sydenham and his party, have collected Rs. 30,00000 from British merchants to fight against us in the cause of home rule. It is therefore in the fitness of things that you Indian merchants should also show your willingness to help us in the cause of home rule.

When in England if I am asked whether the merchants of India are with us and whether they want home rule with us, I will proudly say that the merchant class of India is also behind us and that at such and such a gathering I have been presented with this valuable course for being used in the cause of home rule. (Loud applause).

Mr. Khaparde, Sheth Madhavprasad, Mr. Fatechand Rule and two other Marwari gentlemen then addressed the meeting in Hindustani. In their speeches, they eulogised Mr. Tilak's services to the country and expressed a sincere hope that the deputation would return to India with success in the cause of home rule.

The meeting was then dissolved amidst cries of Vande Mataram.

On behalf of the Lokamanya, Swagat Mandal citizens of Bombay gave an At Home in honour of Mr. Tilak at the China Bagh on Monday the 25th March 1918 at 5:30. Many of Mr. Tilak's upcountry friends who had come to Bombay specially for the occasion were present. Messrs, Tilak, Khaparde and others were photographed.

After light refreshments Mr. S.R. Bomonji thanked, he distinguished guests for gracing the occasion and requested Mr. Jinnah to speak.

Mr. Jinnah enumerated the singular services Mr. Tilak had rendered to the country and said that since their opponents were misrepresenting facts to the British public it was but meet that some of them ought to go there to counteract that misrepresentation.

Mr. Tilak thanked all present and said:

> We are going to England to clear the way for the congress representation that is following us. We are going now because we are convinced that this is the proper time to place our grievances before the British Parliament and the British public. You all are fully aware of what our opponents are doing there. Just imagine what will happen when Mr. Montagu goes to England and places his views before the Parliament. If we are not there to represent our grievances, do not you think that the vedict of the Parliament will be one sided ? No doubt my first object in going there is in connection with my own appeal.

Mr. Bomanji: That is also our work.

Mr. Tilak (continuing): After my work in connection with the appeal is over, I shall be devoting my attention towards ventilating our grievances before the British public. I am going to tell them in plain language that if India is not given home rule the Empire will be in very great danger (Hear, hear). Our demand is cut and dried in the draft of the congress-league scheme. You all must remember that we are not going there to beg something of them but that we are going there to demand what is our birth right. God is on our side. By His grace time will soon come when all of us will assemble here to thank England for having given us home rule.

Mr. Bipin Chandra Pal was then requested to speak. He said:

> Why are we going to England ? Is it because our countrymen want us to go ? No, we are going to England because the Empire's call has dinned into our ears. (Cheers). The Empire at present is in great danger. And we are going to England to show to the British public how they can escape from that danger. (Applause). The manpower of England is now growing feeble and now they cannot do without taking the help of the manpower of India. Such is the state of affairs now. Unless the people of India are satisfied, unless their expectations in the matter of home rule are fulfilled, they will never be ready to fight for the Empire. We are going to say so in plain language to the British public. (Applause).

Messrs. Khaparde and Kelkar then thanked the organisers of the At Home.

The audience then urged on Mr. Horniman to speak and he said:

> Gentlemen, as a loyal Englishman I am of opinion that the grant of home rule is absolutely necessary for the safety and protection of the British Empire. I am one of those who maintain that home rule must be granted to India not only for the safety of the Empire but for the principles of human liberty and justice. As a loyal Englishman and one devoted to the British Empire I would like to see the British Empire to go to rack and ruin rather than to be working against its great principles in any part of the Empire. (Applause).

Mr. Jamnadas Dwarkadas then said:

> I am glad to offer our best wishes to Mr. Tilak and his colleagues on behalf of the younger generation. Mr. Tilak has for the whole of his life been fighting.

A mass meeting attended by about 5000 people was held on Tuesday the 26th March 1918 at 6.30 pm to give a hearty send off to Mr. Tilak and other members of the Home Rule deputation in the compound of Shantaram's Chawl, Kandewadi.

Members of the deputation, Messrs. Tilak, Khaparde, Bipin Chandra Pal, Karandikar and N.C. Kelkar and other born rulers like Messrs. P.K. Telang, Horniman, Jamnadas, Ratansi Dharamsi, Dr. Munje, Hon. Mr. Upasani and others were among those sitting on the platform.

Dr. M.B. Welkar said:

> Gentlemen, we have met here this evening to bid bon voyage and safe and speedy return to Lokamanya Tilak and the other members of the Home Rule Deputation that is going to England shortly, and you will all agree with me, I am sure, when I propose that the President of our Home Rule League, the Hon'ble Mr. Jinnah should preside on this occasion.

Mr. Tuljapurkar in seconding the motion said:

> Gentlemen, I will not take much of your time in seconding the motion. Mr. Jinnah is the President of our Home Rule league and he is the real Jina (ladder) of Swarajya. Had it cot been for such a ladder it would not have been possible for the home rule league to attain that amount of success that it had attained in such a very short time and it is therefore but meet and proper that he should preside on this memorable occasion.

Mr. Jinnah then rose to speak amidst loud cheers and said:

> Gentlemen, I feel sure that I am voicing the feelings of all assembled here this evening when I say that we all wish the members of our deputation most heartily bon voyage safe and speedy return and every success in their mission. I feel sure also that you will all agree with me when I say that no man is more fitted to voice the views of India to the English democracy than Mr. Tilak who has devoted the whole of his life for the

> national cause and whose words would surely carry a great weight in England. Before Mr. Montague arrived in India we were asked to maintain a calm atmosphere and we are maintaining a calm atmosphere because Mr. Montague is at present here and he is investigating the case for home rule for India. And we desire that there should be no bungling. We say so in plain words that let it be clearly understood that the demand for the immediate step towards the transfer into our hands of the control of the Government of this country and for the marking of a clear road to establish self-government is the united demand of the whole of India and not a demand of a particular class or creed. Home rule is the birth of every man and in demanding home rule we are simply claiming our birth right and it is laying down of the principle of self-determination for India. And we feel sure that Mr. Tilak is the man who will be able to place our case in the best possible manner not only before the English Democracy but before the English Nation.

Mr. Tilak on rising to speak was received with deafening cries of Vande Mataram and Tilak Maharaj ki Jai and Tilak Raja ki Jai. He said:

> Mr. Jinnah and gentlemen, I thank you all very sincerely for the honour you have done me and my party and for the good wishes for our success. The principle of self-determination lays down that every nation, every country, has the right to choose the sort of Government they should have and it should precede self-government. We are determined to have self-government in the near future at an early date and to have a substantial instalment to begin with. While the question of self-determination for the European Nations and the African colonies was discussed India was excluded. President Wilson said that Ireland should have self-determination and our Prime Minister convened the Irish Convention to draft a

scheme of their own, but India without any such declaration, formulated a scheme of its own. Mr. Montague came to India and he studied on the spot in consultation with the members of the bureaucracy who were primarily opposed to any sort of self-government in this country. He was to formulate a scheme and act as an umpire and arrive at a settlement, a compromise between the two parties the people and the bureaucracy. We want responsible government which has been agreed to by the bureaucracy except in connection with the steps and the time for establishing the same. The chances or Mr. Montague's scheme, I think, though I am an optimist, are not so bright as many of our people imagine them to be. Our opponents are trying to impress upon the British people that if self-government were granted to India the Empire would go to ruins and that in the interest of the Empire India must be continued to be Government in a despotic manner. A very keen campaign has been undertaken by determined people to defeat our object. We have now to fight two parties, the Cabinet who would have to be convinced and the Sydenhamites (cries of shame, shame) who would have to be—suppressed.

Mr. Tilak (continuing): And the Sydenhamites who would have to be "suppressed" as our President suggests. The way is not so smooth as some of us believe. The question to be determined is whether if Mr. Montague's scheme fell short, our leaders would accept the temptation held out and would be prepared to receive something shadowy but apparently substantial. Some of our leaders might advise it. Surely our Anglo-Indian friends and newspapers might do that. We are going to plead before the British Democracy the cause of self-government for India taking our stand upon the Congress League Scheme. I therefore earnestly urge upon you to stand by us not only now but two months hence like men, like resolute men, and insist upon having nothing less than the Congress-League Scheme. There ought to be no compromise in this matter (Applause). Remember, if you accept any compromise, we shall be left in the lurch in all humiliation and we shall be laughed at by the whole world. (Cries of no, no). The bureaucracy whose interest is sure to suffer if we get home rule, might try to create a split amongst us. The bureaucracy might say that they have done enough by giving us something and that we ought to be satisfied with that something. But I warn you, you will ruin your country if you accept any such compromise.

You must remember that America did not enter the war simply because of German Kaiserdom being substituted by bureaucratic kaiserdom. America did not go to help England simply because England was her mother country or simply to protect England, but America joined the war to put an end to despotism in any and every part of the world. I earnestly appeal to you to be careful, attentive and to act as men, resolute men and to stand by the resolution of the Congress and the Muslim League.

The Hon'ble Mr. Khaparde then addressed the audience. He said:

> Gentlemen, we must remain firm in our demand and must guard against temptation. The bureaucracy will surely try their utmost to put temptations in our way because it is the interest of the bureaucracy which will suffer if we get all that we ask for. The bureaucracy will therefore try to put temptations in our way under any guise and we must be careful not to fall a prey to any compromising attitude, because you must remember that if you fall a prey to any compromise you are sure to lose everything.

Mr. Bipin Chandra Pal said:

> Gentlemen, there is no doubt that we owe a great deal to Mr. Montague for his visit although I am not sure as to what would be the practical result of Mr. Montague's visit. But, gentlemen, I know this much that the sun of Mr. Montague who had risen on the political horizon of India freed us from the mosquitoes and fleas of the C.I.D. (cries of shame, shame) who were following us everywhere. Last year when I came here I was not allowed to deliver any speech. I was even threatened with internment under the Defence

of India Act (cries of shame, shame). Do not cry shame, shame, my friends. Police is all powerful at present and we want to deprive them of this power and we want to put that power into the bands of the people and that is why we are crying for home rule. The whole question before us at present is how to transfer that power from the bureaucracy to ourselves. If you had asked to go to England as one of the deputation years ago I would never have agreed to go. I did not like to go to England to beg alms of the English people. But I see that now the times are changed. We now are going to England not as mendicants to beg for the gift of home rule but we are going to tell the British Democracy that if Home Rule is not granted to India it would be done so at the risk not of the future of India but of the Empire and of the whole civilized world. (Applause). No doubt the hands of India are weak at present but the future of England and of the Empire is at present in the hands of India.

At present there is one nation in the world, in Asia, whose army and navy is invincible. That nation is not affected by the present war but it has enriched itself by furnishing ammunitions to the warring nations. And that nation is Japan. No doubt at present Japan is one of the allies. But sometimes we feel doubtful when we think of her movements in Siberia. If Japan turns into a belligerent nation who will save India from her. It is not possible unless they raise a national army in India. England at present is lacking in manpower. If England wants to use the manpower of India she must at first remove the dissatisfaction among the people and must satisfy the political ambition of the Indian people. If England takes the Indian people into its confidence the national army of the thirty crores of Indians will be on her side. We are claiming home rule from the British Democracy by placing all these things before them.

I thank you all for your good wishes and I hope and trust that day and night you all would be ready to strive and work and suffer for the realisation of our aspirations. I implore you all to work without flinching, without violence and without fear. I appeal to you to hold on to the cause and the banner of home rule and thus proceed to victory.

Mr. R.P. Karandikar then addressed the meeting in Marathi. He said:

> Gentlemen, in the Bible there is a sentence "knock and it will open", and that is the characteristic of the English people. Unless we knock at the door of the British people for Swarajya, they will open the door of home rule for us. We are going to knock at their door and we are sure that with our knocking at their door in England and with your continuing the agitation in India we are sure to reach our goal. (Applause).

Mr. N.C. Kelkar then addressed the meeting in Marathi. He said:

> Gentlemen, I will say what I have to say in three minutes. Wherever we go we are asked. "Why do you go to England ?" Well, I answer we go to England for asking for Swarajya. Well, they say, "Why do you go to England for asking Swarajya ?" Well, I tell them if we are not to go to England for asking for Swarajya, are we to go to Japan ? If our present rulers do not give us Swarajya, perhaps time may come when we may have to go to Japan to ask for Swarajya. But at present we must ask for Swarajya from England and that is the reason why we are going to England. Well, then some people ask, "Why do you go to England?" I say if some one else wants to go we do not want to go. Because others do not want to go we are going. Then others ask "Are you going to England ?" I tell them we are not going there for good but we are going there and coming back.

Mr. Tilak and other members of the deputation were then garlanded amidst cheers.

Mr. S.R. Bomonji in proposing a hearty vote of thanks to the chairman said:

> Gentlemen, I need not say anything more about our Chairman. He accepted the Presidentship of the Home Rule League at a time when some people used to laugh at our movement. And under his presidentship the Home Rule League has attained the status which is well known to you all.

Mr. Jamnadas Dwarkadas seconded the proposal which was carried unanimously.

Mr. Jinnah in replying to the vote of thanks said:

> Mr. Tilak and gentlemen, I assure you all that I feel it a very great honour to be asked to preside over a meeting like this and express our feelings to Mr. Tilak and other members of the deputation. Let me assure you, Mr. Tilak, that the Congress would stand by the principles it advocated for the last 32 years and as clearly embodied in the Congress League Scheme and that the leaders of the Indian National Congress were not likely to be taken into the trap laid by the bureaucracy and that they would not serve from their resolution by one inch or iota.

The meeting was then dissolved amidst the deafening cries of Vande Mataram and Tilak Maharaj ki Jai.

Another Milestone

The yardstick of measuring a year's progress of the Home Rule campaign is the election of Mrs. Besant as president of the 1917 Congress. She was Tilak's nominee, and her success was interpreted as defeat of the Moderates. They had not yet decided to withdraw from the Congress, but their position was no better than that of the Extremists before 1906, with the difference that while the latter were vigorously pushing forward their aims, they themselves were like the setting sun. In 1916, Mrs. Besant had been defeated by 62 to 25 votes of the provincial Congress committees. In 1917, her popularity mainly due to the Home Rule campaign routed the Moderates.

In her presidential address, Mrs. Besant emphasised the point, which Tilak had raised at the Lucknow Congress and which they

Moderates were not willing to concede, that a Bill should be brought before Parliament during 1918, "establishing self-government in India on lines resembling those of the Commonwealth on a date to be laid down therein, preferably 1923, the latest 1928, the intermediate five or ten years being occupied with transference of the Government from British to Indian hands, maintaining the British tie as in the dominions".

The main resolution of the Congress also urged the necessity for the immediate enactment of a Parliamentary Statute providing for the establishment of responsible government in India, the full measure to be attained within a time-limit to be fixed in the statute itself at an early date. The resolution demanded immediate introduction of the Congress-League scheme of reforms by statute "as the first step in the progress". Before the Congress met in December, Gandhi had taken practical steps to popularise the Congress-League scheme among the masses. At his instance, the scheme was translated into Indian languages and explained to the people; up to the end of 1917, over a million people had signified their approval of it by appending their signatures to it.

Again, as in 1916, Tilak spoke on the self-government resolution; that was his only interest. He said that the pronouncement of the Secretary of State for India mentioned the words 'responsible government' and not Home Rule or Self-government. "It is necessary to define responsible government, otherwise the words may be interpreted quite contrary to our intention, and it may said, 'We promised responsible government in which the Legislature ought to be under the control of the executive and the more it is placed under the control of the executive, the more responsible will be the government you get (Laughter). I must tell you frankly that this is not the kind of responsible government we want. We understand by responsible government a government where the executive is entirely responsible to the legislature, and the legislature is wholly elected. When I say that the executive should be under the control of the legislature, I go so far as to say that even the Governors and the Lieutenant-Governors should be elected. That, however, will be the final step. But in the present circumstances, I shall be quite content, and so I think will most of you, if the first step that we demand is granted to us immediately. And by full self-government at an early date, I do not think any sane man will understand more than 10 or 15 years at most".

The other resolution in which Tilak took interest and which he himself agreed to move was the one which urged Government to release Muhammad Ali and Shaukat Ali, who had been in internment since 1914. Calling upon Tilak, to move the resolution, the President said: "We have chosen him because he has suffered seven years imprisonment for his country". The compliment was greeted with loud cheers. On the dais sat, next to the President, the mother of the two internees, listening to the speeches made on the resolution.

Tilak congratulated the mother that she had given birth to two brave sons, and wished that India had many mothers like her. He deplored the policy under which Government imprisoned people without trial.

The 1917 Congress was a damper to Government; the dwindling strength of the Moderates was a cause of great anxiety.

Now when the Congress, the Muslim League, the Home Rule League and other political organisations were all united over the self-government demand, there appeared some disturbing elements. On the one hand, the Hindu Mahasabha, alarmed at the Lucknow Pact, came out with a resolution repudiating the claim of the Congress to speak on behalf of the Hindus; on the other some non-political Muslims took up cudgels against the Muslim League, and saw the Secretary of State on behalf of several organisations which had perhaps came into existence just a short while before.

There were some Ulemas also among them, and the Viceroy Chelmsford, who was present at the interview, asked them a question: "Can you tell your views shortly to the Secretary of State and myself?" Quick came the answer, "We do not want Home Rule". Montagu's Diary records further conversation thus: "Then a delightful old man, with a beautiful beard and a fine profile, told us that he had studied the Quran and all the commentaries, the Bible and the Holy Books, and he could find no sanction for the Congress-Muslim League scheme in them".

Ever since these questionable activities of some people on both sides came to the notice of Tilak, he had been trying to circumvent them. He knew that the disruptionists would invoke religion for their nefarious ends and, therefore, he established contacts with religious-minded people. In January, 1918, he called a private conference of some Hindu nationalists and Muslim Pan-Islamists. Dr. Ansari was also present. Tilak spoke on the desirability of widespread agitation being carried on among the masses, and pointed out that the agitation would not succeed unless it was mixed up with religion. The outcome of the conference were two new movements: One was the revival of the Kirtan among Hindus; the other was the Anjuman-i-Khuddam-i-Kaba. At the gatherings of these two, political songs were to be sung with the religious. It was stressed at the meeting that what appealed to the masses most was a movement ostensibly religious and spiritual.

This was Tilak's unique achievement. Religion which was sought to be used by each community against the other was made by him a cementing force to be utilised for political progress. He used to say that if both Hindus and Muslims lived a true religious life, according to the dictates of their religion, there would be no quarrels between the two, and both would live happily with each other.

But what worried Tilak more than the tiny opposition in India was a carefully organised effort in England of some retired Anglo-Indian bureaucrats against Indian Home Rule.

In 1917, after the August 20 declaration, they formed the Indo-British Association, and started their campaign, which they said should be as vigorous as Tilak's in India. Little was being done on behalf of India by the Congress machinery in England. The paper, *India*, published by the British Committee on behalf of the Congress, was conducted by Moderates of the extreme right. It did not even publish the Congress resolutions. Some positive action was called for to counter the propaganda of the Indo-British Association, and although the question of carrying the Home Rule campaign to England had been in Tilak's mind for many months, he took a decision only after his return from the Congress.

Attitude to War

England entered the Great War of 1914-18 as a champion of democracy, with the vast resources of men, money and material of her dependencies. Her position was apparently anomalous; she was fighting for the cause of democracy, but showing no inclination to give democratic rights to the people of India and other dependencies. Opinion in India was divided as to whether support to the war effort should be willingly given. On the one side were those who had faith in England's good intentions and readily assured their help and co-operation; they belonged to the constitutional school of politics, on the other side were those who were not only opposed to any kind of co-operation in the war effort, but collaborated with the enemies of the Allies, sincerely believing that that method would liquidate the British Empire and liberate India; they belonged to the revolutionary school, and their activities were not confined to India. Among the former were men who asked whether the principles for which Britain was fighting were going to be applied to India. They did not mean that a democratic setup should be brought into existence in the midst of the war or that a full-fledged democracy should be established at one stroke.

They wanted a definite promise, and argued that such a promise would enthuse the leaders and common run of men to contribute to the war effort with greater vigour. Tilak was the leader of this school, and soon after the outbreak of the war came out with a statement saying that "at such a crisis it is the duty of every Indian, be he great or small, rich or poor, to support and assist His Majesty's Government to the best of his ability". This statement was made by one who had for many years fought and suffered for the freedom of his own country. He expected a reciprocal gesture from the authorities believing that for the first time a big Empire like the British was mobilising the forces of a great part of the world in the cause of democracy.

Congress leaders and others of the constitutional school were for unconditional support. They were holding meetings everywhere to encourage the people to enter military service.

The most enthusiastic among them was Gandhi who worked as a "recruiting sergeant". He raised the question to a high moral plane: unconditional support, given at a time of crisis, would yield better results. When the British authorities made no announcement of their policy with regard to India, Tilak broke his silence, and demanded an assurance of self-government as a condition precedent to India's willing support to the war effort. His campaign for conditional support developed side by side with that for Home Rule. The beginning was made with a sarcastic article in the Mahratta (February 27, 1916) which was a comment on a speech of the Lt. Governor of TJ.P., Sir James Meston, in which he had exhorted the Jats to join the army.

His writings and speeches were marked, throughout the war, by more bitter sarcasm, and questioned Britain's right to expect help from India. In the Kesari, dated February 20, 1917, he wrote:

"Without waiting for the introduction of the Defence of India Force Bill, our leaders have gone on holding public meetings everywhere to encourage the people to enter military service. The Viceroy need entertain no misgivings that his call will not be responded to by the Indian public. It is only the Indians who have a misgiving as to whether Government would inaugurate a generous and judicious policy or whether, even at the present critical time, they would still continue to be possessed by the spirit of partiality and would observe invidious distinction between their black and white subjects. Whatever the attitude of Government, our line of action has been definitely settled and our leaders have advised the people to enter military service unconditionally.

It is now to be seen whether Government would grant the prayers made by responsible Indian leaders at various meetings. They have not called upon Government to do any act of extraordinary liberality, but only bare justice which demands equality of treatment to both the black and the white in all matters. If the Government refuses to grant the demand and discontent results and the call for military service does not receive a response from Indians, the blame will not be theirs.

"What is the significance of this throwing open of military service to Indians by Government? We shall indulge in a little plain speaking in interpreting the significance of this step. It simply means that today Government cannot do without our aid. To properly understand the significance of the measure, we must first of all shake off our intellectual dullness brought on by our over-loyalty and free ourselves from the delusion resulting from our excessive love for the Empire. If Government was really actuated by disinterested motives, why did they withhold the boon of military service from us for the last hundred years, and why did they disarm us? What have we done that has rendered us worthy of their trust now? If the possession of arms was the cause of the Mutiny of 1857, what guarantee has been taken from the nation that armed and trained men under the new measure will not raise a standard of revolt in the future? In 1857, there was no demand for Swarajya as at present. Thus, it may perhaps be argued by some that there is a strong motive for rising in rebellion now while there was none formerly.."..

For over two years, Tilak did not put any obstacle in the way of the recruitment. His preoccupation being the campaign for Home Rule, he only casually mentioned the war effort. In the beginning, he even asked students to suspend studies for a year or two and contribute their mite to the war effort. "If age and grey hair", he once said, "are no disqualifications, I am prepared to stand in the fighting line".

While asking the people to help the Government, he sometimes threw in a note of sarcasm here and there in his speeches, but did not attach any conditions. But the behaviour of the Government changed his opinion. The police apparently had instructions to hinder the Home Rule movement, and began to harass and victimise villagers who enrolled themselves as members of the Home Rule League. Obstructions were put in the way of the League workers holding public meetings. The speakers took care to see that by no stretch of interpretation should their utterances be regarded as seditious; and yet the authorities were alarmed, because they did not like the people to be told that since Britain was fighting for the cause of democracy, it was India's right to demand Home Rule. The unanimous resolutions of all shades of political organisations in India, asking the British Government to promise self-government within a specified period, failed to persuade the British rulers to make an unambiguous declaration.

Tilak, therefore, now refused to fall in line with some of the other prominent leaders—the most conspicuous among them being Gandhi—and said that unless he was assured of Home Rule, he would not help in recruitment. He said that Government was not responsive to Indian demands and sentiments. It did not heed the agitation that had been going on against indentured labour for South Africa. Tilak was bitter. At a meeting held at Puna early in February, he said that if Government was not prepared to put an end to the system of indentured labour, the people could easily force it to do so. He advised young men to work together for this object. He asked them to be prepared to give up their studies and make up their minds to suffer hardships and even to go to jail. If the Government was not prepared to stop recruitment of indentured labour, the people should do it themselves. His faith in the Government's good intentions was shaken. He made speeches to young people that he could not honestly ask those who listened to his advice to join the army. The overall effect of the speeches was that Indians would be only wasting their blood if they fought for the victory of the Allied arms. There was no difference between fighting for the Allies and sitting at home.

He was *persona non-grata* with the Government, and was not invited to the War Conference, held in Delhi on April 27, 1918. Gandhi, who had been invited by the Viceroy, Lord Chelmsford, responded to the invitation, but had objections to taking part in it, the principal one being the exclusion from it of leaders like Tilak, Mrs. Besant and the Ali brothers. The Viceroy called Gandhi for a discussion and told him that if he agreed that the Empire had been on the whole a power for good, he should help the British during the critical year. The Viceroy pleaded: "You may raise whatever moral issues you like and challenge us as much as you please after the conclusion of the war, not today".

Gandhi agreed, and participated in the Conference.

The Secretary of State for India, Montagu, did not like the Viceroy's action in ignoring Tilak, according to the entry in his Diary for April 27: "With regard to Tilak, if I were the Viceroy, I would have had him at Delhi at all costs. He is at the moment probably the most powerful man in India, and he has it in his power, if he chooses to help materially in the war effort. If he is not there, it will always be said that we refused to select the most powerful people".

On the eve of the Delhi Conference, a public meeting was held at Delhi, under the combined auspices of the Home Rule League, the Provincial Congress Committee, the Indian Association, and the Muslim League, under the presidentship of Dr. Abdur-Rahman. The only item on the agenda was—'The Imperial War Conference and our duty.' The meeting adopted two resolutions: that the Imperial Government should recognise India's right to full responsible Government and, as a first step, grant the Congress-League scheme of reforms; and that no assembly can be considered representative of the views of the people and can command their confidence which does not include Tilak, Muhammad Ali, Shaukat Ali, Mrs. Besant and Rabindranath Tagore. While the Conference was in session, Tilak, Mrs. Besant and Sir Subrahmaniam Iyer sent a telegram to the Viceroy saying that "any attempt to stop political discussion will be fraught with serious danger to public tranquillity and will be an unheard of inroad on fundamental rights of the people to be resisted by all constitutional means".

After the Bombay delegates return from Delhi, a public meeting was held in that city on May 3, 1918, in honour of Khaparde and Moonje, who were among the invites of the Conference and who raised their voice for Home Rule.

Tilak was in the chair, and in a speech he delivered in Marathi, he said that the Delhi Conference was no doubt a beautiful spectacle, but it had achieved very little. There were thirty representatives of the people at the Conference.

If they had supported the self-government resolution, the Viceroy would have been compelled to take up the question but only fourteen of them signed the requisition asking that the question should be considered, and when the time came to submit the requisition Khaparde was left to do it single-handed. The truth was that these men were not the real representatives of the people. They were merely nominees of Government. The bureaucracy wanted them to sacrifice their lives without making any sacrifice themselves. The Empire's need was India's opportunity, Tilak added. It was their duty to exploit that opportunity as Canada and Australia were exploiting it.

But Tilak was invited to the Bombay Presidency War Conference held on June 10, under the chairmanship of the Governor, Lord Willingdon. The Governor inflicted on the audience a severe sermon on Home Rulers whose *bona fides* he called into question. He said: "Indeed I must frankly say that their (Home Rule Leaguers') object seems to have been at every available opportunity to increase the difficulties and embarrassment of Government whenever and wherever they could. From reading their speeches, the position of those gentlemen seems to be this — 'We quite realise the gravity of the situation; we are all anxious to help, but unless Home Rule is promised within a given number of years, and unless various other assurances are given us with regard to other matters, we do not think we can stir the imagination of the people, and we cannot hope for a successful issue to the recruiting campaign".

Tilak was then called upon to speak. He expressed on behalf of himself and all Home Rulers deep loyalty to the King Emperor. The resolution, however, was defective in one respect, he said, and regretted that the rules of procedure did not allow him to move an amendment to the resolution. The chairman (Willingdon) said that if Tilak wished to move an amendment, he could not allow it, as he had stated at the very outset. Tilak dropped his intention of moving an amendment, and proceeded to say that cooperation with the Government necessitated certain things. There could be no Home Defence without Home Rule. The chairman here called Tilak to order and said he could not allow any political discussion. When Tilak was twice interrupted and called to order, he left the platform and the meeting also. He was followed by his Home Rule League friends. A hurriedly called meeting of the executive committee of the Home Rule League was held, and it was decided that the Home Rule Leaguers would not attend the subsequent meetings of the War Conference. Bhulabhai Desai, one of the invited Leaguers, differed and resigned his membership of the League in order to release himself from the obligation.

Next week, a public meeting was held, under the presidentship of Gandhi, to protest against the Governor's behaviour at the Conference. Gandhi condemned Lord Willingdon's gratuitous insult to the Home Rulers. But he impressed upon the people the necessity of helping Britain in her crisis. On June 22, Tilak made a public speech which was considered objectionable by the Bombay Government. Under his presidentship, a meeting was held in the Kirloskar Theatre at Puna, at which a lecture on 'Conscription' was delivered by K. P. Khadilkar. In his lecture, Khadilkar made some observations on Shivaji's army. Tilak dilated on the subject and compared Aurangzeb's method of recruitment with that of Shivaji.

Then he said: "The British just want you to supply soldiers whom they want for the war. Do not entertain any ambition in your minds. Do not entertain any hope of becoming colonels. They tell us, a calamity is hanging over India".

What is that to us? Why should we come forward to protect that India in which we have no rights, in which we are treated like slaves? If the British really have the good of India at heart, they should declare that Indians would get all the appointments in the army and would have the same rights as Europeans. If proper means are not adopted at this time, if educated citizens of India are not made to feel that this country is theirs, then it is impossible to recruit an army.

Hundred recruits secured for hundred rupees each are equal to one recruit enlisted on his own inspiration. Should not the Government realise this fact? I do not think that in Maharashtra there will be found such people as would say — 'Happen what may to Maharashtra, happen what may to India, we shall remain lolling on our beds in our houses'.

This is not the nature of Maharashtrians,... Government should by positive deeds, infuse in them a spirit so that they may feel and say, 'We would die for our country. Then, I am sure we shall be able to raise an army of a crore of men. But by not conceding the demand of India, the British Government is pursuing a wrong policy. The bureaucracy has overrun the whole nation; and we are not prepared to become soldiers in order to increase the power of these men. Serious notice was taken of this speech. Copies were circulated among the Viceroy and his Executive Councillors and the Governor of Bombay and his Executive Councillors.

The concensus of opinion was that legal proceedings would be inadvisable and might eventually do more harm to the war effort. The Bombay Government, therefore, issued an order under the Defence of India Rules forbidding Tilak to speak in public without the written permission of the district magistrate of the district in which he proposed to speak and, in case of the city of Bombay, of the Commissioner of Police.

The order was not to apply to any speech confined to the subject of constitutional reform which he may make at the forthcoming special meeting of the Indian National Congress. Tilak had some correspondence with Gandhi about his attitude to the war, and hoped to recruit 5,000 person from Maharashtra, if Gandhi could secure a promise from the Government beforehand that Indians would get commissioned ranks in the army. As a guarantee of his good faith, Tilak sent to Gandhi a cheque of Rs. 50,000, the amount to be forfeited if certain conditions were not fulfilled by Tilak. Gandhi's position was that the help should not be in the nature of a bargain and he, therefore, returned the cheque.

The two leaders agreed to differ, and went their own ways. Gandhi went ahead with his recruitment campaign zealously until he was informed one day that the war had ended and that the recruitment had now been stopped. Tilak was preparing to proceed to England on his mission of carrying Home Rule propaganda to that country.

Shivaji Coronation Celebration

The Shivaji coronation anniversary was celebrated in Puna on the 14th, 15th and 16th June.

On the 14th, V. K. Rajwade lectured in the Kirloskar Theatre on " The work and prowess of Shivaji", Tilak was in the chair and, in summing up, said that of late he had been engrossed in the subject of Home Rule and considered they had much to learn on the subject from the manner in which Shivaji conducted his administration. They were told that if Home Rule were granted, the Muslims and the lower Hindu castes would be oppressed by the Brahmins. It would be well if their traducers would study the period of Shivaji's rule: protection was extended to all alike and the Cabinet included Ministers of various castes. Representation of the bugbear of Brahmin tyranny was a selfish dodge on the part of the bureaucracy to deceive the people so that they might keep the power in their own hands.

5

Great Nationalist

Two young students, Bal Gangadhar Tilak and Gopal Ganesh Agarkar, both studying at the Deccan College in Puna, sat engrossed with thoughts on the present and the future in an optimistic and self-confident frame of mind. Both had impressed their teachers with their intelligence and desire to acquire knowledge. While most students wove rosy dreams about their personal life, Tilak and Agarkar thought of their society and the future of their country. They were idealists prepared to dedicate their lives to a noble cause.

Their favourite pastime was to go for walks on a hillock nearby and hold discussions on varied subjects. At times they would get involved in heated arguments particularly when the two differed sharply in their views. However, these differences did not come in the way of their friendship as each was aware of the other's sincerity and earnestness.

Bal Gangadhar Tilak was born on 23rd July 1856, in a middle-class family at Ratnagiri. His father Gangadhar Pant worked in the Education Department of the government. Bal lost his mother at an early age and was, therefore, brought up by his paternal aunt. He had his primary education at Ratnagiri. His father was then transferred to Puna as Assistant Deputy Educational Inspector. During Bal's school days, his father regularly made him recite the subhashitas, shlokas and other verses in Sanskrit and Marathi.

As was customary in those days, Bal got married at a young age in 1871. A year later he lost his father. His uncle Govindrao took charge of the household. On completing his matriculation at the age of sixteen, Bal joined the Deccan College at Puna. Since his father had made adequate provision for him, Tilak could complete his college education without being burdened by economic constraints. He secured a first class in his B.A. examination with mathematics as the main subject. As a student Tilak was known for his razor-sharp intelligence and love for reading.

Agarkar came from a poor family. He had to pass through many hardships, both during his high school as well as college days, that is, while studying at the Deccan College. But that did not deter him in any way. In a letter to his mother, Agarkar wrote:

> "Dear Mother, I know you must be hoping now that your son has passed his high school examination, he would get an officer's job which would enable you to lead a happy life. However, let me tell you frankly, I have decided to earn just as much as is required for sustenance; I shall be satisfied with modest means of livelihood and will spend the rest of my life for the good of the society".

These two young friends had diametrically opposite views regarding the manner in which they would serve their country. Tilak was of the opinion that they ought to devote their energies to the task of liberating their motherland from the British yoke. Agarkar, on the other hand, felt that though political independence was important, it was necessary first to reform the society through social work and then turn one's attention to political work. Tilak, being a student of mathematics, was forthright in his approach and clear in his perception. Agarkar, a student of philosophy, with a rare sensitive mind, was keen to launch a battle against the evils and injustices perpetrated in Indian society. One thing they had in common — both were voracious readers and admirers of two great English thinkers — Mill and Spencer, whose thoughts and ideas greatly influenced them.

Both Tilak and Agarkar had no time for futile talks or sterile discussions. Both were eager to act but according to each one's own ideological convictions. For days together they would discuss India's problems and how these could be overcome. It was through these discussions that their ideas took shape and both came to the conclusion that before plunging into either the political or social field, it was necessary to spread education, an essential prerequisite for laying the foundation for their future work. This was no compromise, but a realistic decision taken after careful thought and serious deliberations.

It was but natural for both Tilak and Agarkar to hold in great regard the then leaders of the society and be influenced by their ideas. Mahadev Govind Ranade was the leader who profoundly influenced their thoughts and ideas. Ranade, a judge to the High Court, was a great scholar with wide vision and earnest desire to serve the society. Even though in government service, Ranade had worked endlessly towards the enlightenment of his people through his words and deeds. He started institutions like the Sarvajanik Sabha, established libraries at different places and started a series of spring lectures, in Puna, for educating the people and making them aware of their rights and duties to the Indian society. Tilak and Agarkar held Justice Ranade in high esteem, but somehow felt that they could serve the society better only if, unlike Ranade, they kept themselves away from the shackles of government service. Interestingly enough, it was during this period that Vishnu Shastri Chiplunkar resigned from his government job to start publishing his inspiring writings. Chiplunkar had a powerful pen and edited a Marathi magazine, Shala Patrak. In 1872, he wrote an article entitled, 'The Mission of a Teacher'. In this inspiring article, Chiplunkar drew attention to the fact that in the hands of idealist teachers, education can become a powerful weapon like a sword sharp, forceful and penetrating.

When Tilak and Agarkar took the decision of devoting their energies to education, it was the ideas put forth by Chiplunkar that made them conscious of the nature of their mission.

When these two young idealists came to know that Chiplunkar had decided to start a high school in Puna, they met him in September 1879 and expressed their desire to join him in his mission by working as teachers in the proposed high school. This gave an impetus to Chiplunkar's project and on 2nd January 1880 started the New English School in Puna. Among those to join the school was Vaman Shivaram Apte, an eminent Sanskrit scholar who took charge as headmaster at the high school.

Another very hard-working, dedicated and resourceful person, Madhavrao Namjoshi, also joined this team of teachers. In those days most students of the Deccan College, on completing graduation from the University of Bombay, preferred to enter into government service or start practising as lawyers. But Tilak and Agarkar chose to shun a stable and secure life and took to the thorny path of idealism. They wanted to create awareness in the young generation regarding the future of the society and inculcate in them the noble values of patriotism. These idealists, scoffed at by the so-called successful persons in society, were determined to accept the challenge of their times. They paid no heed to criticism by the worldly wise because they held a strong belief in the words of the revolutionary Marathi poet Keshavsut, who had said, "There is great substance in the so-called futile ideals and those who seek this substance are generally dubbed as mad men".

The founding of the New English School marked the first step in the path of enlightenment and social service. Thus, also began a new chapter in the life of Tilak and his colleagues. A school which started with only thirtyfive students in the first year, grew in strength with the number of its pupils rising to three hundred and thirtysix in the next year. Prof. Wordsworth, an eminent and a renowned professor in Deccan College, showed his appreciation by writing: "I am surprised at the remarkable success of the New English School. The education imparted in our college to the students has created in them strength and fervour. This school is an expression of that strength". Dr. William Hunter too, who was then the Director of Education, admitted that the standard of education in the New English School was higher than that in the government high schools.

The next step in the field of education was the establishment of the Deccan Education Society on 24th October 1884. Shortly afterwards, the Fergusson College was founded on 2nd January 1885. When Tilak and Agarkar were students in the Deccan College, it had been their dream to start a new college after finishing their studies. This dream became a reality with the starting of the

Fergusson College. Both Tilak and Agarkar, after they had taught in the New English School for about five years, started feeling the need for teaching in a college. During his student days, Tilak's capability in mathematics had been highly appreciated both by his fellow students and professors. Sharangpani, a friend of Tilak, has related the following incident about Tilak. Once he found Tilak walking restlessly in his room. When Sharangpani asked Tilak the cause for his disturbed state of mind, Tilak replied that he was thinking about a problem in integral calculus.

Sharangpani said, "Then why don't you meet Prof. Chhatre?" Tilak replied, "I know the method of solving the problem as stated in our textbook but, I want to solve it by a different method". Next day Tilak could arrive at a new method. He approached Prof. Chhatre with his solution which impressed the latter so much that he remarked, "Tilak's intelligence has the brilliance of the sun".

No wonder, Tilak was eager to make the best of this opportunity to teach at Fergusson College. He greatly enjoyed his work. However, Tilak's teaching was appreciated by brilliant students but the ordinary students had difficulty in keeping pace with him because while teaching, for instance, the binomial theorem, he tended to state the initial steps verbally and to write only the important steps on the blackboard. L.R. Pangarkar, who later earned recognition as a scholar and writer in Marathi, was a student of Fergusson College, and in one of his lectures said "Those who have fine sensibilities, study and enjoy poetry and those who have a dry matter of fact mind, study mathematics and science". When Tilak came to know of this observation made by Pangarkar, he called him and said, "There is poetry in mathematics but it requires a particular type of intelligence to understand the poetic charm of mathematics. Just as you visualise beauty while reading poetry, I visualise beauty while studying astronomy and while making mathematical calculations about the stars during their course". Tilak further added, "I think a person, who does not understand mathematics, has a defective intellect".

Chiplunkar, Agarkar and Tilak enjoyed the work of teaching and coming in contact with young and impressionable students. They, however, did not want to restrict their students' activities to the field of education. They wanted to widen their horizon by teaching them about the people, the political and social problems besides inculcating in them the spirit of patriotism. Realising that the newspaper was the most powerful instrument for educating the people, they decided to launch a newspaper. Here it is necessary to take into consideration the situation prevailing in India and the challenges faced by those who wanted to mould public opinion.

The British had initially come to India for the purpose of trade. The East India Company started trade in different parts of India. After a few years, ambitious persons like Robert Clive began to feel that political power was essential for safeguarding the economic interests of the East India Company and that of Britain. India was ruled in different parts by different rulers. The Mughals were dominant in north India. The Peshwas ruled Maharashtra, the Rajput Princes governed Rajasthan while there were feudal lords spread in other parts of India. Clive with his policy of 'divide and rule', set one ruler against the other and used all means in his power to establish his supremacy in various parts of India, primarily with the help of money-lenders and selfish feudal lords.

Bengal was the first to be brought under British rule. Later, their rule extended to other regions too. Some resistance was offered to the British, particularly by the Santhals in south Bihar. But as there was no combined resistance by the Indians, the British succeeded in crushing the Adivasi revolt and of various patriotic groups in different parts of India. Till the eighteenth century, the Indian society was prosperous. India had a huge section of weavers who helped the country in exporting cloth to many countries in the East. The British could not tolerate this rivalry to their dominance in trade and chose to destroy the Indian handloom industry. Thus, the export trade was destroyed and India soon became impoverished. Further, owing to the caste system of the Hindus, political power was concentrated in the hands of the upper caste Brahmins. As a result, the society was fragmented. The Peshwas, instead of looking after the welfare of their people, acted selfishly, ruling in a tyrannical way. The common people were exploited and the scheduled castes were given in human treatment by being treated as untouchables. They were fed up with the corrupt and decadent regime of the Peshwas and as such the British encountered no difficulty in conquering the Deccan. The common people in India were brave and patriotic while the rulers were corrupt and inefficient, but there was no alternate leadership. Moreover, the British had modern weapons and knew the techniques of modern warfare, whereas the Indian soldiers fought with arms which were outdated.

As a result of these factors political, social and military British hegemony was established.

In 1857, there was a major uprising in which Bahadur Shah Zafar, the Mughal Emperor, Nanasaheb, Peshwa and Laxmibai, the Queen of Jhansi, incited their people to revolt. The Indian soldiers, who had joined the British Army, revolted against the British.

However, the leaders of this national uprising did not get any co-operation from the people in the south, while in the north, Sikhs and many Rajput Princes joined hands with the British. As a consequence, the first war of independence in 1857 was quelled and the British brought the whole of India under their domination. India lost her freedom while the British established imperial rule in India.

The British rulers decided to administer the country with the help of the 'native' people. They started schools and colleges for educating the Indians who could then be recruited for different jobs in administration. Universities were established in Calcutta, Madras and Bombay. This gave the young generation access to modern education.

Many students viewed this opportunity for higher education from a utilitarian point of view and, as expected by the British willingly joined government services. However, some gifted students transcended the limitations imposed by the examination system and started a different pursuit of knowledge which would help in developing a new outlook on life. Raja Rammohan Roy in Calcutta was the first such individual who was proud of his cultural heritage despite being imbibed the modern knowledge through the British system. While many Indians, enamoured of the British way of life, slavishly imitated them, some among the first generation of university graduates, conscious of the strength and the weaknesses in the Indian society, decided to take measures for reforming it. In Maharashtra, Mahadev Govind Ranade, Jyotirao Phule, Lokhitawadi and Bal Shastri Jambhekar were the persons belonging to the latter category with vision and foresight.

They made a fervent plea for social reforms through their writings and boldly analysed the defects and shortcomings of our social system. Jyotirao Phule, an active social reformer who exposed the evils of the caste system, made a strong plea for social equality. He and his wife Savitribai started a school for girls, and a home for destitute women. He welcomed persons belonging to all castes and allowed the scheduled castes to draw water from the well in his house. Mahadev Govind Ranade, a moderate, through his patient and methodical work, shook the tradition-ridden and orthodox Hindu society out of its stupor by giving enlightenment to it. Justice Ranade wanted the spirit of liberalism to permeate the various strata of the society. Many eminent Indians, pained by the state of affairs in India, decided to devote their life to the task of social upliftment. Dadabhai Naoroji of Bombay was the tallest among these worthy individuals to be fired by the spirit of social service. Surendranath Banerjee in Bengal and many others in different parts of India rose up to create a new awareness and enthuse the people to work for social reforms while fighting for political rights. The contributions made by the persons of such high moral and intellectual stature like Dadabhai Naoroji, Justice Ranade, Surendranath Banerjee and others laid the foundation for future political work. The British established the rule of the law and gave people a sense of security.

Universities established by them enabled the young generation to develop close contact with modern ideas and knowledge. Persons like Ranade appreciated these benefits though not at the cost of losing political freedom. Dadabhai Naoroji was the first to point out that though there was law and order, the British rulers were exploiting India of its economic resources and making it impoverished. Jyotirao Phule pleaded for a basic change in the social structure while Ranade favoured a gradual change — first in the way of thinking and then in the way of living.

Vasudeo Balwant Phadke, a young man from Colaba, came to Puna and was so moved by the speeches and ideas of Ranade, that during the 1872 famine in Maharashtra, he chose to tour the famine-stricken districts of the Bombay Presidency. He was appalled at the terrible plight of the people, the numerous deaths due to starvation and the callous attitude of the British government. Phadke was enraged and convinced that India's lot could not improve till the British left the country. The young rebellious Phadke took to the path of armed revolt against foreign rule. Failing to muster support of the educated class, he decided to organise the tribals — Ramoshis and Kolis — amongst whom he had faithful and brave followers, prepared to sacrifice their lives.

Despite his organisational abilities and extraordinary valour, Phadke's efforts at armed rebellion did not succeed. He and his men were overpowered by the British. He was arrested, tried, and sentenced to life imprisonment at Eden where he died in prison in 1883. Phadke's martyrdom not only evoked admiration in the people but kindled the flame of patriotism in the hearts of many a youth.

British domination angered the people, but, owing to continued subjugation, moral degeneration had set in and the people had lost their sense of self-respect. Efforts of leaders like Dadabhai Naoroji and Justice Ranade were directed at the task of reviving the spirit of self-respect in the people. Political work in the first phase entailed efforts at moral regeneration. The first generation of political leaders and social reformers through their spade work paved the way for the next generation of patriotic leaders. In Maharashtra, Chiplunkar, Tilak and Agarkar were the rising stars of the new generation, whose aspirations for a new order in India far surpassed those of the earlier generation.

With tremendous self-confidence, while working in the field of education, they took upon themselves the task of educating the people by starting two journals, Kesari in Marathi and Maratha in English.

Tilak, Agarkar and Chiplunkar had to surmount considerable difficulties in setting up their press. However, obstacles were overcome and the first edition of Maratha, the English weekly, was published on 2nd January 1881. Kesari, the Marathi weekly, saw the light of the day two days later. Tilak was the editor of Maratha while Agarkar was that of the Kesari. The meaning of the Marathi word Kesari is 'a lion' and the Sanskrit verse printed near the editorial, addressed and warned the intoxicated elephant not to stay in the forest, for there was a lion used to tearing the huge rocks mistaking them for elephants.

These young men strove hard at raising financial resources for running the two weeklies.

Both the Kesari and the Maratha evoked an enthusiastic response and within a short time five thousand copies of the Kesari were getting printed. In almost all the major towns of Maharashtra, a single copy of the Kesari was read by many people. This marked the first step in establishing communication with the people of the state. However, it was difficult for the Kesari to become a self-supporting weekly. The Maratha was beset by financial losses but Tilak and Agarkar deemed it necessary to publish a journal in English — the language held in high esteem by the educated.

It was not easy for Tilak, Agarkar or Chiplunkar to shoulder the responsibilities of teaching at the college and of running the two weeklies simultaneously. Moreover, they were inexperienced as journalists. It was, however, their dedication, determination and enthusiasm which enabled them to carry on their mission of educating the young generation as also the others. The zeal and sincerity of their efforts won much support for them. But not for long. Soon they ran into stormy weather when they published some letters in the Kesari and the Maratha. In these letters, an allegation had been made that a conspiracy had been hatched in Kolhapur state to declare its ruler as 'mad' and so dethrone him. It was further alleged that Madhavrao Barve, who was the then Diwan of Kolhapur, was playing a leading part in this sinister plot and was torturing Prince Shivaji II, the ruler of Kolhapur. Unfortunately, these letters given to the editor of the Kesari were fake and as a result Barve, the Diwan of Kolhapur state, filed a case of defamation against Tilak and Agarkar. People were convinced of the innocence of Tilak and Agarkar who owing to their inexperience, had put their trust in Kagalar, the villain, who had duped them by giving forged letters. Tilak and Agarkar frankly admitted before the court how they got the letters and mistook the contents to be genuine. Nevertheless, both were sentenced to four months simple imprisonment. However, the common man was convinced of their honesty and their devotion to the ruler of Kolhapur. They were all praise at the courage of these two young editors who went to jail with a smile on their lips. Principal Wordsworth, Justice V.N. Mandlik and other eminent persons of the town submitted a petition to the government pleading for annulment of the punishment, but the government paid no heed to it.

Tilak and Agarkar were kept in Dongri Jail in Bombay. Agarkar has given a graphic description of his experience in the prison in his small book, A Hundred-and-One Days in Dongri Prison, in Marathi. Owing to the hardships of prison life and the unappetising food served to the inmates, Tilak lost twenty-four pounds while Agarkar lost sixteen pounds in weight. After a month's stay in prison, they were given the permission to read and write. However, the two friends spent most of their time discussing various subjects of their interest. On their release from Dongri Jail, they were given a warm welcome by the people. Lokhande, the editor of Deen Bandhu, and other influential persons belonging to the non-Brahmin community were the first to felicitate Tilak and Agarkar.

Generally, days spent together in prison help to strengthen the bonds of friendship and amity. But with Tilak and Agarkar the ideological differences between them became more and more sharp. In 1884, when a plea was made to the government to pass a law against child marriage, the reactions of the editors of the Kesari and the Maratha were diametrically opposite. While Agarkar, a staunch opponent of child marriage, wrote in the Kesari a signed article supporting the plea against child marriage, Tilak opposed the idea of government interference in social and religious matters. His stand encouraged the proponents of child marriage to raise their voice too. This development widened the gulf between Tilak and Agarkar. Their differences of opinion were echoed during the meeting of the life members of the Deccan Education Society. Agarkar led a group of reformist teachers, while the other group of orthodox and traditionalist teachers supported Tilak's point of view. In the Kesar if articles expressing divergent views on this subject were published. The rift between the editors grew to such an extent that Agarkar resigned from his post as editor of the Kesari to start a Marathi weekly, Sudharak, in order to propagate social reforms and to work whole-heartedly towards carrying them out.

During the meeting of the Deccan Education Society, Tilak was of the view that life members should work as Jesuits and not supplement their income from outside sources.

In one way, this was a reference to Agarkar who had written a book Vidya Mimamsa for which he had received a grant from Holkar, the ruler of Indore. Tilak and Agarkar clashed on the issue of the Holkar grant. Both Agarkar and Tilak were men of principles and had made sacrifices for the Deccan Education Society. However, the differences among them became irreconcilable, forcing Tilak to resign from the Society and the teaching profession. This marked a parting of ways for Tilak and Agarkar.

Tilak in his letter of resignation wrote a long explanation clarifying his ideological position. He stated that "while serving the Deccan Education Society for over a decade, I worked with others in the Society for a noble cause and therefore, it was with a feeling of deep regret that I took the decision to leave the Society". He added, "I assure you that it was only after a great struggle with my own feelings that I came to this conclusion. In fact, I am now giving up my life's ideal with the aim that by separating myself from it, I shall serve it best, and to the best of my satisfaction". Tilak did not just defend his position, but candidly wrote: "I am deeply conscious of my fault, which, I know, has given at times reason to some of my colleagues to be offended by me. The chief fault that I am aware of in me is my manner of expressing myself in strong and sharp language...

But, I can assure you, that if I spoke strongly it was because I felt strongly for the interests of the institutions".

Tilak and Agarkar, who in their college days were close friends and shared each other's ideals and worked together through sunshine and rain, parted company not only on matters of education, but in the field of journalism too. Each had a different set of priorities — Tilak gave importance to political work while Agarkar gave prominence to social reforms. However, apart from these differences, they held similar political views.

Both wanted India to be freed from British rule and both were prepared to make sacrifices to achieve this freedom. However, their contrary philosophical stands came in the way. Agarkar was a rationalist and an atheist. In his speech in the Deccan College in 1895, Tilak admitted that he was an agnostic as he had been brought up in an orthodox family and owing to its influence during his formative years; he had come to respect the traditions of Hindu society. He did not approve of Agarkar's zeal for social reforms.

Agarkar stood for individual freedom but Tilak with his traditionalist approach felt that the individual should conform to the norms of the society. Both worked together in the educational field but on issues like child marriage, they differed sharply and these ideological differences became so acute that parting of ways became inevitable. On leaving the Deccan Education Society, Tilak devoted his energy to political work. He made the Kesari a powerful weapon to fight the British. Agarkar, after resigning from editorship of the Kesari, launched the journal Sudharak, which he used as a powerful instrument to attack the hypocrisy and orthodoxy of the Hindu society. It was a sad day when Agarkar died at the young age of thirtynine in 1895, and there is no way of finding what his views would have been on the political struggle in India which intensified soon after. However, it has to be admitted that Agarkar was a pioneer in his rational struggle for social reforms. Tilak, in his obituary on Agarkar, published in the Kesari, paid glowing tributes to the noble qualities of head and heart possessed by Agarkar.

On leaving the Deccan Education Society, Tilak started law classes in Puna for those appearing for the High Court pleader's examination. This was necessary for earning his livelihood. Tilak had not practised as a lawyer after passing his law examination, but due to his rare analytical mind, his law classes became very popular in no time. He not only coached students for the examination, but also explained the fundamental principles of law in a lucid manner. His lectures on Hindu law, in particular, were so illuminating that Justice Mahadev Govind Ranade, who was senior to Tilak, once quietly attended the class to listen to Tilak's lecture.

Tilak now concentrated his energies on political work. He not only gave expression to the aspirations of the people through the Kesari, but created in them a new awareness of their rights and the path to struggle against the government.

Concept of Swaraj

Tilak was the first Indian leader who enthused courage, confidence, fearlessness, strength and determination amongst the people of India. He declared unequivocally that constitutional agitation would not by itself have any effect on the British government. He, therefore, made it a confirmed political programme to organise the masses under the banner of the Indian National Congress and to make it the real and dependable spokesman of the people. Undoubtedly, it is he who made the people realise of their fundamental rights by ensuring their active participation in Indian politics against the *Raj.*

The celebration of national festivals in a large scale was another shrewd measure of Tilak to engender in the hearts of the people a feeling of oneness, self-respect, and self-sacrifice with a deep sense of national respect and honour. He was also greatly responsible to widen the implications of *Swaraj* and made it a most sacred slogan for realising the goal of independence cherished by one and all. He is rightly called the Father of Indian freedom struggle as he dominated the Indian political scene for about three decades.

Undoubtedly, Tilak was also the first Indian leader, who planned to make his movement mass-based. He himself went down to the masses dwelling in the remote villages and gave them the message of their rights and implications of the freedom struggle. He became the editor of the *Kesari* on 22 October 1887 and of the *Mahratta* on 3 September 1891. With the *Kesari,* he was in his element. A weekly paper and with a circulation of over 35,000, it moulded the national life of Maharashtra. The *Kesari,* as the name indicates, stood for manliness, strength. Its style was like the physiognomy of its illustrious editor, plain, blunt and aggressive. It was 'reason fused and made red-hot with passion.'

Tilak's release in 1914 gave a new twist to the existing nationalist politics of India. If was a common belief earlier amongst the bureaucracy that he would not be able to survive the oppressive sentence he had to undergo in Mandlay. Though nearly broken in health, he maintained a most formidable spirit which was yet to launch an anti-Raj movement. He was in receipt of numerous messages from his followers and well wishers from India and abroad. *Tilak-Ki-Jai* and Long Live Tilak were the spontaneous slogans of people, who happened to accord him a warm welcome on his release. He declared in an assembly of thousands of people, 'I can only assure you all that separation for six long years could not diminish my love for you and that I am ready and willing to serve you in the same manner, in the same relation and in the same capacity as I did before although I may perhaps have to modify the course a little.'

Precious Opinions

Mahatma Gandhi: Mahatma Gandhi reminisced about Tilak thus: 'I admire Lokamanya like millions of his countrymen for his indomitable will, his vast learning, his love of country, and above all, the purity of his private life and great sacrifice. Of all the men of modern times, he captivated most the imagination of his people. He breathed into us the spirit of Swarajya. No one realised the evil of the existing system of government as Lokamanya did.

Motilal Nehru: Pandit Motilal Nehru opined, 'I was always stuck with his remarkable grap of the intricacies of difficult situations and the clear judgement he brought to bear on the subjects under discussion. I must however confess that I never found myself on the same plane of thought with him.

C.R. Das: C.R. Das opined, 'Was Tilak a revolutionary ? Was Lokamanya Bal Gangadhar Tilak, the idol of his people, the implacable foe of the bureaucracy, an anathema to it, the worshipper of Shivaji, the greatest Maratha, since Shivaji, was a revolutionary ? A passionate devotion to work, an energy that never wavered or halted, a supreme mastery of details, a grit, an utter callousness to, or disregard of, difficulties or dangers gave indeed to all his action a sharpness and an edge.... He was by temperament incapable of the big jump, and a spirit that would take what it gets and fight for the rest cannot harbour that restlessness, that impatience, which is at once the habit and instrument of the born revolutionary. He was conservative by instinct, compromise was the essence of his politics, but he never lost sight of the ideal to which his whole being moved.... Action gave him the impulse of his life and it bred in him the will to suffer.... Tilak won and laid the beginning a greater India reborn for self-fulfilment and the service of humanity.

Rabindranath Tagore: Rabindranath Tagore greatly praised the services of Tilak: 'He had more faith in Truth than in method. His ideal of the fulfilment of India's destiny was vast, and therefore, it had ample room even for a dreamer of dreams, ever for "music-maker". He knew that freedom had its diverse aspects, and, therefore, it could be truly reached if individuals had their full scope to use their special gifts for opening out paths that were diverse in their directions.

C. Rajagopalachari: C. Rajagopalachari stated, 'His plans remind one of Napoleon. He would be in his natural element in the fierce battlefield, amidst blood and ruin, and stand unmoved amidst physical pain and intensest suffering. On the other hand, Lokamanya Tilak who spoke the doctrine of Force, really could not beat to see a fly hurt, and would break down if he saw any slaughter of human beings whatever might be the end in view.... His philosophy did not urge asceticism for politicians but he himself was an ascetic and saint as well as politician.

Madan Mohan Malaviya: Pandit Madan Mohan Malaviya reminisced about Tilak thus: 'Mr. Tilak made it clear so far back as the beginning of 1907 that self-government on colonial lines sufficed for him as a thing to work for. That was his attitude when he started the Home Rule movement in 1915 and joined hands with Mrs. Annie Besant for its realisation. One may safely say, that was his attitude to the last. The means by which he sought to bring about self-government on colonial lines was the creation of a vigorous, clamorous public opinion in India which would not be satisfied until it saw self-government established, and continued agitation in England to make the English people realise the wisdom and justice of helping to establish it.

Annie Besant: Annie Besant indeed had high opinion for him. 'He was a man filled with passionate and never weakening love for India, for whom every sacrifice for her was joy, every suffering was welcome. No physical bondage could bind that free spirit... In my own relations with him, I found him absolutely straight and loyal to his word".

M.A. Jinnah: M.A. Jinnah opined, 'Mr. Tilak was a shrewd practical politician.... He rendered yeoman services to the country and played a very important part in bringing about the Hindu-Muslim unity, which ultimately resulted in the Lucknow Pact in 1916. Subsequently he was one of the pioneers of the Home Rule League movement and established the Indian Home Rule League... He felt that we must work the Constitution so far as it went and fight for more. He actually prepared a definite policy and programme of electioneering campaign and advised the people to be ready to see that our best representatives were returned to the various legislatures.... He was an unique figure both in the political and social life of the country.

T. Prakasam: T. Prakasam stated, 'It was Lokamanya Tilak that laid the real foundation of *Swarajya* in India at a time when the rest of the people, educated as well as uneducated, were asleep; that he fully foresaw the trend of events that must follow the causes at work in full force in his day. His teachings and selfless work and devotion were based upon his undaunted courage, unbending patriotism and ungrudging suffering for the freedom of his country..'

J.M. Sen Gupta: J.M. Sen Gupta stated that he was.. 'a dauntless soldier in freedom's battle... Living a life of solemn consecration, he endeavoured to create in the nation a resolute will to be free and a dauntless determination to face all difficulties and sufferings that a struggle for freedom brings in its train. Pre-eminently, a man of action, with a supreme capacity for splendid organisation, he taught by his life that it was by action more than anything else that the will of the people could be trained and strengthened'.

Ideology behind Indian Home Rule League

In an article published in the *Maharatta,* Tilak put forward cogent reason for the necessity of the foundation of the Indian Home Rule League. 'It was generally recognised that the time had positively come for an organisation to be started for educating public opinion and agitating for Home Rule throughout the country. The Congress was the body which naturally possessed the greatest authority for undertaking such a work with responsibility. The scheme of self-government which the Congress is supposed to be intending to hatch, served as a plausible excuse for most of moderates to negative a definite proposal to establish a Home Rule League. But the Congress, it is generally recognised, is too unwieldy to be easily moved to prepare a scheme for self-government and actively work for its practical success. The spade work has got to be done by someone. It can afford to wait no longer. The League may be regarded as a pioneer movement and is not intended in any sense to be an exclusive movement.

Tilak's speeches amongst the masses of western and central regions of India had direct and homely appeal which made him a hero of the people. His name became a household and this kind of popularity earned him the epithet of Lokamanya revered by the people. He became to be liked, praised rather worshipped like a god. Whenever he happened to tour, he was accorded a right royal reception. He, on his part, earned their love and affection and appealed to them to imbibe the virtues of fearlessness, sacrifice of any kind and patriotism and advised them to hold out the national hero Shivaji as their model.

In a meeting Tilak happened to address at Puna, he stated 'The British just want you to supply soldiers whom they want for the war. They tell us a calamity is hanging over India. What is that to us ? Why should we come forward to protect that India in which we have no rights, in which we are treated like slaves ?... The bureaucracy has overrun the whole nation; and we are not prepared to become soldiers in order to increase the power of these men. What are we to tell our men ? Join the array to strengthen the *Zulm* of those English people?'

On the occasion of Shivaji Coronation Festival, Tilak presided over a lecture on conscription. In his speech, he called the army as mercenary one which consisted of foreigners ready to shoot the people without compunction.

At another occasion Tilak observed. 'History and reason are against the difficulties created by the bureaucracy, and we must triumph in the end. Be prepared to say that you are a Home Ruler. Say that you must have and I dare say when you are ready you will get it. There is nothing anarchical in this demand... Home Rule is the only remedy. Insist on your rights. India is your own house.'

Tilak defined *Swarajya* during the course of his speech delivered at Belgaum on 1st May 1916". "What is *Sawarajya* ? Many have a misconception about this. Some do not want it. Thus, there are many kinds of people. The idea *of Swarajya* is an old one. Of course when *Swarajya* is spoken of it shows that there is some kind of rule opposed to *swarajya,* i.e. ours and that his idea originates at that time. This is plain. When such a condition arrives, it begins to be thought that there should be *Swarajya,* and men make exertions for that purpose. You are at present in that sort of condition. Those who are ruling over you, do not belong to your religion, race or even country. The question whether this rule of the English Government is good or bad is one thing. The question of 'one's own and alien' is quite-another. Do not confuse the two at the outset.'

For the first time after 1907, extremists happened to attend the session of the Indian National Congress at Lucknow. It was a significant phenomenon to note when 'A Home Rule Special' carried Tilak and the members of his party to the Lucknow Congress in 1916 and when they received unique ovations all along the way. At Lucknow, their reception all over was proverbial in manner and style. It was indeed a royal reception. The tyres of his car were cut in order to force Reception Committee to put him in a carriage which was unauthorised and dragged through the main bazars and streets of the town and the wild acclamation of a huge procession. So far so when he arrived at the pandal of the Congress, he was virtually carried on shoulders by his numerous followers and admirers. His speech, which was fairly comprehensive and effective in contents touching upon various crucial political facts of the time, I was greeted with deafening cheers.

In supporting the resolution on self-government at the Lucknow Congress, Tilak severely criticised the bureaucracy in India and put forward demand for self-government. 'We have to get these rights from powerful bureaucracy, an unwilling bureaucracy, naturally, unwilling because the bureaucracy now feels that these rights, these privileges, this authority, will pass out of their bands. I would feel the same if I were in that position, and I am not going to blame the bureaucracy for entertaining that natural feeling. But whatever the character of that may be it is a feeling which we have to combat against: it is a feeling that is not conducive to the growth of self-government in this country. We have to right against that feeling. When we have to fight against a third party, it is a very important thing that we stand on this platform united, united in race, united in religion, united as regards all different shades of political creed. That is the most important event of the day.

'Let us glance. As I said, ten years ago when Dadabhai Naoroji declared that *Swaraj* should be our goal: its name was *Swaraj.* Later on it came to be known as self-government or constitutional reform and we nationalists style it Home Rule. It is all the same, in three different names. It is said that as there is objection raised that *Swaraj* has a bad odour in India and Home Rule has a had odour in England, we ought call it constitutional reform. I don't care to call it by any name. I don't care for any name. If you style it as A.B.C. reform scheme or X.Y.Z. reform scheme, I shall be equally content; I don't mind for the name, but I believe we have. But I believe you have hardly realised the importance and character of that scheme of reform. Let me tell you that it is far more liberal than the Irish Home Rule Bill, and then you can understand what possibilities it carries with it. It will not be complete Home Rule but more than a beginning of it. It may not be complete self-government but it is a far better than local self-government. It may not be *Swaraj* in the widest sense of the word, but is far better than *Swadeshi* and boycott. It is in fact a synthesis of all Congress resolutions passed during the last 30 years, a synthesis that will help us on to proceed to work in a definite, in a certain responsible manner'.

In a Home Rule conference held at the Aminabad High School, Lucknow on 30 December 1916, Tilak gave vent to his feelings about the functions of bureaucracy, concept of liberty and on the need of Home Rule for India. 'The fight at present is a triangular light, you have to wrest the whole Self-Government from out of the hands of a powerful bureaucracy. This body has already commenced to work in order to retain power in its own hands. It is but natural. You would do the same thing yourself if you were in possession. Possession is nice points of law. Bureaucracy in possession is nine point of law. Bureaucracy is in possession of power and why should it part with it ? Rights cannot be obtained by yearly resolutions. There are difficulties in the way of carrying out these resolutions, but these difficulties must strengthen us in our beliefs and in our actions.

'We now want liberty. Similarly, we educate our children and expect them to take our position later on in life. So is the case with Englishmen. They have united us, they have educated us and they must expect us to take the position we are fit for. History and reason are against the difficulties created by the bureaucracy and we must triumph in the end. The only thing that comes in our way is that we are not yet prepared. No shilly; shallying will do. Be prepared to say that you are Home Ruler. Say that you must have it and I dare say when you are ready, you will get. work for it?

'Home Rule is the synthesis of all Congress resolutions. Home Rule is the only remedy. Insist on your rights. India is your own house. Is it not ? Then why not manage it yourself ? Our domestic affairs must be in our own hands. We do not want separation from England.'

The Lucknow Congress in 1916 led to the unity of Tilak and his associates on one side and the moderates on the other. Besides, the Congress and Muslim League jointly sponsored resolutions which had full support of the cause of self-government. In fact, the agreed resolutions aimed at the establishment of provincial autonomy, the provision of election of about four-fifths of the members of central and provincial legislatures, the introduction of the clement of responsibility in not less than half members of executive and foreign affairs in the hand of the central government, and last but not the least, the grant of Dominion Status for India. Over the Muslim representation, it was agreed that they should have separate electorates. While in the centre, their representation was to be one third, in the provincial level, they should have 50 per cent in Bengal, 25 per cent in Bihar and Orissa, 33. 13 per cent in Bombay, 30 per cent in U.P., 15 per cent in C.P. and 15 per cent in Madras.

With this kind of understanding between the Hindus and Muslims, and moderates and extremists, the tempo of the Home

Rule Movement was greatly exhilarated. The *Kesari* observed 'Friday 29th December, 1916 is a day in India British relations worthy to be written with golden letters. On that day on the banks of the sacred river Gomati, the standard of Indian *swaraj* was unfurled. The resolution of *swaraj* passed on that day was an act of historic importance, the aspirations of India were crowned on that day, so I speak, and all her subjects came there to pay their homage to Mother India. Case distinctions, differences of opinion, personal jealousies and everything that was gross and went to destroy the unity of the nation was finally drowned in the waters of the Gomati and India assumed a new sacred form.

At Yeotmal, Tilak clarified a few significant points about Home Rule Movement. 'We tell the Government that we are no longer minors, nor are we lunatics, and we are able and competent to look after our affairs, our "home" and we will rule the "home"; we have got a right to say that we want this agent or that and we will guide the "Home policy". This demand for "Home Rule" is not a new one; Congress and the other older and younger institutions in the country have been demanding it.

Our opponents say we are not fit; but that is not true. Every one who is an adult and not a lunatic is fit to manage his house. We may commit mistakes in the beginning; but who is so perfect as to be beyond human feelings ? Even great men err. We want the right to commit mistakes also; we will commit mistakes and ourselves rectify them even the great *Avatars* commit mistakes. The Government does not lay down any standard of fitness; if they will lay down any, we will try to attain that standard. Government are not at all definite; those who ask us to be first fit and then demand *Swaraj* have no mind to give it to us at all. It is as good as to ask a boy to learn swimming and then to go into the river. You cannot separate Home Rule from us, as you cannot separate the quality of "heat" from fire; both are inseparably bound up; let your ideas be clear; let your motives be honest; let your efforts be strictly constitutional, and I am sure your efforts are bound to be crowned with success; never despair, be held and fearless and be sure that God is with you. Remember "God helps those who help themselves".

In a largely attended public meeting at Akola in January 1917, Tilak expressed his feelings about the Home Rule for India thus.

'The ideal of Home Rule has passed through trials and ordeals, and stands today perfectly vindicated as both loyal and practical. It is now conclusively proved that the gain of the one is the gain of both, and in India's Self-Government lies the future stability and safety of the British Empire. Since Home Rule became an ideal vindicated in courts of law as legal and loyal, it had to proved by arguments that India stood in immediate need of it, that India should demand it, that the demand was justified by defects in the method of the working of the existing mode of Government which could not be remedied except by Self-Government and that it was also proved that we were fit for receiving and handling the rights of *Swaraj* when they came to us.

Self-Government as I told you, means Representative Government in which the wishes of the people will be respected and acted upon and not disregarded, as now, in the interests of a small minority of civil servants. Let there be a Viceroy and let him be an Englishman if you like, but let him act according to the advice of the representatives of the people. Let our money be spent upon us and with our consent. Let public servants be really servants of the public and not their masters as they at present are.

None will be more unlucky and unfortunate than yourselves if you lag behind at this critical moment. You have the ideal of *Swaraj*, you have the legal methods to work for it, and you know what the ideal means. The Almighty helps you in His inscrutable divine ways by offering a unique opportunity. Now it is for you to say whether you will answer by vigorous efforts or sit silent and let the opportunity slip through your fingers. By allowing this golden opportunity escape, you are incurring the just blame of those that will be borne hereafter. Your daughters and sons will be ashamed of you and future generations will curse you. Take courage, therefore, and work now. Strike the iron whilst it is hot and yours shall be glory of success.

It is quite clear from Tilak's ideology that he was determined to take full advantage of the government's involvement and helplessness in the war. He was not to wait the conclusion of the war. So far so he sent Joseph Baptista to London on 14 July 1987 with the advice to propagate the ideal of Home Rule on the basis of the Congress-League Scheme.

Tilak travelled over two thousand miles and collected about fifty thousand rupees. With his weak ailing physique, he delivered as many as thirty-two speeches which were largely attended. He once remarked, 'People cannot possibly realise that I feel so weak. When the moment comes I make a speech. But the body is all the while under the strain. The speech over, I return from the crowds and sleep over my fatigue. Only my will to live sustains me.'

'Home Rule is my birthright

There are higher powers that rule the destiny of things and it may be the will of Providence that the cause I represent may prosper more by my suffering than by my remaining free.

For the success of his Home Rule Movement, Tilak was fairly mobile. His movements tinged with propaganda work for the movement covered a huge area in north India. The terrible unrest in the Punjab engendered by the anti-government activities by the workers of the Ghadar party had made the whole administrative machinery much engaged in establishing law and order. At this point of time, Tilak intended to enter the Punjab for the political propaganda work amongst the people, and when the government got the information that Tilak had planned to inaugurate a branch of the Home Rule League in the Punjab, it at once issued a notice to him under the Defence of India Consolidation Rules 1916 prohibiting his entry in the Punjab. Similarly, the police chief of Delhi prohibited the entry of Tilak in the city.

The personnel sufferings of Tilak during the long drawn political battle against the *Raj* were phenomenal. He had to face prosecution and hardships in the jail. 'He made life in jail for the political leaden in subject India an honourable and unavoidable service. His sufferings made blunt the edge of the hardships of jail life of political prisoners in India, and he served as the leader of sappers and miners in the life of the national army *of Swaraj.* By his ceaseless actions, his fearlessness, his selflessness, he infused courage into a generation that came forward to follow him, to support him, and to die for the cause of the motherland.

Undoubtedly, Tilak was a born rebel and his impatience with the prevailing structure of foreign rule made him raise the banner of revolt during his life. His relations with the revolutionaries was cordial although he did not participate in their violent activities. He opined that an armed revolt was also constitutional provided it was result-oriented. He had much sympathy with Senapati Bapat, Wasudeo Chapekar and other leaders engaged in revolutionary activities. He in fact strove hard to galvanise the Congress into a militant constitutional movement.

By his incessant linkage with the hectic political activities, Tilak had endeared himself so much amongst the people that he was called by them Lokamanya, i.e. adored by the people. Whereas Valentine Chirol described him as the 'Father of Indian Unrest', C. Vijayaraghavachariar called him, 'a great son of India whose manhood was a life of selfless suffering in our country's cause in a spirit of dedication rarely surpassed in the annals of national struggle for freedom.'

Tilak used his paper, the *Kesari* as the best organ for the propaganda of his political creed. Through his writings in it, he could influence a major portion of the population in the western region. He apprised the people of their fundamental rights and enjoined on them to prepare themselves for the grim battle of freedom. He wrote that the only way to settle the Indian problem was a proclamation by the King of England declaring that the ultimate object of the British government was to grant *swaraj* to the people of India and that the first fundamental step by the government should be to grant it after the war.

Time and again Tilak told the British bureaucracy that his countrymen were trying in India as the Irish Home rulers have been doing in Ireland for a reform of the system of administration. His main argument centred round the idea that if Ireland could put a fight for their demand of Home Rule, why could a similar demand be not put forward by Indians. In this regard he wished to get a parliamentary bill moved so that Indians could manage their domestic affairs in a better shape. By doing so, he did not wish to severe ties with the British Empire, but he propagated *swaraj* within the Empire.

The government watched the political propaganda made by Tilak amongst the masses with doubt and suspicion. Plans were made to muzzle his Home Rule propaganda. So in July 1916, a case was instituted against Tilak for certain seditious speeches which he had delivered during his tour of various regions. On 22 July 1916, an order was passed by the District Magistrate of Puna under Sections 108 and 112 Criminal Procedure Code requiring Tilak to show cause why he should not be ordered to execute a bond for the sum of Rs. 20,000/-with two sureties each in a sum of Rs. 10,000/- to be of good behaviour for a period of one year. In pursuance of this order, Tilak was bound down on 12 August 1916 for a period of one year and was to enter into a bond in a sum of Rs. 20,000/-with two securities, each in a sum of Rs. 10,000/- in consequence of certain speeches delivered by him on the 1st, 21st May and 1st June 1916. On appeal by Tilak, the High Court Bombay reversed the order of the District Magistrate, Puna ordering Tilak to execute a bond to be of good behaviour. These pinpricks did not cripple the political activities of Tilak, rather he continued his work with great enthusiasm and patriotic fervour.

On Economic Front

On the economic front too Tilak did not show a progressive outlook, particularly regarding the restrictions on the money-lenders. He wrote an editorial under the title, 'The Money-Lender is killed and the Farmer too is killed'. In this article, Tilak argued that as long as the loan was not given to the farmer, it was futile to impose restrictions on the money-lender. In another article, Tilak opposed the legislation regarding land revenue. In sharp contrast to the progressive attitude of Mahatma Phule, Tilak took a rigid, traditionalist view. The fact was that he belonged to the family of Knots, who were money-lenders in Ratnagiri district. Instead of supporting the plea for giving more rights to farmers who tilled the land, Tilak chose to defend the privileges enjoyed by the money-lenders, who were looked upon as exploiters. At a time when he was fighting for political rights for the Indian people, he failed to uphold the rights of the farmers who tilled the soil. Instead, he chose to support the rights of the class to which he belonged. In this regard Tilak, who was expected to be ahead of his times, failed to show the farsightedness expected of him.

Meanwhile in the political field, he was gaining in popularity. Upto 1898, his field of activity was confined to Maharashtra. After 1900, however, he realised the need for spreading the political activity to every nook and corner of India and directed his efforts towards doing so. He did not approve the moderate stand of the Indian National Congress because he felt that it would not help to achieve political rights. He decided to give a radical orientation to the Indian National Congress by creating a greater awareness among the people through their participation in political activities. He wanted a militant struggle against the British government which was responsible for economic exploitation and impoverishment of the Indians. Tilak pointed out that due to foreign domination people had lost their sense of self-respect which had led to moral degeneration in the society. He was agonised at the slavish mentality that had come to stay with the Indians; he decided to make a determined bid to put a stop to this rot and generate a new enthusiasm among the masses. He realised that sacrifices were necessary in order to kindle the flame of patriotism. Convinced that not words but deeds alone could bring about a change in the attitude of the people, he organised cadres of active and devoted young men, willing to make sacrifices. Though he himself worked within the framework of law, he wanted the young men to pave the way for revolutionary action.

He gathered a few young idealists, who came out with novel ways for acquiring political freedom. Krishnaji Prabhakar Khadilkar, an intelligent young man, who worked with the Kesari, also thought on similar lines. Tilak and Khadilkar went to attend the Indian National Congress at Calcutta in 1900. There an elderly woman known as Mataji, invited Tilak to the school run by her. They went to see the school and were surprised to hear "Mataji speaking in Marathi". This woman, a widow, had some years earlier gone on a pilgrimage to Nepal. At the Pashupati temple in Kathmandu, the Maharaja of Nepal saw her and both started living together. After the Maharaja's assassination, she settled down in Calcutta and started a school. She came to be known as 'Mataji'. She maintained her contacts with Nepal through a colonel, Kumar Narsinha Rana. Mataji told Tilak that he would get all co-operations for his work in Nepal from Colonel Rana. Tilak accepted the offer and accompanied by Khadilkar went to Patna. But they failed to get the permit to enter Nepal and perforce had to return to Puna. However, Khadilkar decided to use this contact for revolutionary activities. He went to Nepal under the pretext of setting up a factory for manufacturing tiles, though his intention was to manufacture rifles covertly.

Through Colonel Rana, he established contacts with a representative of the German firm JCruppa, for the manufacture of arms. Ḳhadilkar stayed in Nepal as Krishnarao upto 1903. He was accompanied by one Vasudeo Limaye and some others. However, his efforts did not realise much and Khadilkar returned disappointed to Puna. Tilak knew about Khadilkar's activities but in no way was involved with him.

Vasukaka Joshi, another young associate of Tilak, went to Afghanistan under the pretext of seeing the Mahnubhav math, a religious place of a particular Hindu sect at Kabul. His intention was to establish contacts with the Amir of Afghanistan, but, as he failed to do so, he had to return disappointed. Tilak helped and encouraged some young men who wanted to go abroad to study science. He helped Vishnu Ganesh Pingale, a brilliant student, to proceed to America to study chemistry. Pandurang Sadashiv Khankhoje was a bright student from Wardha, whom Tilak gave financial assistance for going to America to study modern agriculture. Both these young men after completing their studies, joined the revolutionary party — the Ghadar Party.

Japan was then a developing nation, and when in the Japanese-Russian war Japan defeated Russia, all Asiatic countries were filled with pride, because never before had an Asiatic country defeated an European nation. Japan emerged as a symbol of the aspirations of the people of Asia. Some youths in Maharashtra went to Japan surreptitiously to get training in the use of arms. There is, however, no evidence to prove that these young men got support from Tilak though they had his blessings.

During this period, Tilak had to pass through a great deal of torment in personal life.

He wanted to keep the promise which he had made to his friend Baba Maharaj Pandit before the latters death; and he did what he thought best. However, his enemies and those whose interest was at stake hatched a conspiracy to destroy his public life by character assassination. The humiliation which Tilak suffered due to this unfortunate incident must have taken a toll of a few years of his life.

This episode had its beginning when Tilak was prosecuted in 1897. With his release on bail on 4th August, he returned to Puna on 5th August Shri Baba Maharaj Pandit, suffering from cholera and aware that he was not likely to recover, made a will requesting Tilak to become one of the trustees of his estate. Tilak deemed it his duty to respect the last wishes of his friend and agreed to become a trustee. Baba Maharaj died the next day.

At that time, Baba's wife Tai Maharaj was pregnant. Baba Maharaj had stated in his will that if Tai Maharaj were to give birth to a son then he would be the legal heir. However, if she did not beget a son or if the son died at an early age, then Tai Maharaj with the consent of the trustees could adopt a suitable boy as a son. Tai Maharaj gave birth to a son but unfortunately he died in 1898. At that time, Tilak was undergoing his term of imprisonment.

After his release, Tilak called a meeting of the trustees. The trustees reviewed the income and expenditure of the Maharaj family and made the necessary arrangements. On 18th June 1901, at the next meeting of the trustees, it was decided that Tai Maharaj would adopt a boy belonging to a Brahmin family and who was living with his parents in a village near Aurangabad. Accordingly, Tilak and Dadasaheb Khaparde accompanied Tai Maharaj to Aurangabad where she approved of the boy and agreed to adopt him as her son. The adoption ceremony was performed according to the shastras in the presence of respectable citizens. Tilak felt relieved that he had kept his promise and discharged his obligation accordingly. Little did he know that a conspiracy was afoot against him. Tilak, too keen to return to political work, wanted to fulfil his promise made to a friend as soon as possible.

Meanwhile, Tai Maharaj changed her mind and turned hostile. On 6th July 1901, she served a legal notice on the trustees that henceforth they should not interfere in her affairs. Nagpurkar, one of the trustees and two others declared that the adoption ceremony had not taken place and wanted Tai Maharaj to adopt one Balamaharaj Pandit of Kolhapur as her son. The adoption ceremony was scheduled to take place on 13th July.

However, Tilak stepped in and took prompt and firm action to prevent further mischief. The proposed adoption ceremony did not take place and Balamaharaj returned to Kolhapur on 15th July. Tai Maharaj then decided to perform the adoption ceremony at Kolhapur. Tilak tried to prevent this but his efforts proved of no avail. The second adoption ceremony was performed at Kolhapur on 18th August 1901. Tilak, as a trustee of the estate of the late Baba Maharaj Pandit, filed a suit in the court, in order to prove that the adoption ceremony at Aurangabad was legal and the second one at Kolhapur illegal. Tai Maharaj in the meanwhile filed an application to revoke the probate. Aston, the District Judge, heard the suit filed by Tai Maharaj and held the Aurangabad adoption ceremony invalid and revoked the probate. He found Tilak guilty of criminal offence and recommended his prosecution. Tilak appealed to the High Court against the decision. The High Court reversed Aston's order of revocation but strangely enough allowed the criminal proceedings against him to continue. The magistrate sentenced him to eighteen months' rigorous imprisonment with a fine of two thousand rupees. Tilak was released on bail. In the Sessions Court, the judge reduced his sentence to six months and revoked the fine. The news of Tilak's conviction shocked the people. However, Tilak maintained a calm and dignified silence. S.B. Tambe, counsel for Tilak, in his reminiscences has written: "Tilak's peace of mind was never disturbed in spite of the fact that the conviction was to be a permanent blot on his character".

While the case was going on, an unfortunate incident occurred in Tilak's family. His eldest son Vishwanath, who was twentyone years old, died of plague. Tilak, however, maintained his composure. Tilak used to dictate his editorials to Appaji Vishnu Kulkarni, who in his reminiscences has written: "On the day following Vishwanath's death, Tilak brought reference books from the library and dictated to me an editorial under the title, 'The Resignation of Maharaj Holkar has been sanctioned'. I was disturbed at Vishwanath's death, but Tilak dictated the editorial with his usual composure as though nothing had happened".

Meanwhile after the decision of Lucas, the Sessions Judge, Tilak appealed to the High Court. The appeal was heard on 24th February 1904. On 3rd March, the two judges who heard the case acquitted Tilak and set aside the sentence passed by the Sessions Judge.

They also ordered that the fine, if already paid, should be refunded. The original adoption at Aurangabad was held valid. Thus, Tilak's stand was fully vindicated and the blot on his character removed. There was great jubilation all over the country on Tilak's victory.

The Amrit Bazar Patrika wrote: "Tilak's character has shone forth more brilliant, like gold after being exposed to fire". The Advocate of India, while welcoming the judgement of the High Court, said that the judges in the lower court and the Sessions Court were prejudiced against Tilak and that their partiality had given a blow to people's trust in the British mode of justice. Over two hundred telegrams congratulating Tilak were received by him. There was a public meeting in Puna in which he was felicitated.

Tilak spoke, "I did not show any extraordinary courage. Public opinion was on my side that was why I withstood the ordeal". Tilak was acquitted in the criminal prosecution, but the civil litigation continued. In 1906, the magistrate gave a verdict in which each of Tilak's contentions was accepted.

Tilak's opponents appealed to the High Court. The judge' of the High Court declared the Aurangabad adoption invalid and passed strictures on Tilak. Against this judgement, Tilak filed an appeal before the Privy Council. In 1915, the Privy Council gave its verdict unequivocally in favour of him. Thus, Tilak's moral stand was at long last vindicated.

However, he had to suffer mental tension for many years and had to spend over fifty thousand rupees as expenses for filing suits, both civil and criminal. Tilak regarded his promise to his friend Baba Maharaj Pandit as sacred and courageously faced harrowing experiences in order to keep his word and discharge his obligation.

Jagannath Maharaj Pandit, the boy adopted as her son by Tai Maharaj at Aurangabad, became the legal heir. In his reminiscences, he wrote: "When I expressed a desire to give Tilak fifty thousand rupees, he told me that he would not accept a pie from me. When I insisted on giving something Tilak said, 'If it will make you happy, give me some land behind your bungalow; I shall donate the land to the New Puna College, an institution which takes pride in our nation and works enthusiastically in the field of education'".

Four-point Programme for Swarajya

The struggle for liberty is a way of asserting the dignity of human life. When a nation loses freedom and is ruled by another nation, the subject nation develops a feeling of inferiority and the people lose their sense of self-respect. The Indian leaders were deeply disturbed over this moral degradation afflicting large sections of the people and thus, using the platform of the Indian National Congress, they appealed to the people to join hands to preserve India's dignity and integrity. Lokamanya Tilak started the Shivaji festival with the hope that the noble life and heroic deeds of Shivaji would provide inspiration to the people and instil self-respect in them. At this time, Swami Vivekananda gave a brilliant exposition on the noble qualities present in Hinduism to an international conference on religion. He made the world realise the glorious nature of India's tradition and devotion to noble values in life. In September 1893, while addressing the World Conference of Religions, he declared, "Hindu religion is based on tolerance and accepts the existence of other religions. I regard truth as God. The entire world is my country".

Owing to his broad outlook and wide vision, Swami Vivekananda won worldwide acclaim. His speeches enthralled his Western listeners. He convinced the world that though India had lost its political freedom, it was not in bondage, the soul of the nation was still free. He helped create a noble image of India in the world, and during his tour, conquered the hearts of many with his simple and austere life, his brilliant intellect and his noble character. These rare qualities of his filled the hearts of Indians with joy and respect for him. When Vivekananda returned to India, he was given a tumultuous welcome. He then embarked on a tour of different parts of India. He delivered innumerable speeches, made people conscious of their glorious heritage and identity and appealed to them to bring about reforms in all spheres of life. His emphasis was on removal of poverty and inequality, establishment of ties of brotherhood among all sections of the society and the need for unity to build a new India. Lokamanya Tilak held him in high respect and deeply appreciated his work. He had great expectations from Swamiji, but unfortunately, Swami Vivekananda died prematurely in 1902. In an obituary on

Vivekananda, Tilak published in his journal an inspiring character-sketch of the noble preacher, and appealed to the people to practise what Vivekananda had preached. He also wrote that India's glory could be revived if Indians were to act according to the inspiring message of Swami Vivekananda.

In 1904 during the Bombay session of the Indian National Congress, it was decided to depute a representative of the Congress Party to explain to the British rulers the political aspirations of the Indian people. Accordingly, Prof. Gopal Krishna Gokhale was sent to England. Lala Lajpat Rai, who was then in England, assisted Gokhale in pleading for India's cause. Gokhale was not only intelligent but had an uncanny control over the English language. His thinking was logical, his manner persuasive and he could present facts with a rare skill. He pleaded India's cause in an effective and forceful manner. He placed before the British a correct picture of the state of affairs in India and exposed the Machiavellian policy of Lord Curzon. He also made the demand for home rule in India.

In one of his public speeches, he said, "The Indian people are getting united to work for a political ideal. They are making preparations for fighting against the government. If justice is denied to the Indian people and if their legitimate political aspirations are thwarted, then there can be an uprising and the 'people would try to win swarajya in their own way. Under such circumstances, you must guard against the eventuality of sending British troops to India to crush the Indian uprising".

Tilak was very happy when he read the report of this speech. He wrote an editorial in the Kesari showering praise on Gokhale. He congratulated him for the excellent work done while presenting India's case in England. On Gokhale's return, a mammoth meeting was held in Puna to felicitate him. Tilak moved a resolution thanking Gokhale and praising him for his patriotic spirit and excellent work in England. On 12th December 1905, Tilak published in the Kesari a photograph of Gokhale with an artistically designed border. In the same issue a special interview of Gokhale given to the Kesari was also published.

India's plight under the British made many Indians restless and incited the sensitive and the idealist to strive for freedom.

Barrister Shyamji Krishna Varma was one such idealist who had started his activities in England. He had an extraordinary career before he took to active politics. An eminent scholar of Sanskrit, Shyamji Krishna Varma had helped Monier Williams in the preparation of his English dictionary before leaving for England to become a barrister. On his return to India, owing to his fine legal acumen, he was invited by the Prince of Junagadh state to work as the Dewan for him. In Junagadh state, his activities made the British suspicious of him and so he left for England in 1897.

There he started practising as a barrister and within a short time acquired fame and fortune. He then decided to work for India's freedom and started a journal, Indian Sociologist to give expression to India's political aspirations and put forth his radical views to the British. In the first issue, he announced the scheme under which he proposed to give scholarships to Indian students. He wanted to help brilliant students to study in different departments of the world's universities. He also wanted to inculcate in these promising young men a spirit of patriotism so that they could take a lead in the freedom movement. He was prepared to spend all his fortune on building up a cadre of revolutionary young men. In the Indian Sociologist, he fearlessly wrote incisive articles demanding India's freedom from the British and in 1905, founded the India Home Rule Society. He also founded a hostel for Indian students which later became the rendezvous for Indian revolutionaries. Tilak lent support to Shyamji's activities besides giving advice and guidance. Shyamji sent the Indian Sociologist to Tilak regularly. Tilak asked Shyamji to draw up a plan for building up a group of political missionaries who could work for India's freedom. It was decided to call the organisation 'Deshbhakta Samaaj'. Bipin Chandra Pal was chosen as the first political missionary, but as he was arrested in Bengal, the scheme could not progress any further.

Lokamanya Tilak was of the opinion that a nation striving for freedom had the moral right to use all means and methods in its struggle. He knew the significance of the contribution made by Swami Vivekananda in India's freedom struggle by trying to mould world opinion. He also appreciated Gokhale's fervent advocacy of the Indian cause and his concerted efforts at convincing the British of the need for giving political rights to the Indians. He was also aware of the importance of the spade work done by Shyamji Krishna Varma in building up a revolutionary cadre. He strongly supported all these efforts carried out in different corners because all aimed at the single ideal of winning freedom. His ideological stance was to accept the sudra which called for adoption of all kinds of means for the realisation of the goal of swarajya.

Tilak was eager to give a radical twist to the political movement so that feelings could be roused to such a pitch as to encourage all to participate in the freedom struggle. Lord Curzon's autocratic rule presented the necessary impetus for building up the political movement in India. Curzon was a diehard imperialist with contempt for the Indians.

Towards the end of 1900, in a confidential letter to the Secretary of State for India, Curzon wrote: "The Congress is tottering to its fall and one of my greatest ambitions, while in India, is to assist it to a peaceful demise".

Curzon, intoxicated with the might of the British Empire, took one unjust decision after another. This deeply hurt the Indians and Tilak felt the need for challenging Curzon's tyrannical rule. He fearlessly took certain steps in that direction. When Curzon declared his resolve to partition the country, Tilak wrote a fiery editorial in the Kesari entitled, 'The Moment of Crisis'. He said, "Like Ravana, Lord Curzon wants to dance frantically all over India. Power has gone to his head to such an extent that reason has ceased to function and like a wild elephant he is trampling on public opinion in Bengal".

Tilak, while arguing that the people ought to react strongly to Curzon's high-handedness, wrote: "Unless we take some stringent action to hurt the government's pride, Lord Curzon's arrogance will not get checked". In the end, Tilak wrote that mere speeches by leaders of Bengal were not enough and would not serve any purpose either.

In the editorial of 22nd August, Tilak wrote: "Instead of submitting petitions and making requests, the people should resort to some extreme measures which would be an eye-opener for the autocratic and arrogant British rulers... National boycott is a measure of this kind". Tilak described how Italy, China and America had used such a weapon effectively in the past and history has proved that even the unarmed people, if united and determined to act courageously, emerge strong and can defy a powerful opponent without resorting to arms.

Once Tilak made up his mind to pursue a particular course of action, nothing could halt him or make him falter. On 29th August 1905, he wrote an highly inflammatory editorial under the heading, 'The Rule of Lord Curzon'. He strongly attacked the tyrannical deeds of Curzon and compared him to Aurangzeb. In the concluding paragraph, he wrote: "Just as in the solar system there are some comets, similarly among the galaxy of politicians, who surround the King Emperor, there are some who resemble the comets. Lord Curzon is a person of this kind".

Tilak was always serious in everything he did. He was never shallow or superficial in manner. Once he had decided on the path to be taken, he took every step firmly and resolutely. When he made a plea for using boycott as a weapon, he wrote an editorial, 'Boycott-A Yoga', in order to explain the nature of the strategy he wanted to adopt. He emphasised the need for boycotting foreign goods and viewed it not merely as a movement to be carried on for some time but a yoga which should pervade the Indian's way of life. He even made a reference to the teachings of the Bhagavad Gita which said that taking action was the best form of yoga.

On 16th October 1905, Bengal was partitioned. Bengal was a politically conscious state where the people were dead against the partition. The government clarified that Bengal was being partitioned for administrative convenience, but the leaders of Bengal knew fully well that Lord Curzon's intention was to attack and destroy the unity of the people of Bengal and permanently create a rift between the Hindus and the Muslims. The Hindus were in majority in West Bengal while in East Bengal the Muslims were more in number. Curzon's shrewd plan and evil intentions were clearly reflected in his speeches during his tour of East Bengal. In order to strengthen the rule of British Empire in India, Curzon adopted the 'divide and rule' policy. His devious plan, however, did not succeed.

The people of Bengal acted in a concerted manner to oppose the partition. The movement gathered tremendous momentum within a short time. On 7th August 1905, before the announcement of the partition, a large demonstration was held in Calcutta, the like of which the people of Bengal had not witnessed before in their life. In a public meeting it was decided to boycott British goods and a committee was appointed to chalk out the future plan of action. People from different strata of society joined the anti-partition movement. Fearing that the movement might remain restricted to Bengal, radical Indian leaders, in a rare political foresight, gave it a broad base by organising the struggle on an all India basis. Tilak and Lala Lajpat Rai made the people aware that partition of Bengal was not a regional issue but an attack on the self-respect and dignity of all Indians. In this movement, the trio — Lal, Bal and Pal, i.e. Lala Lajpat Rai, Bal Gangadhar Tilak and Bipin Chandra Pal — emerged as the accredited leaders of India's freedom struggle, blessed with political foresight. By chalking out a practical and realistic programme of action, they displayed their capacity for giving the people a correct lead and their determination to strengthen the bonds of unity among the Indians. It was no mean task to take the political movement to every corner of a vast country like India. Tilak with his strong sense of realism knew that once the wrath of the people had been sufficiently aroused against British rule, it would be necessary to give it the right direction. He came forth with a four-point programme of swadeshi, boycott, national education and swarajya, thus, involving the people in different activities and enabling them to contribute their bit to the freedom struggle.

Bengal's agitation against its partition helped in forging intimate ties of friendship between it and Maharashtra. Of course, this did not happen suddenly. A few years before the partition, Sakharam Hari Deuskar from Maharashtra had gone and settled down in Bengal. He not only mastered the Bengali language but wrote a book too in Bengali. The book contained stories of heroes drawn from Indian history and due to the patriotic fervour of his tales; it soon captivated the imagination of the youth in Bengal. Many felt an irrepressible urge to fight for the freedom of their motherland and decided to take recourse to revolutionary means. Aurobindo Ghosh was the fountain-head of inspiration for the

Bengali youth at the time, of the partition of Bengal. Ghosh had his education in England and was a brilliant young man with strong patriotic feelings. While studying at Cambridge University, he took to revolutionary ideas and felt that India could be liberated only by means of an armed revolution. On his return to India, he started working as a professor of English at a college in Baroda. He began writing a series of articles for a weekly in Bombay called Indu Prakash under the heading, 'New Lamps for Old'. He severely criticised the moderate methods of the Congress and advocated the need for giving a radical orientation to the party. This created a sensation in political circles and drew Tilak's attention to the writer of such articles. Tilak appreciated these articles for their radical ideas and patriotic fervour. Aurobindo published a pamphlet, Bhavani Mandir, in which he put forth his plan for preparing for a revolution. He planned to collect a group of young idealists and train them in an ashram to promote all-round development of their personality. These young men, with fine physique and sharp intellect, would also have the capacity for independent and original thinking. According to Aurobindo, they would be karmayogis who would renounce the pleasures of life and devote their energies to the task of liberating their motherland. He, with his brother Barindra Kumar and another associate Keshavrao Deshpande, began training and building of a cadre of revolutionaries.

The first meeting between Tilak and Aurobindo took place in 1902 when both attended the Ahmedabad session of the Indian National Congress. Tilak took Aurobindo outside the Pandal and both had a long discussion in the open ground for quite some time. This was not merely a discussion between two political stalwarts; it was a confluence of two streams, a meeting of two forces in the country's freedom struggle.

They exchanged views and resolved to make a united bid to break the chains of slavery which had stifled the spirit of the Indian people. Both felt that the efforts of the moderates were not leading the nation anywhere. Aurobindo felt that politics of petition and prayers only helped to take away the edge from the movement. His aim was to train and organise young revolutionaries who could help in obtaining freedom. Tilak felt that the liberal leaders who had put their faith in the fairness of British justice were completely mistaken because with their moderate methods they were incapable of leading the struggle towards swarajya. He felt that a radical orientation of India's political struggle under the aegis of the Congress was a necessary prerequisite, Aurobindo, though blessed with a sharp intellect was highly emotional. Tilak too had a sharp intellect, but seldom got carried away by emotions. His approach to problems was always rational. Aurobindo was a dreamer with the capacity to involve people in his dreams about an ideal world. Tilak knew that a determined effort would have to be made to educate the people politically and make them participate in the freedom struggle. A mass movement at the grassroot level, according to Tilak, was a prerequisite of radical politics. Nevertheless, both regarded swarajya as their common goal and both were eager to co-operate with each other. Tilak was aware of Aurobindo's capacity to touch the chords of the young hearts by arousing them, and urging them to sacrifice their all for a noble cause. With faith in Aurobindo's inspiring personality, Tilak decided to join hands with him to take the political movement on a radical path.

The struggle against the partition had begun when Aurobindo was working as a professor in Baroda. He soon resigned from his teaching job and along with his brother Barindra reached Calcutta. He launched a journal, Vande Mataram, which in no time became very popular with the youth. His powerful pen and wonderful command over the English language helped inspire the youth to action. 'National education' was not just an empty slogan during the anti-partition movement. The leaders of Bengal wanted to practise what they preached. They, therefore, started the National College in Calcutta with Aurobindo Ghosh as its Principal. As an eminent scholar with a knack for teaching English literature, Aurobindo inculcated in his pupils the noble values of life by placing lofty ideals before them. He became a hero for many who became revolutionaries and dedicated their lives to the service of motherland. Tilak, despite his admiration for the rare qualities which Aurobindo possessed, however, did not want the youths to live in a world of dreams. Once some youths in Maharashtra who had joined the 'Abhinav Bharati' — an organisation started by the revolutionary, Veer Savarkar came to meet Tilak to seek his advice on the action to take. They told Tilak that they were prepared to die for their motherland but he, in his characteristic manner, remarked, "It is equally necessary to live and work for the motherland". He asked them whether they had read the writings of Dadabhai Naoroji and told them to first prepare themselves adequately for participating in the struggle. He warned them not to get carried away by emotions as there was no place for adventures or any rash action in a political struggle. He explained his views to Aurobindo too and told him that it was necessary to initially create a mass base for their political movement. In his bid to involve as many people as possible in the struggle against Bengal's partition, Tilak insisted on the implementation of his four-point programme of swadeshi, boycott, national education and swarajya. Though Aurobindo held Tilak in high esteem, he believed that freedom could be won only through revolutionary methods. He thought that the four-point programme, though a step ahead of the plans of the moderates, was not a bold move. Tilak, on the other hand, was confident of building up a mass base through his programme. This led to a difference of opinion between them though Tilak was aware that he could not afford to ignore Aurobindo's charismatic personality. Therefore, despite the differences in approach, he maintained a cordial relationship with Aurobindo and often sought his co-operation. He decided to utilise Aurobindo's extraordinary abilities not merely for the anti-partition movement, but for the realisation of his goal of swarajya.

It was due to the three leaders — Lal, Bal and Pal — that the four-point programme became popular during the anti-partition agitation. Lala Lajpat Rai observed, "Swadeshi is the road to freedom; only then can we become self-reliant. We shall have to mobilise man power and other resources in India. We shall have to collect capital, then only can we make the swadeshi movement a success in the interest of our country". While advocating boycott, Tilak and Bipin Chandra Pal said that boycott was just the first step and that the movement should culminate in the boycott of the British government. In Bengal, the people in a demonstration of unity collected all cloth manufactured in Manchester as also clothes made out of British cloth, and made a bonfire of them. This act created a wave of enthusiasm among the youth who realised the symbolic significance of burning foreign cloth. They knew that this marked the beginning of the process of destroying British rule in India.

Tilak, Lajpat Rai and Bipin Chandra Pal, in order to prevent the anti-partition movement from becoming negative in character, therefore, while encouraging the boycott of British goods, gave an impetus to the swadeshi movement by persuading resourceful businessmen to start mills for weaving cloth indigenously apart from factories for manufacturing soap and matchboxes. National banks were set up for collecting the capital required for establishing different industries. In the institutions founded for imparting national education, arrangements were made for providing technical education.

Concerted efforts were made to promote among the youth the need for a healthy physique, intellectual curiosity and spirit of patriotism. A number of young men became teachers in such schools and colleges to make the national education programme a success.

Tilak felt it necessary to involve people of all the states in his four-point programme.

He wrote editorials in the Kesari on swadeshi and boycott and appealed to the people to participate wholeheartedly in the programme. At Pandharpur, devotees of God Panduranga had gathered in large numbers on the day of Ekadashi (11th day in the first fortnight) in the month of Kartik. Tilak decided to utilise the occasion for exhibiting swadeshi goods and hold a meeting of those involved with the swadeshi movement. In such programmes, Tilak did not allow his political differences to come to the fore. He invited even liberal leaders and both Gokhale and Tilak were present at the meeting at Pandharpur. In Bombay, Tilak collected a number of industrialists and businessmen and started the Swadeshi Co-operative Stores Ltd., which evoked an enthusiastic response from all sections of the society. For this purpose, he collected a fund of two and a half lakh rupees from eminent persons like Tata, Dwarkadas Dharamsi, Khatau Makanji and others.

The swadeshi movement was instrumental in imparting impetus to some enterprises which had been started before the anti-partition movement. He launched the paisa fund in Maharashtra, under which one piece was collected from every person for starting some business. Many young men came forward to collect for the fund and the money thus collected was utilised for setting up a glass factory at Talegaon in Puna district.

In 1905, at the venue of the Banaras session of the Congress, an exhibition of swadeshi goods was organised. In the Banaras session of the Indian National Congress, the movement for national education and the idea of establishing the Banaras Hindu University were mooted. Pandit Madan Mohan Malaviya placed before the delegates his concept of founding a Hindu university and this found strong support from Tilak. The proposed university received donations to the tune of nine lakhs rupees. At this juncture, the Nagari Pracharini Sabha organised a meeting which was addressed by Tilak. In his speech, Tilak pleaded for adoption of the Devnagari script all over India. He realised that it could not be done immediately particularly in south India, so he suggested that a beginning could be made by printing textbooks for primary schools in the said script.

The movement for national education soon gained momentum. In the 1906 Congress session at Calcutta, it was announced that the Rashtriya Shiksha Mandal which had already started a school and college, would start giving degrees to its students. In Puna, a new institution, the Maharashtra Vidya Prasarak, was established and under its auspices the Samartha Vidyalaya was started at Talegaon. Prof. Vijaypurkar, who drew inspiration from Tilak, threw himself headlong into the national education movement and was appointed Head of the Samartha Vidyalaya. Before taking any action, Tilak always clarified his ideology. He defined national education as education which promotes love for one's nation and in an editorial in the Kesari under the title, 'The Responsibility of Private Institutions in Imparting National Education'; he elucidated his theoretical concept in a convincing manner.

While participating in the movement Tilak did not lose sight of the political issues. He wrote two informative articles on the cotton-yarn industry and the weaving industry. On 12th December

1905, he wrote an editorial in the Kesari repudiating the arguments levelled against the swadeshi movement. In between all this, Tilak never refrained from making a dig at Morley, who had just taken over as Secretary of State for India in the British Cabinet. Morley, a liberal, called himself a disciple of the great liberal thinker John Stuart Mill. Morley had written a book on Compromise. His assumption of office was hailed by the liberals in India as they had great expectations of him. Tilak regarded this trust in Morley as an act of political naivety. Within a short time of assuming office, Morley declared that Bengal had to be partitioned for administrative convenience. Tilak in an editorial entitled, 'Bluff has been Called Off" wrote that it was a good thing that Morley had shown his true colours and dealt a blow to the foolish hopes harboured by moderates. Tilak's editorial on Morley under the title, 'A Philosopher or a Diplomat' was one of the finest pieces of political criticism. Tilak argued that Morley might be a liberal for England's internal affairs, but vis-a-vis India, he was in no way different from any other imperialist ruler. He then listed instances of Morley's hypocrisy by proving how, while acting as a diplomat, he was doing his best to protect and promote the interests of the British Empire under the garb of liberalism. Tilak's arguments were logical and convincing. He strongly criticised Gokhale and other moderates for expecting concessions from Morley.

In 1905, Prof. Gopal Krishna Gokhale presided over the session of the Indian National Congress at Banaras. Tilak had earlier praised Gokhale for the work done by him in England; he also favoured Gokhale's nomination for presidentship of the Congress. In his presidential speech, Gokhale severely criticised the autocratic rule of Curzon and made a plea for swadeshi. In this session, Tilak put forth a resolution regarding famine, poverty, land revenue and the economic survey of India. While moving his resolution, he drew a devastating picture of India's poverty and argued that it was the responsibility of the government to remove poverty by conducting a survey of representative villages to identify the causes of poverty before suggesting ways of removing it. Tilak believed that emphasis on economic issues and the demand for removal of poverty would give a fillip to the struggle for swarajya. He feared that a weak-kneed policy of the moderates would result in destroying the tempo of the anti-partition movement. He advocated that the reins of the Congress should be given to the hands of radical leaders. He and his colleagues started working towards bringing about a change in leadership. Gokhale, Pherozeshah Mehta and moderate leaders considered it undesirable to give a radical orientation to the swarajya movement. Gokhale and his colleagues frowned on Tilak and his radical associates. They feared that the common man's participation in the fight for swarajya might give the movement a wrong and undesirable turn. The moderates wanted India's case to be pleaded only by a handful of intellectuals who could put forth their views in a persuasive manner to which the British ruler might respond favourably and hence grant political rights to the Indians. The moderates had failed to understand the character of the British Empire whose sole aim was to exploit colonial nations economically. They had implicit faith in the British sense of justice. Tilak, on the other hand, had correctly gauged the character of the British Empire and was convinced that only political pressure on the British rulers could bring about fulfilment of India's demands. Thus, even though the moderates and the radicals had the same goal of swarajya, there was a sharp difference in their approach to realising the goal. A conflict between the moderates and the radicals became inevitable. It was a conflict regarding the leadership of the political movement in India. Though it was evident as to who would control the Indian National Congress and carry on the political movement, Gokhale, Pherozeshah Mehta and others did not want to be led by Tilak, and therefore decided to keep the reins of the Congress in their own hands.

After the Banaras session, it was decided to hold the next session of the Congress at Calcutta. The radicals, led by Bipin Chandra Pal and Tilak wanted to select a new president for the Congress to impart momentum to the struggle. On the other hand, Gokhale and the moderates desired that someone who toed the moderate line of action should be made the leader. Tilak proposed the name of Lala Lajpat Rai for the presidentship, while Bipin Chandra Pal and other Bengali leaders proposed the name of Tilak. Gokhale and his colleagues were opposed both to Tilak and Lala Lajpat Rai.

However, Gokhale realising that the political atmosphere in Bengal was favourable to the radicals, decided to come to a compromise and suggested the name of Dadabhai Naoroji, the grand old man of Indian politics, for the presidentship. In a way, this was a moral victory for the radicals. Dadabhai Naoroji was not just the grand old man; he was very clear in his thinking and forthright in his opinions. His deep study of the political and economic problems, his integrity and upright behaviour and, above all, dedication to the service of the country, inspired great respect among the Indians.

Thus, Dadabhai Naoroji was unanimously chosen president of the Indian National Congress. Immediately after this Tilak wrote an editorial in the Kesari under the title, 'What would be the Advice of Dadabhai?' In this editorial, Tilak gave a correct evaluation of Dadabhai's contribution to India's struggle. Tilak wrote: "Alexander, Muhammad Gori, Taimurlane and Nadir Shah invaded India and looted and plundered its wealth but the economic exploitation of India by the British is far more harmful to us. The British rulers, while establishing peace in India, have impoverished and sucked our blood. Due to British rule, moral degradation has set in among us and our abilities in different fields have been thwarted.

To Dadabhai Naoroji goes the credit for making us and also the world conscious of all this. He has substantiated his thesis on India's exploitation by the British Empire with relevant facts and statistical data. Dadabhai was the first leader to state emphatically that British rule would ruin India completely. He made convincing arguments while making this serious observation.

Tilak paid glowing tributes to Dadabhai's contribution as member of the British Parliament and quoted the following statement of Dadabhai: 'It is not enough to put a check on the economic exploitation of India by the British. It is absolutely necessary that Indians should be given the rights of swarajya.' Tilak reiterated in the end that Dadabhai Naoroji, who had given expression to such radical thoughts, was bound to support the political movement started by the radicals. Tilak's prognostications came true. Dadabhai Naoroji in his presidential address stated: "We do not ask for any concessions or favours. We want justice. To state this in brief, we want self-government, i.e. swarajya". Dadabhai Naoroji was the first leader to utter the word swarajya from the platform of the Congress party and give sanctity to it. Thus, came to be sown the first seeds of swarajya in the minds of the Indians. On 8th January 1907, Tilak through the Kesari commented on what had taken place in the Calcutta session of the Congress. He gave extracts from Dadabhai Naoroji's address and wrote: "The ideal of the Indian National Congress is to get swarajya. The duty of the Congress is to work for achieving this goal. This has been proved and established in an unequivocal manner in the Calcutta session of the Congress".

Different resolutions were moved at the Calcutta session and there were heated debates on them. Tilak, though an ardent advocate of the radical line of action, did not stretch the differences too far as it could have led to a split in the Congress. However, he did not compromise on his principles. The resolution on boycott stated: "Since at present the people of India have no say in the administration, the Congress is of the opinion that the boycott in Bengal was legal and justified". He expressed satisfaction over the sanction given to the boycott by the Congress. In the resolution on swadeshi, it was stated that the programme would be undertaken even if it was to be at the cost of some sacrifice. Tilak pointed out how Pherozeshah Mehta's views on swadeshi were wrong and how the sacrifices made by the people while accepting the creed of swadeshi had given a new orientation to the country. There was no difference of opinion on the resolution regarding national education. In brief, the Congress set its seal of approval on Tilak's four-point programme.

Dadabhai Naoroji's speech and the tenor of the resolution was a victory for the radical leaders — Lal, Bal and Pal. However, the Congress organisation continued to be dominated by the moderates. Tilak, therefore, felt it necessary to start a wing within the Congress which would work towards radicalising the programme of the party. His suggestion was accepted by other radicals and the younger section of the Congress. Tilak constituted a new party which would function under the aegis of the Congress. Some leaders described it as a 'ginger group' while some journalists dubbed it as a 'pressure group'.

After the Calcutta Congress, in a public meeting presided over by Bipin Chandra Pal, Tilak delivered a speech on 'The

Tenets of the New Party.' He said, "Self-government is our goal. What the new party wants you to do is to realise the fact that your future rests entirely in your own hands. If you mean to be free, you can be free; if you do not wish to be free, you will fall and remain forever fallen... You need not use arms; but have you not the power of active resistance, have you not the power of self-denial and self-abstinence so as to prevent this foreign government to rule over you? This is boycott, and this is what is meant when we say, 'Boycott is a political weapon'. We shall not give them assistance to collect revenue and sit peacefully. We shall not fight wars outside India with Indian blood and money. We shall have our own courts, and when the time comes, we shall refuse to pay taxes. Can you not do this with your combined efforts? If you can, then you are free from tomorrow".

In politics, politicians, though vanquished, continue to show dissent. Prof. Gokhale had to beat a retreat at the Calcutta session of the Congress, but he did not accept defeat.

He decided to put forth his point of view before the people and undertook extensive tours of important cities. Tilak wrote articles in the Kesari refuting Gokhale's views. In the editorial entitled, 'The Confusion of Hon'ble Gokhale', Tilak specifically pointed to the contradictions in his stand. Tilak began his article by appreciating Gokhale's efforts to make India progress but followed it by criticising his self-contradictory stand when Gokhale started opposing the boycott movement which he had initially favoured. Tilak felt that this contradiction was due to Gokhale's moderate stand in politics.

Boycott was a powerful weapon which Gokhale was not willing to use against the British. Tilak praised Gokhale for starting the Servants of India Society for training young men who would dedicate their lives to the service of India. At the same time, he pointed to Gokhale's misplaced support to government service because it was in strong contradiction to the ideals of the Servants of India Society. In an editorial published on 19th February 1907, Tilak exposed the weak links in the ideological stand taken by Gokhale and profusely quoted from the latter's speeches. The title of the editorial was, 'It is good that he has spoken'. Tilak remarked that Gokhale's views centred around two assumptions, viz. 'We should not oppose this government because we cannot do without it' and that private schools should help the government in the education programme and that there was 'no point in opposing the government'. Tilak wanted universal education but did not approve of education merely to serve the British administration. He feared that Gokhale's moderate approach would render his efforts futile and take the edge off the political movement in India.

The editorial which Tilak wrote on 5th March 1907 was especially significant as it threw light on his ideological stand. In another editorial entitled, 'Constitutional or Legal', Tilak's criticism of Gokhale was far from personal. The two leaders differed sharply in their views and Tilak strongly opposed Gokhale's statement that "the political movement in India should be constitutional". He felt that the political movement could be constitutional only in those countries where the people had won a charter of their rights.

He observed that in countries where the ruler enjoys unlimited powers, a political movement cannot be considered constitutional. Tilak wrote: "When people in England say that there is constitutional monarchy in their country, it means that the people through their movement have curbed the authority of the monarch and won political rights for themselves. In countries where the powers of the King are unlimited and where people have no political rights, the Constitution does not exist.

In England, people have won their rights through political movements and have gone to the length of deposing their monarchs and even beheading one of them. In England, the constitutional rights of the Parliament and those of the King are clearly demarcated. But, a Constitution does not exist in India; the powers of the British Parliament and those of the King Emperor vis-a-vis the Indian people are unlimited. This means that in India, the government does not function in accordance with the wishes of the people. In other words, the government in India is unconstitutional". Tilak clarified that India was administered according to the laws formulated by the British government and under these circumstances, the question whether our movement is constitutional or unconstitutional does not arise. The only question that remains is whether the movement is legal or illegal. He further added: "At present we cannot make the laws for ourselves. Therefore, even if our efforts are in consonance with the natural rights of the people and the historical process, and have a moral and ethical basis, the British rulers alone decide whether they are legal or illegal. It is probable that our legitimate efforts made for a right cause might be dubbed as illegal. In such a case, instead of conceding that our efforts are illegal, we should state that the laws are tyrannical". In the end Tilak concluded: "We must only see that our efforts are just moral and are made in order to achieve progress. We need not bother whether our efforts conform to the laws made by the government or whether they transcend the limits imposed by law. After all laws in India are made and interpreted by an alien government. It is true that punishment should be given for breaking a law, but if the law is unjust we must defy it and suffer punishment for our action because there can be no other alternative when the law is divorced from morality".

The culmination of Tilak's ideal was seen in the Satyagraha movement in which Gandhiji openly asked the people to flout the laws made by the British because they were divorced from morality.

Lord Curzon, the autocratic Viceroy who was responsible for partitioning Bengal, had to resign because of his differences with the commander-in-chief. However, the sufferings of the people did not end with Curzon's resignation. After the partition of Bengal, Fuller was appointed Lieutenant-Governor of East Bengal. Fuller was a tyrant who tried to crush the movement against Bengal's partition through repressive measures.

While fomenting trouble between the Hindus and the Muslims, he showed partiality towards the Muslims as became obvious through his perverse remark, "Muslims are my favourite mistress". Meanwhile a political conference was called at Barisal, where a Muslim leader presided. Fuller was enraged at this and he insulted leaders like Surendranath Banerjee. A brutal lathi-charge was made on students who took out a peaceful procession, shouting "Vande Mataram". He imposed a ban on the use of Vande Mataram but many students defied the ban and though mercilessly flogged, suffered the beating bravely. Bankim Chandra, the pioneer of modern Bengali literature, had in his novel Anand Math, composed the words for the song Vande Mataram. Vande Mataram got recognition not because of its poetic excellence, but because many young people had to suffer imprisonment for singing it. As a result of this, Vande Mataram came to be regarded as a holy song and became the national anthem. It became the slogan of the freedom fighters. The words Vande Mataram inspired the youths to make the supreme sacrifice of their lives.

After a long and arduous struggle by the people of India and of Bengal in particular, the British government revoked the decision to partition Bengal. This marked a victory for the mass movement organised by Lal, Bal and Pal. The success of this movement was first major step on the path to swarajya.

6

Significant Speeches

Swaraj is My Birthright, I Will Have It

The Surat fiasco made it clear that the Moderates were not in a mood to yield to the other party an inch of land in which to plant extremism. They knew that once planted, it would grow. They were not prepared for any compromise, but Tilak continued to make offers and gestures of a reunion. He was ridiculed, abused and even called a traitor, and yet he stretched out his hand in friendship. After the abandonment of the Congress at Surat, a Moderate-sponsored public meeting condemned 'Tilak's behaviour'.

The Moderate press indulged in wild abuses: "Tilak had been feeding the flames which have burnt the Congress to ashes. He is not a patriot, but a traitor to the country, and has blackened himself. May God save us from such patriots". This is typical of many leading articles in the Moderate press; they seemed to vie with each other in abusing Tilak. He ignored them, and in a reasoned article in the Kesari pleaded with the Moderates to accommodate the Extremists. He said: "It is a mistake to suppose that a difference of opinion as to ultimate ideals should prevent Indians from co-operating with one another, for gaining a common end.

We see that Radicals, Socialists, Democrats and others, though labouring for widely different ideals, are able to co-operate with one another in Parliament in advancing the interests of their country as a whole. With this example before our eyes, does it not betoken a lack of liberality to insist that the representatives of a certain school of Indian politicians should alone be admitted to the National Congress? The duty that lies before our politicians is not to seek to eradicate all differences of opinion, but to secure the co-operation of men holding divergent views for the accomplishment of comments. Whatever our differences may be about the ideals, we Moderates and Extremists, should unite in carrying on the work of the National Congress. The rise of a new party necessarily produces friction with the old, but it is the duty of wise men not to make much of this friction but to carry on national work in co-operation with the new party".

The Moderates did not relent. The Extremists were not prepared to recede; they, in fact, had decided to go ahead with their programme with redoubled vigour. The whole of Maharashtra had gone extremist, and a considerable part of political Bengal was in favour of the politics of Tilak and Aurobindo.

A few months after Surat, both the provinces demonstrated their faith in the extremist leadership. Maharashtra did it repeatedly.

Soon after his return from Surat, Tilak sent round his lieutenants all over the district of Puna to establish Taluka associations. This was the first attempt of its kind in the history of Maharashtra; there were no political organisations in the countryside, and having established a network of them, Tilak convened the first Puna District Conference which held its lively sittings for three days. All those resolutions over which a battle was fought at Surat were passed here. Tilak moved the resolution on National Education, and in the course of his speech said: "The question of national education is peculiar to India as being a country in which the interests of the rulers and the ruled are conflicting. The name of Swarajya is forbidden in the schools set up by the Government. Under the name of discipline, everything likely to teach boys about national salvation is denied to them, both in Government and aided schools. Textbooks in other countries taught that it was glory to die for one's nation; it was not so in the case of textbooks in India".

At the district conference also, a Moderate wished to substitute "boycott of foreign goods" for "Boycott Movement", in the resolution on the Swadeshi and boycott movement; his amendment was defeated by an overwhelming majority.

One of the fourteen resolutions adopted at the conference appealed to the leaders of various parties to sink their differences and restore unity in the Congress. It was done at the instance of Tilak who had, on the eve of the conference, again expressed, through the columns of the Kesari, a pious hope of unity: "It is the fear of the Extremists that has induced Government to coquette with the Moderates and not any love for the latter. If at such a juncture Government grant any rights to the people simply with a view to please the Moderates, the Extremists will not grudge to accept them, for they will be for the good of the country as a whole. But at the same time the Moderates should take care to remember that it was the activity of the Extremists that ultimately secured the rights and should not therefore break away from them".

After the district conference, Tilak proceeded to seek the approval of the Bombay Provincial Conference to his political programme. The year's provincial conference was held at Dhulia in the last week of April, under the presidentship of a Rao Bahadur G. V. Joshi. Surprisingly enough, he showed the enthusiasm of an extremist. When Tilak entered the pandal a vociferous reception was accorded to him and, by loud gestures, his victory was assured. The unwholesome treatment he received at Surat sent up a wave of enthusiasm for him in Maharashtra, and many people, who had kept themselves away from politics, came under his banner. There was aroused an overflowing zeal for Swadeshi.

Thus, the Dhulia Conference promised to be a brilliant success for Tilak. The speech he made there was received with thunderous applause. He said: "It is now over 90 years that the British have been ruling over us and the time has, therefore, arrived to consider whether we are now better off than formerly. It is a fact that we have been reduced to poverty under the British rule. How has this poverty entered our homes? Formerly, our rulers, both Hindus and Muslims, used to look to the welfare of their subjects. If a ruler does not care for his subjects, how can he be a sovereign? For what are we to pay him taxes? What right has he to expect them from us? The bureaucrats who take our money without caring for us are only taking wages of inequity. The first days of the British rule dazzled us by its glamour, but we have now come to see its deceptiveness. The Government has granted us liberty to drink, but other liberties we do not enjoy. The present Government of India is a mighty government but, if our own people who carry out its behests refuse to help it, it will not be able to go on. If a rule becomes unbearable, it is everyone's duty to obstruct its operation".

Continuing he said: "He who has set his face towards the temple of the Goddess of Independence will never approve of independence under British suzerainty. A powerful bureaucracy is oppressing and impoverishing the people. The Government desires to provide for the Whites alone; that was not the policy of the Muslim rulers. The people, it is true, should not be guilty of treason to their King, but is it proper for the King to turn traitor to his own subjects? The King who does so, forfeits his authority. We are fighting amongst ourselves as Moderates and Extremists, but they are prepared to throw both of us overboard. Therefore, let us unite and give them a bit of our mind. Let us call upon them to account for the crores of rupees, they take from us. Let us put a check upon the King who is robbing us with both hands".

Tilak got the reception committee of the Conference and the Conference itself to adopt a resolution demanding full autonomous status for India. A delegate of moderate leanings moved an amendment which would have had the effect of excluding from the Congress those whose avowed aim was the attainment of an autonomous status unfettered by English rule. The amendment got only three votes and was rejected.

The entire-moderate press was shocked by the resolution which virtually aimed at terminating the British rule, and yelled out angry comments: "Now that the proceedings of the so-called Provincial Conference are before the public", one paper wrote, "it is easy to see how Mr. Tilak's professions of his desire to work in a united Congress cannot be relied upon.

Is a reunited Congress possible on the basis of such slippery principles and methods?" Another paper suggested: "From its inception, it has been the aim of the Congress to carry on its work by constitutional means, and for such a body to entertain other ideals is as good as courting the charge of treason.

Some of those who have been thinking of attaining Swaraj, untrammelled by British rule, have been misled into imitating the methods of anarchists. These people can never be received into its fold by the Congress". The moderate press did not even like the Conference resolutions on swadeshi, national education, etc. It characterised as 'deplorable' president Joshi's address in which he attributed the Surat fiasco to the failure of the Moderates to see the signs of the times.

Again, as if to avenge Surat a mammoth public meeting was held at Dhulia in honour of Tilak. The organisers did not allow the police to loiter in the compound. In a long speech, Tilak described the condition of India and her peasantry under the British rule. After the showdown, the Nationalists formed themselves into an association called the Surat Nationalists Association. The Moderates having gone on a year's retirement, the Nationalists carried on their work from day to day. They held public meetings on every Sunday and spoke on Swadeshi and Swaraj.

As if the whole burden of preparing the country for Swaraj, which he had desired the Congress to carry, had been shifted to his shoulders, Tilak knew no rest after Surat. Single-handed, he launched a many-sided struggle, and kindled the fire of patriotism in every nook and corner of the Bombay Presidency. He made whirlwind tours, collected money for starting a Marathi daily (Rashtramat), and to make self-supporting the Samaratha Vidyalaya which had been started to impart national education of his conception. In the numerous speeches he made, he exhorted the people to work for Swaraj and be ready for suffering. That was the subject of his speech at the Shivaji celebrations also. "We are at present clamouring for Swarajya", he said, "and therefore the Shivaji festival is the most fitting one for us to celebrate. If Shivaji was able to establish Swarajya two centuries ago, we too may expect to achieve it some day. Swarajya belongs to us by birthright. The Moderates can be compared to Shivaji's father Sahuji, who always used to advise his son not to take up arms against the mighty Muslim monarchies of the Deccan. But Shivaji, who can be compared to the Extremists of the present day, gave a new turn to events. We are masters of our fortunes and can govern them if we only make up our minds to do so. Swarajya is not far off from us. It will come to us the moment we learn to stand on our own legs".

At every meeting, at every function, that he attended, he gave this slogan: "Swarajya is my birthright; I will have it".

Historic 21-hour Speech

When the trial opened on July 13, the Advocate-General proposed, on behalf of the prosecution, that cases in respect of the two articles, which constituted two separate charges, might be tried together; it would be more convenient.

Tilak objected to the amalgamation both on the grounds of law and of prejudice which might be caused to him by the confusion in his own mind as well as in the minds of the jury.

But Davar disagreed with him. "It is not fair", he said, "that the accused should have the charge hanging over him". He, therefore, ordered the two charges to be tried at the same trial.

Now, the proceedings began with a brief address for the prosecution—it was so brief that Tilak had to point out that "in the opening address for the prosecution nothing was said, and I do not know specifically the points upon which I have to reply". Apparently, the prosecution cleverly reserved the points for the second address which the Advocate-General was to make after Tilak had addressed the court. Tilak had hoped that at that stage he would only put in documents on which he was to build up his arguments, and make his reply after listening to the arguments of the Advocate-General against him. And when he pointed this out, the Advocate-General circumvented him saying, "I do not want to weary the jury".

This answer was a subterfuge, for after Tilak's address, the Advocate-General did "weary" the jury with a long speech.

His stand was upheld by the judge also who told Tilak: "I warned you yesterday that if you put in documents, you would lose the right of reply. The Advocate-General is not entitled to anything more." Tilak, therefore, had to make his speech without knowing what the prosecution had to say against him.

He dispensed with the services of his lawyers, and himself addressed the jury for 21 hours; it was a record-breaking speech.

At the outset, Tilak sounded a note of warning that the original articles had got perverted in the translation, and that any insinuations based upon the translation "would be likely to be unsafe. It is unsafe, nay dangerous, to adjudge me guilty merely because the words, as conceived by you from the wrong translations, are, in your opinion, calculated to produce feelings of hatred and contempt in a community of which probably you know nothing". (Seven of the jurymen were Europeans.)

Tilak questioned the method by which justice was sought to be administered. That was to tell the jury to read the article, judge its effect as a whole, and give their verdict. It was unsafe, Tilak contended to draw any inference by reading an article alone. That doctrine was now much discredited in England, and the English juries drew their own conclusions not merely from the character of the writing itself, but from all the surrounding circumstances. The law of sedition being the same in England as in India, Tilak pointed out, the jury would be failing in their duty if they left the surrounding circumstances out of their consideration.

The question was whether Tilak really offended against Section 124-A, which said: "Whoever by words either spoken or written or by visible representation or otherwise brings or attempts to bring into hatred or contempt, or excites or attempts to excite disaffection towards His Majesty or Government established by Law in British India, shall be punishable.

Tilak contended that there was no evidence adduced before the court that any excitement had been caused by the articles in question, and therefore the case did not come within the first part of the section; His Majesty or the Government was not brought into contempt or hatred nor was disaffection excited. Now the question was whether an attempt was made towards that end. Tilak said: "Attempt is actually an offence minus the final act of crime. When it fails it is only an attempt at the crime. There must be everything necessary to make it an offence except success under the particular circumstances. It must be shown that if I have failed in this attempt, it was from circumstances beyond my control. Now that kind of evidence has not been put before you. The mere fact that a certain article is published will not make it an attempt when attempt is so defined. Attempt definitely means that a man intends to do something; the act must be present in his mind.

This has been stated by Justice Stephens in his History of the Criminal Law of England, Vol. II. Publication is brought in to show intention, but I maintain that mere publication cannot prove any intention. When there are other circumstances which are shown to exist, then it is the bounden duty of the jury to take all the circumstances into consideration and then to decide whether certain intention was in the mind of the accused or not. It is the duty of the prosecution to prove intention. The burden of proving all this is thrown upon the defence. The prosecution does not take into consideration the fact that this article was written in the heat of controversy, that this article was intended as a piece of advice, and that it is written in reply to certain criticisms already published. But the prosecution says, It is not any business of ours to enquire into these circumstances. We only place the article before you and if the accused does not reply, the best course for you is to return a verdict of guilty'".

Tilak then proceeded to narrate the circumstances under which the articles were written, but prefaced his narrative by the remark that the jury should be able to understand those circumstances, and must therefore be selected from the people.

The jury in this case had not that advantage. Tilak pointed out another disadvantage: "In England, if one man out of the twelve disagrees, the jury is discharged, and another jury is empanelled; and if this happens two or three times, the man is ultimately acquitted". In India, opinion of the majority was considered enough to secure conviction.

"We often misunderstand each other, Tilak said. "If I draw an inference as to your intention without knowing the state of your society, it is not likely to be correct. In the same way if you wish to draw an inference from the Marathi writing as to the effect it would produce on the Marathi-knowing community, you have to consider the feelings and the general state of that community. Without doing that you cannot say whether the writing will excite any particular feelings or not.

The prosecution ought to have produced evidence before you to show what the state of the Marathi-speaking people is and how are they likely to be affected,... I am not here to ask you any grace. I am prepared to stand by the consequences of my act. There is no question about it. I have written the articles believing it my duty to write in the interest of the community. It was both in the interest of the people and the Government that this view should be placed before them. If you were placed in my position and if you had been impelled by my circumstances to take up the defence of your community, what would you have done? You must place yourselves in my position and then judge of my motives and my intention.

There must be a distinct criminal intention to justify a verdict of wicked intention. This intention cannot be inferred from merely the fact of publication, but from surrounding circumstances; and between these two lies the liberty of the press".

Tilak invoked a number of English judgements in his support, and contended that if the law was interpreted in the same way as they did, he was innocent. "Today I am in the dock", he told the jury, "for opinions which I have promulgated. If you want reform, you might be in the dock tomorrow. It is not seditious to find fault with Government or to advocate the reformation of administration". He claimed that it was his right to fight for the liberty of his people, for a change in the Constitution, for a reform of Government, and therefore expected a verdict of 'not guilty'. By writing on the cult of the bomb, he discharged a duty he owed to the people:

> "Khudiram Bose had just been sentenced; and I had to express myself on the subject; that was my duty, whether the times were excited or peaceful; and if the times are times of unrest, it becomes the duty of a newspaper man to impress upon the Government the causes of that unrest. It is a very hard duty—a very thankless duty and sometimes a very risky duty.

> If the newspaper is to go on for the benefit of the people and the interest of the Government, you cannot allow any other consideration to interfere with your duty. A critic may find fault, but to question the writer's motive is extremely ungenerous".

What exactly were the surrounding circumstances when he sat down to write his article on the bomb? Anglo-Indian papers like the Pioneer, Englishman, The Times of India, had repeatedly suggested in their columns that the bombs were the outcome of the agitation of Congressmen, and that Government should put a stop to the Congress and everything of the kind. The London Times carried on the same campaign in England. And Tilak asked the jury: "Now, gentlemen of the jury, if you were the representatives of your community as I am of mine, what would you have done under these circumstances? Evidently you would have done what I did". What, therefore, Tilak did was only to give expression to public feeling in order to inform the Government. "That is my Defence and you have to judge of it from that point of view.

If you want to stop bombs now it will not do to put down the Congress agitation; but you ought to put down the bureaucracy first or reform it". He claimed the same liberty for the Indian press as was enjoyed by the Anglo-Indian press.

The Pioneer, Englishman, The Times of India, etc. made a general attack on Indians, and mentioned Tilak by name. "So what ground is there to suppose", Tilak asked, "that this is not a reply to the Pioneer? That I am not entitled to convey the view of the Marathi-speaking population? Of course there are some Indians on the side of the bureaucratic press just as there are Conservatives and Liberals in England. Would you hold anybody seditious under Section 124-A, for writing as I have done in England? There are two parties in England, and it is the duty of each party to represent its own views.

If the vernacular press should continue to exist, it should exist only for this. I was bound to criticise the abuse of the Pioneer and to express my views couched in decisive terms. I do not speak here with the object of making you converts to my views, but when one party goes on like that and abuses the other, it challenges the other party".

Tilak then brought home to the court how Government exercised discrimination in favour of the Anglo-Indian press:

"I know that some of you will say, 'Yes the Pioneer has said so and so, why don't you file a suit?' If we want to charge the Pioneer, we must file a complaint under Section 153-A.

But to do so we must obtain the sanction of the Government.

The Government must sanction the prosecution, but it is not likely to give that sanction. A question was asked in Parliament as to whether the Government would prosecute the Pioneer for making certain statements; no reply was given.

The questioner, O'Grady, made a similar demand in respect of some other Anglo-Indian papers. I do not want them to be prosecuted. I do not wish that any other editor should be in the same predicament as I am today. I do not wish it even for my enemies. I do not want to be vindictive, but I think it is an instance of the Government's partiality towards Anglo-Indian papers.

"I might mention the case of Captain Hearsay who was libelled by the Pioneer. He did not waste any time in filing a suit. He went to the office and horsewhipped the editor. That is how you, gentlemen of the jury, would proceed if insulted like that. The people of the Punjab once requested the Government to prosecute the Civil and Military Gazette for certain libellous statements made against them, but the Government refused to do so. If the Government believes that those papers are actuated by honest motives, though their language may be very strong, how can they believe that this article written in much milder language by me is seditious? It is only a reply to the advice tendered by the Anglo-Indian papers to the Government. As a matter of fact, we are entitled to greater latitude than the Pioneer since the Penal Code says that what is done in self-defence is not an offence. That refers to property and I maintain that property includes reputation.

We have referred to the article in the Pioneer in very mild terms; we have replied with arguments only. Are we to allow the Pioneer to go on abusing the mass of our readers and of the people in this country? In that case, it would be much better to abolish the vernacular press, and leave the Pioneer in the field alone. It is my duty to reply to such vilification".

Here are some samples of the kind of writing in Anglo-Indian papers which Tilak produced before the court. After giving a coloured version of what were the views of the Moderates and the Extremists, the Pioneer wrote in its issue dated May 7, 1908: "Below the Extremist come the lecturer and the vernacular editor, the latter of whom has been steadily at his work for the last thirty years and more, the former a new development, and both having for their aim the direct inflammation of the minds of the people.... Who can wonder that in the last grade come the bomb-maker and the wretched, infatuated student whom he gets to do the work? They are the logical outcome of the whole movement as it stands. The nexus from top to bottom is complete".

The Englishman published a letter in which the writer said:

> "Were a few of these worthy agitators flogged in public by the town sweepers and their presses confiscated, much of the glamour of the righteousness of their agitation for the people would be destroyed and their dupes would see them as they are, and not in the kaleidoscopic light which they endeavour to attract to themselves".

The Asian directly suggested shooting of Indians: "Mr. Kingsford has a great opportunity and we hope he is a fairly decent shot at short range. We recommend to his notice a Mauser pistol with the nick filed off the nose of the bullets or a Colt's automatic which carries a heavy soft bullet and is a hard hitting and punishing weapon. We hope Mr. Kingsford will manage to secure a big bag and we envy him his opportunity. He will be more than justified in letting daylight into every strange native approaching his house or his person, and for his own sake we trust he will learn to shoot fairly straight without taking his weapon out of his coat pocket".

The Times of India charged the 'native' press and 'well-known nationalist speakers' with the responsibility of working "ferments in the yeasty brains".

The law did not discriminate between the 'native' and the Anglo-Indian papers, but apparently the Government allowed the latter freedom to excite Europeans against Indians and their agitation and aspirations. Tilak said that whatever he wrote in his paper was in self-defence in answer to the broadside of the Anglo-Indian press. His answer was intended to be informative and helpful to the Government in understanding the situation as it obtained at the time. He did not want the same privilege as the Anglo-Indian papers possessed, to abuse his opponents. He owed a duty, in the circumstances created by the Anglo-Indian press, to his people and to the Government which he discharged with all the restraint at his command. On the spur of the moment, he said, he might have made wrong choice of words here and there, as generally happened in newspaper writing, but his motive and intention were pure.

He asked the jury to understand the distinction between the bureaucracy and Government, "Bureaucracy is not the Government. To criticise the bureaucracy is not bringing into contempt or hatred the Government established by law in this country. Every writer in India has made a distinction between Government and the administration; it is now recognised that to contend for the right of self-government (as ruled in ILR 34 Calcutta) is not seditious. How can you demand a share in the administration unless you can show that the present administration has some defects? If you cannot find any defects you have no claim for reformation. It may be unpleasant to the bureaucracy, but there is nothing in it which brings contempt or hatred upon Government—I mean Government in the abstract".

Tilak refuted the suggestion that he welcomed the cult of bomb, and drew attention of the jury to his earlier writings in which he had clearly said that bomb-throwing was not the method of obtaining Swarajya; that it was not a logical method; that it was not sanctioned by morality. What, however, he emphasised was that outrageous conduct was one of the effects of a bad system of administration, and the remedy was to reform it, and not to tyrannise the people, as had been suggested by the Anglo-Indian press. Tilak's position was that he condemned the outrages, but he condemned the repressive measures also; he could not be taken to task for the latter.

That he claimed as his right. What he had written in his articles, Tilak showed by referring to a large number of writings and speeches, had many times been said by eminent Englishmen themselves and by Members of Parliament. For instance, Tilak had said in one of the indicted articles that the bomb could not be suppressed by military power; and he read out a similar extract from the writings of Major Evans Bell.

Tilak then came to the translation, and dwelt at length on how, at many places, it gave a wrong meaning, entirely different from the text. For instance, there was a sentence in the text which said it was "calling a rope a snake". It was a very common proverb in Marathi for expressing the idea of mistaking an innocent thing for an offensive one. The sentence was so translated that the prosecution drew the inference that the writer, by the word "snake" referred to the Government.

"That kind of translation", Tilak said, "will make anything seditious". It was for this reason, Tilak reiterated, that he wanted a Marathi-speaking jury which would have been better fitted to judge whether the articles really offended against Sections 124-A and 153-A of the Indian Penal Code.

At this stage, the Judge intervened and pointed out that two of the jurymen were Marathi-knowing, and they would doubtlessly correct their colleagues where the translation gave a different sense from the text. But Tilak again stressed that the words used in the translation seemed to suggest that there was an anxiety to make it look like an actionable article.

The same want of appreciation and understanding and the same anxiety was discernible about the ill-fated card which was found in the search of his house; it contained names of handbooks on modern explosives. The insinuation drawn from it by the prosecution was that Tilak was engaged in manufacturing bombs or other explosives. His answer to the charge was: "After I wrote this article, we wanted to criticise in detail the provisions of the Explosives Act, which had just then been enacted, and especially the definition of an explosive, which according to the Act, includes even ordinary kerosene oil. It was necessary to collect material to see whether the definition given in the Explosives Act tallies with the definition given in the works on explosives. The only reference book we had was the Encyclopaedia Britannica and that was not enough, and naturally the first impulse was to refer to the catalogue to see whether there was any work on explosives".

He also characterised as vague the charge under Section 153-A which said he "promoted or attempted to promote feelings of enmity or hatred between different classes of His Majesty's subjects". That phrase again showed that malicious intention was intended, and again no evidence had been produced to show that the effect of the article would have been or actually was promotion of hatred or enmity. But the vagueness consisted in the fact that "there are no classes mentioned in the article. A whole page of that article is full of criticisms on the Explosives Act and the Press Act. It could only be contended remotely by straining the words that, in criticising the provisions of the Explosives Act, it was intended to incite persons to throw bombs at the other community. I do not think that that meaning could be put upon that article. It is further doubtful whether bureaucracy comes in the definition of this section as a class of His Majesty's subjects".

Judge: "Let me see the charge".

Tilak: "I do not think the classes are mentioned. They are not in the copy I received".

Judge: "I see that the words are as follows: By printed words promoted or attempted to promote feelings of enmity and hatred between classes of His Majesty's subjects.'"

Tilak: "That is all; the classes are not specified".

Judge: "No, the classes are not specified".

Tilak: "So I am labouring under a disadvantage. I cannot say whether it is between Europeans or whether it is between Hindus and Muslims or between Jains and Sikhs. Of course, if I mention some particular class now, the prosecution may take up some other class afterwards. That defect in the charge I would ask your Lordship to make a note of as it places me at great disadvantage in answering it, and the charge".

Judge: "Certainly, if there is any new point you have not touched upon, I will give you a chance of replying".

Tilak: "My Lord and gentlemen of the jury, I have again to thank you for the great patience with which you have heard me".

On Political Situation

The *Mahratta* publishes the following summary of a public lecture recently delivered by Mr. Tilak at Allahabad on "Our present Situation":

"My first accusation against the Government was that it had done nothing to help the indigenous industries of this country to live. On the other hand, it had helped to kill them by the neglect of industrial education..............It is not enough merely to encourage indigenous industries; it is obligatory on the state to preserve them by giving industrial education to the artisan class. This obligation is recognised by the Government in England, but it has been invariably neglected by the Government of India. Indian industries have been ruined in consequence. If we wish to preserve and promote them, we should establish a protective tariff of our own by the boycott of foreign goods. I accept the declaration of Anglo-Indian papers that the British are here by the right of conquest and that they hold India by the might of the sword a Government holding that position is not likely to yield any part of its power by speeches and petitions. There is no example in the whole range of history of a foreign Government, which had established its supremacy by conquest giving complete or a large measure of self-government to the subject people of its own accord. It is not in human nature to do so. The rulers look after their own interest, not that of the ruled. Philanthropy has no part in politics. It is undeniable that the British Government have given peace to the country and a certain amount of liberty. I do not deny that Indians have received some benefits from their rulers.

But they naturally aspire to improve their position. A nation must either progress, or it must fall back. It could not stand still. The desire to advance is perfectly natural, but would Government ever, of its own motion, concede to the people all that they desire ? The positions of the Government as well as the people are natural. The Government do not want that we should proceed beyond a certain point; we want to proceed all along the line. And it is not by petitions that our desires can be fulfilled.

Continuing Mr. Tilak declared that the clear object of the Government was to maintain a dead level in this country. The encouragement given to the backward classes was to bring them up to this level and no higher.

The education imparted in Government schools and colleges was intended to qualify the people for a number of subordinate offices and the administration. The Government wanted clerks, lawyers, judges, engineers and doctors, and the course of instruction stopped there. That is why nationalisation of education was wanted, Mr. Dadabhai Naoroji, the President of the last Congress, had declared that our goal was Self-Government. For years it might be only a subject of academic interest, but that was the end we must keep in view. What would the reform or expansion of Legislative Council avail? In place of half-a-dozen Honourables, we might have a dozen. Their speeches would be published in the Government Gazette, but they would be as powerless as they are now. The bureaucracy had not the slightest intention of giving up any portion of their power, and they were too powerful either for Parliament or the Secretary of State for India. The House of Commons passed a resolution that simultaneous examinations for the Indian Civil Service should be held in England and India but the resolution has remained inoperative because the bureaucracy in India were opposed to it. Even Mr. Morley himself had declared that the Government in India must remain absolute. So far as India was concerned, Liberals and Unionists were alike. In order that there should be a growing organisation and a public opinion growing in power, it was necessary, proceeded the speaker that the educated classes should work among the masses. The masses understood what the Swadeshi movement meant; they did not understand such abstruse principles of politics as that of no taxation without representation. They know that village industries were dying out, and any scheme for the protection and revival of those industries would have their support.

Above all, we must clearly understand that it is not by waiting upon the pleasure of a bureaucratic Government or by reasoned petitions to Parliament that our salvation would be achieved. "There is a saying" said Mr. Tilak in conclusion, " that Heaven helps those who help themselves. Is the British Government greater than God almighty that it will help us if we do not help ourselves?" Repeated rounds of delighted applause greeted this effective sally.

On National Education

(Extract from the Speech delivered in 1908, Barsi- Original in Marathi).

I shall speak here this evening on national education. We are not accustomed to this term, hence it needs a little explanation. To be able to read and write alone is no education. These are simply the means of its attainment. That which gives us a knowledge of the experiences of our ancestors is called education. It may, however, be through books or through anything else. Every business needs education and every man has thus to give it to his children. There is no business indeed which does not require education. Our industries have been taken away by other people, but we do not know it. A potter knows how to shape a pot of China-clay but does not know what this clay is made of; hence his industry is lost. Similarly, is the necessity of religious education. How can a person be proud of his religion if he is ignorant of it ? The want of religious education is one of the causes that have brought the missionary influence all over our country. We did not think of it until very lately, whether we get the right sort of education or not. The tradesmen who are present here this evening send their sons very reluctantly to school and some of them do not send at all; because they do not get their education which they need. Besides their sons educated in the present-day system turn out fashionable. They wish to become clerks. They feel ashamed to sit on the *gaddi* where their fore-fathers earned the whole of their estate. The reason of this is that the education which they receive is onesided. The Government wanted Engineers, Doctors and clerks. It therefore started such schools which could supply its need. The students therefore who came out of these schools at first were bent upon services. It was the state of things sometime back that after passing three or four classes in school one could easily get on in life, but it has now become absolutely difficult, even to live from hand to mouth. We have therefore become conscious. It has become now almost clear that it is not the fault on our part that even after getting so much education we remain unable to satisfy our bare necessities; but the fault goes direct to the education stood before us. If the Educational Department had been under our control we could have effected in it any necessary changes immediately. At first we asked the Government to transfer it to our control—the selection of the textbooks for schools, for example. We feel now the necessity of such education which will prepare us to be good citizens. His Excellency the Governor of Bombay also admits the necessity of reforms in the present system of education. But he says that the Government is short of funds. I do not think this excuse reasonable, it may be true or otherwise. It is, however, true that the Government cannot think of religious education; and it is well that they are not doing it; because they are not our co-religionists. We are not given such education as may inspire patriotic sentiments amongst us. In America, the Proclamation of Independence is taught in V or VI classes. In this way, they train their children in politics. Some eighty or ninety years ago the industries of Germany declined on account of the rivalry between England and that country. But the German Government at once started scientific and mechanical education in that country. In this way, Germany became so powerful in commerce that she has now become an object of dread to other countries. Properly speaking these things ought to be done by the Government itself. We pay taxes to the Government only that it may look after our welfare. But the Government wants to keep us lame. There is conflict between the commercial interests of England and India. The Government therefore cannot do anything in this matter.

There being no convenient schools in the villages, our villagers cannot train their children. We must therefore begin this work. There has been a good deal of discussion over this matter. And in the end we have come to the conclusion that for proper education national schools must be started on all sides. There are some of our private schools but owing to the fear of losing the grant-in-aid, the necessary education cannot be given there. We must start our own schools for this education. We must begin our work selflessly. Such efforts are being made all over the country. The Gurukul of Haridwar stands on this footing. Berar and Madras have also begun to move in this direction. Our Maharashtra is a little backward. A few efforts are being made here also; but they need encouragement from you. Money is greatly needed for this work. I am sure, if you realise the necessity and importance of this subject, you would encourage the organisers generously. So far I have told you about the subject, now I turn to tell you what we shall do in these schools of national education.

Of the many things that we will do there religious education will first and foremost engage our attention. Secular education only is not enough to build up character. Religious education is necessary because the study of high principles keeps us away from evil pursuits. Religion reveals to us the form of the Almighty. Says our religion that a man by virtue of his action can become even a god. When we can become gods even by virtue of our action, why may we not become wise and active by means of our action like the Europeans ? Some say that religion begets quarrel. But I ask, "'Where is it written in religion to pick up quarrels ?" If there be any religion in the world which advocates toleration of other religious beliefs and instructs one to stick to one's own religion, it is the religion of the Hindus alone. Hinduism to the Hindus, Islamism to the Musalmans will be taught in these schools. And it will also be taught there to forgive and forget the differences of other religions.

The second thing that we will do, will be to lighten the load of the study of the foreign languages. In spite of a long stay in India no European can speak for a couple of hours fluent Marathi, while our graduates are required as a rule to obtain proficiency in the English language. One who speaks and writes good English is said, in these days, to have been educated but a mere knowledge of the language is no true education. Such a compulsion for the study of foreign languages does not exist anywhere except in India. We spend twenty or twenty-five years for the education which we can easily obtain in seven or eight years if we get it through the medium of our vernaculars. We cannot help learning English; but there is reason why its study should be made compulsory. Under the Muslim rule, we were required to learn Persian but we were not compelled to study it. To save unnecessary waste of time we have proposed to give education through our own vernaculars.

Industrial Education will be the Third Factor: In no school this education is given. It will be given in these schools. It is an important thing. During the whole of this century, we have not known how a match is prepared. In Sholapur, matches are manufactured from straw; and straw is found abundantly in our country. If therefore this industry is taken into our hands the importation of matches will largely decrease in India. It is the same with the sugar industry. We can procure here as good sugar-cane as is found in Mauritius. It is seen by scientific experiments that the sugarcane found in the suburbs of Puna can produce as much sugar as is found in the sugarcane of Mauritius. Six crores of rupees are drained out every year from this country only for sugar. Why should this be? Well, can we not get here sugarcane? Or the machinery necessary for its manufacture ? The reason is that we do not get here the education in this industry. It is not so in Germany. The Department of Industry investigates there as to which industry is decaying, and if perchance there be any, in a decaying state, substantial support at once comes forth from the Government for reviving it. The British Government, too, does the same thing in England. But our Government does not do it here. It may be a mistake or the Government may be doing it knowingly, but it is clear that we must not sit silent if the Government is not doing it. We are intending to start a large mechanical and scientific laboratory for this purpose. Sugar produces *Rab* and from *Rab* is extracted liquor, but the Government does not permit us this extraction. Hence, we cannot get here cheap sugar. Mauritius imports to this country twenty thousand tons of sugar every year. All this is due to the policy of the Government, but we do not know it. The Government will be obliged to change it if we put pressure upon it. We have come to learn these things not earlier than twenty-five years after leaving the college. Our young men should know them in their prime of life.

Education in Politics will be the fourth factor: We are not taught this subject in the Government schools. The student must understand that the Queen's Proclamation is the foundation of our rights. The Government is trying to shut our young men from these things. What has been proved by our revered Grand Old man—Dadabhai Naoroji, after a ceaseless exertion for over fifty years, should be understood by our students in their youth. Every year some thirty or forty crores of rupees are drained out of India without any return. We have, therefore, fallen to a wretched state of poverty. These things, if understood in the prime of life, can make such a lasting impression over the hearts of our young men, as it would be impossible in an advanced age. Therefore, this education should be given in school. Educated men of the type of Prof. Vijapurkar, have come forth to devote their lives in the cause of this education. The educationists are helping with their learning and experience, and it now remains with the well to do to help them with money. It is a matter of common benefit, if the future generation come out good, able to earn their bread and be true citizens. We should have been glad if the Government had done it. If the Government cannot do it, we must do. The Government will not interfere with us and if at all it does so, we should not mind it. And the dawn of the Sun cannot be stopped so it is with this. Our poverty has not yet reached its zenith. In America, such work is done by a single man. But if no one man can venture to do it here, let us do it unitedly, for we are thirty cores of people. A sum of five lakhs of rupees goes out every year for liquor alone from Sholapur. Can you not therefore help us in this work? The will is wanted. Let the Government be displeased We hope the Government will never deter us—we must do our duty. If the Government prohibits us from marriages, do we obey it? The same is the case with education. As men do not give up building houses for fear that rats would dig holes, so we should lot give up our work for fear of Government displeasure. If perchance any difficulty arises our young men are to face it. To fear difficulties is to lose manliness. Difficulties do us immense good. They inspire in us courage and prepare us to bear them manly. A nation cannot progress if it meets no difficulties in the way. We do not get this sort of education for want of self-government. We should not therefore await the coming of these rights, but we must get up and begin the work.

The famine which broke out in Bombay in 1896 was seriously viewed by Tilak. There was much loss of life and he sufferings of the people were greatly aggravated. The fear was expressed about the immediate availability of food to the people. The famine spread to Sholapur and other areas and seriously effected the socio-economic life of the people. Tilak formulated a viable scheme by which local committees were required to cooperate with the government in providing relief to the suffering people. He was critical of the famine policy of the Bombay government, and through the good offices of the Puna Sarvajanik Sabha, he acquainted the people regarding serious lapses on the part of the government. The Sabha sent several memorials to the government and Tilak took the leading part in these efforts. Inspite of critical remarks by the government, Tilak acted fearlessly and went on pursuing the cause of the famine-stricken people.

In Puna, the plague took a heavy toll and thus became a serious menace the human life. Tilak at once came out for help in this social problem, collected funds and started a plague hospital. He established a free kitchen for the needy people besides being in constant touch with the local officials and the Governor of the Presidency. He organised a band of dedicated workers who could do humane service to the suffering people. Indeed, Tilak was critical of the upper class which began to leave Puna *en masse* leaving their brethren in difficulty.

His public life had several complexities by which he suffered a lot. But any kind of hardship did not deter him to relax his efforts in any sense. Rather it enthused him to renew his efforts towards new channels of solutions. In 1895, the public enthusiasm towards the repairing of the *samadhi* of Shivaji at Raighur was shown. After it was done, it was decided to celebrate his birthday in the next year. Owing to plague in the region, the festival was not held. But on his coronation day falling on 13th June, a festive programme combined with hymn-singing, prayers, and sermon-preaching was gone through the Kesari published this programme in a comprehensive way in its issue of 15 June. This kind of celebration generated a spirit of partiotism among the people of Maharashtra and elsewhere and it made Tilak a hero of the public. But the government watched these proceedings with the bureaucratic angle and viewed in differently.

A week later, a serious incident took place on 22 June which involved Tilak, leading to his conviction. Some unknown person murdered Mr. Rand and Lieutenant Ayerst and there was much resentment in the Anglo-Indian community of Puna and Bombay.

The government of Bombay gave orders for Tilaks' arrest. Tilak applied for bail which was contested by the government. At High Court level, the application for bail was rejected, with permission to apply again for review of the case.

The case, however, took a serious turn in due course of time. On appeal, Mr. Justice Strachey presided at the trial. The Jury consisted of six Europeans, two Hindus and one Parsee. The six Europeans returned a verdict of guilty and other three of not guilty. As a result, Tilak was sentenced to eighteen months' rigorous imprisonment.

On 17 September 1897, an application was filed to the High Court with the request that the case was a fit one for appeal to the Privy Council and the leave was refused. An appeal was made to the Privy Council and Rt. Honourable Mr. Asquith argued appeal on behalf of Tilak on 18 November, but the application was rejected. At this point of time, when all avenues of justice were closed for Tilak.

Professor Max Muller and Sir William Hunter sent a signed petition to the Queen praying for mercy to Tilak on the plea that he was a renowned scholar and he deserved to be released. Tilak was consequently released on 6 September 1898. This case made him more popular as a public man and his reputation travelled in every nook and corner of the Presidency as well as in our subcontinent.

7

Golden Words of Tilak

- God has created you, God knows how to conduct his own creation.
- Swaraj is our birth-right
- Unless Swaraj is achieved, India will not prosper. It is required for our existence.
- Will is everything. Will power makes you as strong as you can and the material world around you cannot drive you from attaining the object which you will attain.
- Freedom is the very life of the individual soul, which Vedanta declares not to be separate from God but identical with Him.
- Man strives to gain union with God; and when this union is achieved the individual Will merges in the mighty Universal Will.
- Home Rule agitation has been started to make you masters in your house and not servants.
- Home Rule is nothing else, but to be masters of your houses.
- The words swarajyam, vairagyam, were actually seen in the Shastras. Of course, the word "Swaraj" or "Home Rule" has got a limited meaning today.

- Karma Yoga has been our sacred heritage, from times immemorial, when we Indians were seated on the high pedestal of wealth and lore. Karma Yoga or to put it in another way, the law of duty is the combination of all that is best in spiritual science, in actual action and in an unselfish meditative life.
- We are not all born for Government, that we should so much care for it. The Government is for us and not we, for Government.
- Whole world is changed and it is impossible that there could not be a change. When the world is changed, if you propose to remain stationary, possibly you will be wiped off speedily.

8

Tilak's Life at a Glance

1856: Bal Gangadhar Tilak was Born in a well-cultured Brahmin family on July 23, 1856 in Ratnagiri, Maharashtra.

1866: At the age of 10, Bal Gangadhar went to Puna with his family as his father was transferred. In Puna, he was educated in an Anglo-Vernacular school. After some years he lost his mother and at the age of 16 his father too. He got married to a 10-year-old girl named Satyabhama while he was studying in matriculation.

1877: Tilak completed his schooling and continued with studying Law. Later, he became a lawyer.

1891: He opposed the Age of Consent Bill.

1893: Tilak, reshaped the annual Ganesh festival from private family celebrations into a grand public event.

1896: A plague epidemic spread from Bombay to Puna.

1897: Tilak was accused of sedition and sentenced to an eighteen month imprisonment.

1905: Tilak bought Kesari at Wada from Sayajirao Gaikwad. The Wada still has the offices of Kesari, and mementos of Tilak, including his writing desk original letters and documents, and the first Indian national flag unfurled by Madame Cama.

1906: Tilak along with eminent industrialist Manmohandas Ramji gestated the idea of The Bombay Swadeshi Co-operative Stores Co. Ltd.

1907: Congress Party's annual session was held at Surat (Gujarat). Trouble broke out between the Moderate (Soft) and the Extremist (Hot) factions of the Congress party over the selection of a new President. The Congress party split into two factions. The extremists were led by Lala Lajpat Rai, Bal Gangadhar Tilak, Bipinchandra Pal (known as Lal-Bal-Pal).

1908: Detained and sent to Mandalay jail.

1914: Released from jail.

1916: Founded All India Home Rule League.

1916: The British Government took serious notice of the utterances of Bal Gangadhar Tilak on July 22, 1916, asking him to show cause why he should not be ordered to execute a bond for a sum of Rs. 20000 with two sureties in a sum of Rs. 10000.

1917: Tilak urged the British Government that it must promise the self-government to the Indians in lieu of the help that India has rendered to the British Empire.

1920: Tilak passed away on 1st August 1920. 'With the death of Bal Gangadhar Tilak the voice of India was hushed; the vigilant watchman of her cause had gone to his rest—the beacon light of freedom was extinguished. With Tilak passed away a whole era in Indian History'. Lakhs of people joined the funeral procession. The prominent pall bearers were Mahatma Gandhi, Lala Lajpat Rai, NC Kelker, Maulana Shaukat Ali, Saifuddin Kitchlew and several others.

Bibliography

Annie, Besant: *Lokmanya Bal Gangadhar Tilak*, Asian Educational Services, 2007.

Bakshi, S. R.: *Indian Freedom Fighters: Struggle for Independence*, Hardcover, 2002.

Benneaejea, Surendranath: *A Nation in Making: Being the Reminiscences of Fifty Years of Public Life*, London, 1925.

Bhagwan, V.: *Indian Freedom Movement and Constitutional Acts*, Atma Ram, 1999.

Bhattacharya, B. K.: *India's Freedom Movement: Legacy of Bipin Chandra Pal*, Deep and Deep, New Delhi, 2007.

Bose, Subhas Chandra: *The Indian Struggle*, 1920-1934, London, 1935.

Chakravarty, Shachi: *Quit India Movement: A Study*, New Century Publication, 2002.

Chandra, Bipan: *India's Struggle For Independence*, Penguin Books India (P) Ltd., New Delhi, 1989.

Chandra, Shailesh: *90 Years of India's Struggle for Independence: 1857-1947*, Alfa Pub, 2008.

Cotton, Henrey John Stedemen: *New India or India in Transitio*, London, 1904.

Couchman, M. E.: *Account of Plague Administration in the Bombay Presidency from September 1896 till May 1897*, Government Central Press, Mumbai 1897.

D. D. Karve: *The Deccan Education Society*, The Journal of Asian Studies, Ann Arbor, 1961.

D. Mackenzie Brown: *The Philosophy of Bal Gangadhar Tilak: Karma vs. Jnana in the Gita Rahasya*. Journal of Asian Studies, Ann Arbor, 1958.

Das, Chitta Ranjan, *India for Indians*, Madras, 1921.

Gandhi, Mahatma: *His life, Writings and Speeches*, Madras,1918.

Ganjoo, S.: *Muslim Freedom Fighters of India*, Anmol Publication, New Delhi, 2002.

Ghosh, Ratna: *Netaji Subhas Chandra Bose and Indian Freedom Struggle (2 Vols-Set)*, Deep and Deep, 2006.

Goyal, P. K.: *Battle of India's Freedom Movement*, Vista International, 2005.

Gupta, Shantinath: *Great Freedom Fighters of India*, Anmol, 2006.

Hari Hara Das: *The History of Freedom Movement in India (1857-1947)*, National, 1998.

Indu Dave: *Indian Personality in Its Developmental Background*, Himanshu, 1991.

Iyengar, A. S.: *Role of Press and Indian Freedom Struggle: All through the Gandhian Era*, APH, 2001.

Joglekar, Jayawant D.: *Veer Savarkar Father of Hindu Nationalism*, 2006.

Kailash Khanna: *History of Indian Freedom Struggle*, Commonwealth Publication, 2004.

Kaushik, A. S.: *Great Freedom Fighters of India*, Indian Publication, 2007.

Khairul Anam, Md.: *Indian Freedom Movement and Murshidabad District 1905-1947*, Bagchi, K. P., 2008.

Krishan Mohan: *Encyclopaedic History of Indian Freedom Movement (4 Vols-Set)*, Book Enclave, 1999.

Kumar, Prafulla Pattanaik: *The First Indian War of Independence: Freedom Movement in Orissa, 1804-1825*, APH, 2005.

Kumar, Raj: *Essays on Indian Freedom Movement*, History and Culture Series, Discovery, 2003.

Kumar, Ravindra: *Champaran to Quit India Movement*, Mittal, 2002.

Kumar, Sirisa Shadangi: *The Prisons of South Orissa and the Freedom Fighters in Incarceration, 1900 - 1947*, Punthi Pustak, 2005.

Lion Agrawal, M. G.: *Freedom Fighters of India (4 Vols-Set)*, Isha Books, 2008.

M. K. Singh: *Bal Gangadhar Tilak*, Anmol, 2008.

M.V.S. Koteswara Rao: *Communist Parties and United Front - Experience in Kerala and West Bengal*, Prajasakti Book House, Hyderabad, 2003.

Majumdar, R. C.: *History of the Freedom Movement in India (3 Vols-Set)*, Firma KLM, 1997.

Malhotra, Sumiti: *Thoughts of Great Personalities in 20 Century*, Raj Publishing, 2003.

Manju Verma: *The Role of Women in the Freedom Movement in Punjab (1919-1947)*, Abhijeet, 2003.

Maulana Syed Mohammad Mian: *The Prisoners of Malta (Asira'n-E-Malta): The Heart-Rending Tale of Muslim Freedom Fighters in British Period*, Manak, 2005.

Mazhar Kibriya: *Gandhi and Indian Freedom Struggle*, APH, 1999.

Michael, Edwardes: *A History of India*, Farrar, Straus and Cudahy, New York, 1961.

Muthaiah, S.: *Women Freedom Fighters*, The Hindu, 2004.

Nanda, S. P.: *Freedom Movement and Constitutional Development in India*, Dominant, 2004.

Om Prakash: *Encyclopaedic History of Indian Freedom Movement (12 to 21 Vols)*, Anmol, 2003.

Omesh Saigal: *Shaheed Bhagat Singh: Unique Martyr in Freedom Movement*, Gyan Publication, 2002.

Parashar, Parmanand: *Kashmir and the Freedom Movement*, Sarup, 2004.

Pradhan, K. B.: *Freedom Movement in India*, Arise Pub, 2007.

Rafiya, Nisar: *Shaikh-Ul-Hind Maulana Mahmud Hasan and Indian Freedom Movement*, Manak Pub, 2008.

Ram Sharma, S.: *Education of Women and Freedom Movement*, Discovery, 1996.

Ram, S. and Kumar, R.: *Encyclopaedia of Indian Freedom Struggle (10 Vols-Set)*, Commonwealth Pub, 2008.

Ramanathan, K. V.: *The Satyamurti Letters, Vol. II: The Indian Freedom Struggle Through the Eyes of a Parliamentarian*, Dorling Kindersley for Pearson Longman an Imprint of Pearson Education, 2008.

Ramu, P. S.: *Azad Hind Fauj (I.N.A.) and The Freedom Movement*, Freedom Movement Memorial Comm, 1998.

Ranbir Vohra: *The Making of India: A Historical Survey*, M.E. Sharpe, Armonk, 1997.

Rand, W. C.; Lamb R. A.: *Supplement to the Account of Plague Administration in the Bombay Presidency from September 1896 till May 1897*.. Government Central Press, Mumbai, 1897.

S. R. Sharma: *Life and Works of Bal Gangadhar Tilak*, Book Enclave, 2007.

Savarkar: *Associates in Hindutva Movement*, 2009.

Sharma, S. K.: *Eminent Indian Freedom Fighters (2 Vols-Set)*, Anmol Publication, New Delhi, 2004.

Sundaram, V.: *Great Crusader for Women's Emancipation*, News Today, 2005.

Sundararaja, Saroja: *March to Freedom in Madras Presidency, 1916-1947*, Lalitha Publication, Chennai, 1989.

Taneja, Anup: *Gandhi, Women and the National Movement, 1920-47*, Har-Anand Publications, Delhi, 2005.

Vohra, R.: *Encyclopedia of Asian History*. "Tilak, Bal Gangadhar," Charles Scribner's Sons And MacMillian Publishing Company, New York, 1988.

Waugh, Dr. Dattatraya; Kulkarni, Prof. Sadhana: *Our Freedom Struggle:* Maharashtra State Bureau of Textbook Production and Curriculum Research, Pune, 2006.

Index

A

All India Congress Committee, 97, 100, 103, 107, 161, 173, 179, 181.

All India Home Rule League, 296.

Anglo-Indian, 42, 53, 66, 67, 68, 77, 82, 85, 106, 137, 148, 202, 278, 279, 280, 281, 284, 291.

B

Banaras Hindu University, 260.

Birth, 1, 78, 79, 85, 89, 95, 193, 199, 201, 208, 247, 293.

Bombay University, 10, 69, 73.

British Army, 225.

British Empire, 166, 179, 181, 199, 210, 241, 243, 253, 255, 261, 262, 263, 296.

British Government, 20, 36, 52, 80, 85, 91, 120, 138, 152, 166, 169, 171, 181, 213, 217, 227, 232, 243, 245, 259, 267, 268, 284, 285, 289, 296.

British India, 92, 99, 120, 275.

British Rule, 19, 20, 21, 35, 36, 46, 52, 56, 83, 102, 114, 119, 120, 121, 126, 127, 132, 133, 164, 174, 179, 224, 231, 255, 259, 263, 271, 272, 273.

C

Cabinet, 172, 186, 188, 202, 261.

Cambridge University, 256.

Central Legislature, 122.

Christianity, 49.

Civil Service, 21, 99, 169, 285.

Conference, 23, 42, 43, 44, 45, 46, 47, 50, 73, 75, 99, 100, 102, 103, 109, 118, 123, 139, 149, 153,

154, 160, 163, 164, 165, 166, 167, 176, 177, 178, 179, 182, 183, 184, 187, 194, 209, 213, 214, 215, 216, 238, 250, 268, 270, 271, 272, 273.

Congress, 13, 14, 15, 17, 36, 37, 38, 43, 45, 46, 47, 48, 64, 71, 75, 76, 80, 89, 96, 97, 98, 99, 100, 101, 102, 103, 104, 105, 121, 124, 125, 126, 127, 129, 130, 131, 133, 134, 139, 140, 143, 152, 153, 154, 155, 157, 158, 159, 160, 161, 162, 163, 165, 166, 167, 168, 169, 170, 172, 173, 174, 178, 179, 180, 181, 182, 194, 197, 198, 199, 203, 206, 207, 208, 209, 210, 211, 214, 217, 232, 236, 237, 238, 239, 240, 242, 243, 245, 250, 251, 253, 256, 257, 260, 261, 262, 263, 264, 265, 269, 270, 271, 272, 273, 278, 285, 296.

Congress Leaders, 134, 158, 167, 211.

Congress Party, 162, 163, 251, 267, 296.

Congress President, 169.

Constitution, 5, 121, 157, 158, 160, 161, 162, 165, 166, 235, 266, 277.

D

Deccan Educational Society, 71.

Dominion Status, 239.

E

Early Life, 1.

East India Company, 187, 188, 224.

Education, 1, 4, 8, 10, 11, 24, 25, 26, 28, 29, 30, 45, 47, 57, 58, 59, 63, 64, 70, 71, 82, 95, 127, 135, 144, 149, 150, 153, 154, 155, 160, 219, 220, 221, 222, 223, 225, 227, 229, 230, 231, 255, 256, 258, 259, 260, 264, 266, 270, 273, 284, 285, 286, 287, 288, 289, 290.

Emperor, 32, 169, 215, 225, 254, 266.

English Language, 251, 257, 288.

Englishman, 47, 199, 241, 278, 280.

F

Family Background, 10.

Foreign Affairs, 239.

Freedom, 18, 31, 33, 52, 60, 70, 94, 116, 119, 123, 211, 225, 226, 231, 232, 234, 235, 243, 245, 250, 252, 253, 255, 256, 257, 258, 268, 281, 293, 296.

G

Government, 1, 3, 4, 7, 10, 12, 14, 16, 18, 19, 20, 22, 23, 24, 27, 28, 30, 31, 32, 33, 34, 36, 41,

42, 43, 44, 45, 46, 47, 48, 49, 51, 52, 59, 60, 63, 66, 67, 68, 70, 71, 72, 74, 79, 80, 81, 82, 83, 84, 85, 86, 87, 88, 89, 91, 92, 95, 97, 98, 99, 100, 101, 102, 103, 104, 106, 107, 120, 121, 122, 123, 126, 127, 129, 130, 133, 135, 136, 137, 138, 140, 141, 142, 144, 145, 147, 148, 150, 151, 152, 153, 154, 156, 157, 158, 162, 164, 165, 166, 168, 169, 170, 171, 172, 173, 174, 175, 176, 177, 178, 179, 180, 181, 182, 185, 186, 197, 201, 202, 203, 207, 208, 211, 212, 213, 214, 215, 216, 217, 219, 221, 222, 225, 227, 229, 232, 233, 234, 236, 237, 238, 239, 240, 241, 242, 243, 245, 251, 254, 259, 262, 264, 265, 266, 267, 268, 270, 271, 272, 275, 277, 278, 279, 281, 282, 284, 285, 286, 287, 289, 290, 291, 292, 294, 296.

Government of India, 7, 30, 42, 46, 49, 74, 88, 89, 100, 152, 174, 176, 177, 181, 182, 186, 272, 284.

Governor-General, 23.

Gram Panchayat, 128.

H

High Court, 11, 21, 31, 72, 75, 79, 87, 88, 89, 93, 98, 99, 156, 175, 180, 221, 231, 244, 248, 249, 292.

Higher Education, 28, 225.

Hindu Community, 135, 171.

Hindu Mahasabha, 208.

Hindu Society, 8, 60, 125, 142, 226, 231.

Home Rule, 80, 82, 94, 95, 96, 97, 98, 99, 100, 101, 102, 103, 104, 105, 147, 162, 164, 167, 172, 173, 174, 175, 176, 177, 178, 179, 180, 181, 182, 183, 184, 185, 186, 187, 188, 189, 190, 191, 192, 193, 194, 196, 197, 198, 199, 200, 201, 203, 204, 205, 206, 207, 208, 209, 210, 211, 212, 213, 214, 215, 216, 217, 234, 235, 236, 237, 238, 239, 240, 241, 242, 243, 244, 251, 252, 293, 296.

I

Independence, 3, 80, 128, 154, 220, 225, 232, 272, 287.

Indian Community, 171, 291.

Indian Government, 178.

Indian Jail, 34.

Indian Languages, 36, 73, 117, 207.

Indian National Congress, 17, 43, 45, 64, 126, 127, 134, 154, 206, 217, 232,

237, 245, 250, 251, 256, 260, 261, 262, 263, 264.

Indian Nationalism, 127.

Indian Social Reformer, 39.

Indian Society, 125, 220, 221, 224, 226.

Indian State, 52.

Indian States, 51, 56.

J

Jalianwala Bagh, 40.

K

Kesari, 11, 13, 41, 43, 49, 50, 51, 53, 54, 55, 56, 59, 60, 62, 64, 65, 67, 70, 73, 75, 82, 83, 84, 86, 88, 89, 105, 108, 120, 121, 123, 125, 143, 150, 156, 211, 227, 228, 229, 230, 231, 232, 240, 243, 245, 251, 252, 253, 259, 260, 261, 263, 264, 265, 269, 271, 291, 295.

Khudiram Bose, 81, 277.

L

Legislative Council, 43, 66, 73, 131, 169, 178, 187, 285.

Liberty, 23, 31, 32, 61, 87, 89, 144, 152, 191, 199, 238, 239, 250, 272, 277, 278, 284.

Literature, 51, 63, 77, 112, 117, 118, 121, 257, 268.

Local Government, 42.

Lok Sabha, 152.

M

Mahatma Gandhi, 40, 233, 296.

Marriage, 10, 134, 135, 229, 231.

Mughal Emperor, 225.

Muslim, 19, 31, 36, 102, 104, 126, 131, 135, 137, 162, 168, 169, 171, 179, 181, 203, 208, 209, 214, 239, 268, 272, 273, 288.

Muslim Community, 171.

N

National Assembly, 132.

National Congress, 17, 43, 45, 64, 75, 89, 103, 126, 127, 131, 134, 139, 140, 154, 165, 194, 206, 217, 232, 237, 245, 250, 251, 256, 260, 261, 262, 263, 264, 270.

National University, 150.

Nationalist Party, 154, 158, 170.

Newspaper, 11, 31, 65, 89, 144, 146, 224, 277, 278, 281.

P

Parliament, 20, 31, 83, 89, 90, 95, 96, 128, 134, 164, 180, 188, 189, 191, 198, 207, 263, 266, 270, 279, 282, 285.

President, 28, 35, 71, 80, 97, 102, 105, 125, 130, 133,

136, 154, 155, 163, 164, 167, 168, 169, 180, 194, 196, 200, 202, 206, 208, 262, 263, 273, 285, 296.

Prime Minister, 202.

Provincial Conference, 42, 44, 46, 47, 50, 73, 99, 103, 149, 160, 163, 165, 167, 271, 272.

Provincial Legislative Councils, 130, 169.

R

Rajagopalachari, 234.

S

Salt Satyagraha, 48.

Sarojini Naidu, 116.

Scholar, 1, 72, 73, 77, 108, 109, 110, 112, 113, 118, 120, 121, 221, 222, 223, 252, 257, 292.

Servants of India Society, 266.

Social Conference, 75, 139, 194.

Society, 8, 11, 18, 21, 27, 33, 45, 57, 58, 59, 60, 62, 63, 64, 71, 76, 80, 121, 125, 127, 128, 142, 196, 219, 220, 221, 222, 224, 226, 229, 230, 231, 245, 251, 252, 255, 260, 266, 276.

Speeches, 14, 36, 38, 43, 44, 67, 68, 95, 96, 98, 99, 120, 122, 124, 125, 140, 145, 147, 164, 174, 175, 197, 208, 211, 212, 213, 215, 226, 236, 242, 244, 250, 251, 253, 255, 266, 273, 282, 284, 285.

Swadeshi Movement, 31, 107, 145, 147, 148, 149, 258, 259, 260, 261, 285.

T

Tilak's Attitude, 74, 137.

Tilak's Counsel, 87, 92, 93.

Tilak's League, 97, 178.

Tilak's Role, 73.

Tilak's Social and Political Philosophy, 74.

Tilak's Speech, 71, 146, 154.

U

United Congress, 160, 167, 169, 272.

United Kingdom, 31.

United Provinces, 168, 171, 175.

University of Bombay, 59, 222.

W

World War, 35.

Writings, 14, 36, 84, 114, 117, 120, 121, 122, 175, 211, 221, 226, 243, 258, 281, 282.

❑❑❑

teaching them about the people, the political and social problems besides inculcating in them the spirit of patriotism. Realising that the newspaper was the most powerful instrument for educating the people, they decided to launch a newspaper. Here it is necessary to take into consideration the situation prevailing in India and the challenges faced by those who wanted to mould public opinion.

The British had initially come to India for the purpose of trade. The East India Company started trade in different parts of India. After a few years, ambitious persons like Robert Clive began to feel that political power was essential for safeguarding the economic interests of the East India Company and that of Britain. India was ruled in different parts by different rulers. The Mughals were dominant in north India. The Peshwas ruled Maharashtra, the Rajput Princes governed Rajasthan while there were feudal lords spread in other parts of India. Clive with his policy of 'divide and rule', set one ruler against the other and used all means in his power to establish his supremacy in various parts of India, primarily with the help of money-lenders and selfish feudal lords.

Bengal was the first to be brought under British rule. Later their rule extended to other regions too. Some resistance was offered to the British, particularly by the Santhals in south Bihar. But as there was no combined resistance by the Indians, the British succeeded in crushing the Adivasi revolt and of various patriotic groups in different parts of India. Till the eighteenth century, the Indian society was prosperous. India had a huge section of weavers who helped the country in exporting cloth to many countries in the East. The British could not tolerate this rivalry to their dominance in trade and chose to destroy the Indian handloom industry. Thus, the export trade was destroyed and India soon became impoverished. Further, owing to the caste system of the Hindus, political power was concentrated in the hands of the upper caste Brahmins. As a result, the society was fragmented. The Peshwas, instead of looking after the welfare of their people, acted selfishly, ruling in a tyrannical way. The common people were exploited and the scheduled castes were given inhuman treatment by being treated as untouchables. They were fed up with the corrupt and decadent regime of the Peshwas.

sentenced to four months simple imprisonment. However, the common man was convinced of their honesty and their devotion to the ruler of Kolhapur. They were all praise at the courage of these two young editors who went to jail with a smile on their lips. Principal Wordsworth, Justice V.N. Mandlik and other eminent persons of the town submitted a petition to the government pleading for annulment of the punishment, but the government paid no heed to it.

Tilak and Agarkar were kept in Dongri Jail in Bombay. Agarkar has given a graphic description of his experience in the prison in his small book, A Hundred and One Days in Dongri Prison, in Marathi. Owing to the hardships of prison life and the unappetising food served to the inmates, Tilak lost twenty-four pounds while Agarkar lost sixteen pounds in weight. After a month's stay in prison, they were given the permission to read and write. However, the two friends spent most of their time discussing various subjects of their interest. On their release from Dongri Jail, they were given a warm welcome by the people. Lokhande, the editor of Deen Bandhu, and other influential persons belonging to the non-brahmin community were the first to felicitate Tilak and Agarkar.

Generally, days spent together in prison help to strengthen the bonds of friendship and amity. But with Tilak and Agarkar the ideological differences between them became more and more sharp. In 1884, when a plea was made to the government to pass a law against child marriage, the reactions of the editors of the Kesari and the Maratha were diametrically opposite. While Agarkar, a staunch opponent of child marriage, wrote in the [illegible] supporting the plea [illegible] child marriage, Tilak opposed the idea of government interference in social and religious matters. He strongly criticised the proponents of child marriage [illegible]. This development widened the rift between Tilak and Agarkar. Their differences of opinion were [illegible] during the meeting of the life members of the Deccan Education Society. Agarkar led a group of reformist leaders [illegible] group of orthodox and traditionalist leaders supported Tilak's point of view. In the Kesari articles expressing divergent views on this subject were published. The rift between [illegible] grew to such an extent that Agarkar resigned from h[illegible]